Thurso

Wick

Firth

Aberdeen

Dundee

Edinburgh

OASIS OF THE NORTH

DAWN MACLEOD

Oasis of the North

A HIGHLAND GARDEN

Decorations by
WILLIAM McLAREN

HUTCHINSON OF LONDON

HUTCHINSON & CO. *(Publishers)* LTD
178–202 Great Portland Street, London, W.1

London Melbourne Sydney
Auckland Bombay Toronto
Johannesburg New York

★

First published 1958

*This book has been set in Bembo type face. It has
been printed in Great Britain by The Anchor Press,
Ltd., in Tiptree, Essex, on Antique Wove paper and
bound by Taylor Garnett Evans & Co., Ltd., in
Watford, Herts*

With love and gratitude to my
mother (Mrs. E. N. Mooney),
who made it possible for me to
write this book; and to Monica
Brooks and The Hall School at
Wincanton, where between cock-
light and rising-bell much of it
was written.

Note

Characters in this book who are still living and working in and around Inverewe have been given fictitious Christian names. Attempts to indicate pronunciation of Gaelic words and place-names are to be taken as only rough guides.

Contents

Foreword

In July 1953 I lost the dearest of friends. Many other people the world over felt the same when they heard that Mairi Sawyer of Inverewe was dead. To the folk of Wester Ross, where in her famous gardens she worked so hard and so successfully, the news seemed to mark the end of an epoch.

During her last years I was in almost daily contact with her, and my strongest recollection (which would please her) is of the fun we had together. She loved to observe and retail all the amusing little quirks of the Highland character, and to make quizzical remarks about the dear and trusted Gaelic speakers who served her so long and so faithfully; about me; and (most important of all) about herself. No one need have qualms about my references to such matters as her quaint spelling, for anything which evoked kindly mirth delighted her. If the laughter sometimes concealed heartache it was none the less welcome; and surely one would not grudge her a few gentle chuckles.

As *The Times* of August 3rd 1953 put it: 'For the last eight years of her life Mairi Sawyer strove alone and valiantly with the worries and anxieties of a Highland laird.' But always calm and ever ready to be gay, she had no truck with self-pity or gloom. At the last she went out suddenly—a powerful light switched off —and it seemed very dark afterwards. Now I am happily remembering the light, and in the following pages trying to recapture and record some of the fun we had in that wonderful place between the hills and the sea, for others to share and—I hope —enjoy.

Thanks are due to The National Trust for Scotland for their co-operation; to Mr. Milton Waldman, Literary Executor of the late Robert Nichols (for permission to use verses from *Ardours*

Foreword

and Endurances); to Dr. W. Douglas Simpson, M.A., D.Litt., and The Aberdeen University Press Ltd. (for an extract from their *Guide to Dunvegan Castle*); to Messrs. Martin Secker and Warburg Ltd. (for Lady Margaret Sackville's poem *The Slayers*); to *The Daily Telegraph* (for the quotation from Peter Simple); to Messrs. Geoffrey Bles Ltd. (publishers of Osgood MacKenzie's book *A Hundred Years in the Highlands*); to Miss Ann Munro of Laide (for help with some Gaelic spelling); to Mr. Alfred Wilson (for examining the manuscript); to my friend Enid, now Mrs. Wigram Money (for her constant interest and encouragement); and to my wartime colleague Mr. John Betjeman (for blessing the work, and for not minding what I said about him).

DAWN MACLEOD

1. *Up North*

THE cottage is a wee one—really ½ of the gardiner's house devided into 2—but I can get it let for 3 gins a week to summer visitas. There is plenty wood and you could have milk from the farm and eggs and veg. free from the gardins here, in return for the help I need in the afternoons with shruberys and boarders round this house.

No letter has ever given me such surprise as this one—not because of Aunt Mairi's spelling, to which I was accustomed, but because the unsought offer of a home on the remote and wild west coast of Ross-shire in Scotland fulfilled my dearest but unspoken wish. How did she guess? Or was it just a chance suggestion thrown out on sudden impulse without thought? The letter might not even be meant for me to take seriously. A grisly dungeon of disappointment loomed at the back of this idea, but it was soon dismissed by remembrance of my adopted aunt's quiet reliability and the warmth of goodwill in her steady blue eye.

All my friends in England thought me crazy. Why leave a comfortable urban home and well-paid work in order to stagnate a hundred miles from a cinema and forty from the railhead, with only a tiny cottage and some vegetarian rations to count on?

'How in the world will you get clothes?' asked one.

'Think of the long, dark winter nights!' said another.

'Why throw up a safe and profitable job and forfeit your pension?' exclaimed everyone. 'At your age you should be settled in life.'

I knew that without being told, but as the life I was leading irritated and depressed me it seemed wise to settle into something more congenial—and this was my chance. Aunt Mairi's offer came out of the blue. She had need of me, and I wanted to go. Some way of supplementing the rent-free cottage and veg. would surely be provided. I felt in my bones that I was meant to go, and having long since discovered that bones were best obeyed, go I did.

My resignation was quickly written out, but not so easily accepted. Senior Civil Servants do not look kindly on wartime stop-gaps who have been honoured with permanent post-war appointments which they happily relinquish after a few months. I began to feel like a criminal on trial, but explained that I had Highland blood from a MacLeod grandmother, and could not resist the call of the wild. This remark at once transformed the reproaches of my superior officer into unmistakable relief. (Wild creatures are not suitable material for the Civil Service.) Nevertheless, after ten years spent under the benevolent tutelage of a Government Department, I felt apprehensive and almost naked as I stepped out of the office building for the last time—now free and entirely dependent on my own efforts in sickness and in health.

I did not even know my adopted aunt very well, and had never visited her home with its famous sub-tropical gardens, but brief holidays in Skye and Morar had already shown me that the West Highlands would always be my Promised Land; and all that I had seen and heard of Aunt Mairi made me conscious of some hidden well-forged bond linking us.

I travelled up to Inverness in a third-class sleeper overnight from Euston. The bunk was apparently stuffed with gravel, and a charming old lady on the berth below kept me awake with conversation and the crackling of bullseyes, which I declined to share as I am allergic to peppermint. So influenced by emotions are we, that I can now sniff the hated smell with fond appreciation of the happy memories it revives. For gravel and peppermint did nothing to diminish the rapture I felt as the long train squeaked and jolted us over the Border.

Aunt Mairi had promised to meet me on the station platform, but was nowhere to be seen, and I stood alone by the empty carriage feeling rather disconsolate as I watched everyone else greeted by friends or relations. I went out to the front of the station where the cars waited, and asked a porter if he had noticed a black Standard with a silver Highland warrior on the bonnet, but he couldn't say. As I finished speaking I became aware of a third person beside us, and turned quickly, and there she was: her blue eyes bright with amusement at standing so close to me undetected. She had the trained stalker's gift of quiet movement, and seemed able to withdraw her personality on occasion so that no waves from it made you aware of her presence until she wished you to be.

She drove me out of the town of Inverness by the Ness bridge, and away north and west through Muir of Ord towards the mountainous skyline ahead. It took us over two hours to pass between those ancient hills of Torridon red sandstone, along the single-track road through miles of uninhabited rock and heather-clad peat hags to the grand old pine trees on the shores of Loch Maree. As we came down from the awesome Glen Docherty I heard a murmur in my right ear: 'That is *Slioch*.[1] This is my country.'

Soon we left Bridge of Grudie and the great lump of a hill she had named behind us, passed the Loch Maree hotel—half buried in a tangle of rhododendrons beside the loch of many islands—and coasted down a steep hill past Kerrysdale falls and the old MacKenzie house (*Tigh Dige*) to the imposing hotel of Gairloch, with its stretches of sandy foreshore now empty of visitors. Out to

[1] Pronounced 'Slee-ock'.

15

sea the northern end of Skye stood up like the blunt head of a giant sperm whale. Then our road turned inland again, climbing the long hill of Achtercairn to a high plateau and the windswept Tollie Loch.

Aunt Mairi looked at me and said: 'Tollie is a name your grandmother's clan has good reason to remember.'

'Yes,' I replied, with vague memories of dark deeds five hundred years before, when a MacKenzie slew—was it six MacLeods before breakfast?

She nodded towards the silver figure on the bonnet of her car. 'That is my ancestor, Hector MacKenzie, who "shortened the MacLeods by the head", as we say in Gaelic. You and I are deadly enemies, you know! And you've got MacLeod written all over you.'

'I daresay we shall live down the shady past,' I said laconically; an amused flash of her eye seemed to register assent. Having been warned by others that I should find myself driven about Wester Ross behind a statuette of our clan's greatest foe, I was prepared for Hector and had already decided to lose no sleep over him.

Presently we came to the village of Poolewe, with its stout bridge where the salmon river rushes out into the sea, and as our road swung away round Loch Ewe in the direction of Ullapool and Cape Wrath, I saw at last the big white house of Inverewe with its attendant Gate Lodge beneath the dark wooded brae.

'That is my home,' said a voice at my ear; and then, 'I know! *I remember it all so well!*' I heard myself shout, quite involuntarily. The car stopped in a passing-place to make way for a lorry, and I caught a sharp gleam from the blue eye of my companion. 'But you have never been here before!'

Most people would have attributed my strange behaviour to fatigue—or even mental disorder—but not Aunt Mairi. She accepted the rational and the fantastic with her usual calm as so many differing threads in the warp and weft of existence, which provided a texture to interest but not astonish her. It was easy in her company for many sorts of people, feeling thoroughly confident of her understanding, to be at their happiest and best. Yet with all her power of making and keeping friends, she would say with her little shy laugh that she preferred plants to people.

As we went through the big gates into the drive and I had my first glimpse of eucalyptus and Himalayan lily on good terms with heather and pine, I began to see that the same gift had created harmony among plants as diverse as her friends. The power to combine alien growths from sub-tropical climates with a wild and austere northern landscape, in such a way that each complemented the other and produced a balanced whole, seemed to me a creative art so subtle that it might easily escape notice.

Not that the master-gardener would have cared for a pedestal; she had more than a dash of the shrewd practical outlook of the crofters amongst whom she had spent most of her life, where the ability to live and get a living in rough, remote country is the basis for judging the worth of men and women. Even the poets and musicians of this land are working crofters, shepherds and fishermen whose ideas, springing from their labours, must wait to be recited or played until night comes and the peat fire glows. The lady of the Big House had earned the respect of the people for the skill with which she would catch and cook a trout or salmon, spin and weave a plaid, or work with her men in any sort of weather, and this contented her.

No sooner had the house door opened to us and my overnight case been taken upstairs by Janet, the young maid, than Aunt Mairi exchanged jacket and beret for an ample blue-checked apron and went into her kitchen to prepare a high tea. Meantime I wandered through back ways to the garden, and it would be hard to find a greater contrast anywhere than that between the rich variety and lush growth of flower and foliage discovered in the next fifty minutes, and the bleak expanse of mountain and tumbled rock which the day's motoring had shown us.

The garden soil—acid and peaty, and the climate—a mild, wet and very windy one—were obviously determining factors in the choice and disposal of plants and trees; but admiration mounted as I saw how skilfully items of practical necessity, such as shelter belts, had been used to enhance the effect of the whole design.

Our native rhododendron (*ponticum*—whose hybrids produce the gorgeous blossoms seen *en masse* in southern gardens such as Leonardslee and Longleat) has a short flowering season and is not attractive as a foliage plant. But here, used as a wind-break and background to the hundreds of natural species of rhododendron from China, Turkestan and northern Burma, it was admirable. In places it was lightened by gleaming boles of silver birch, and in others shrouded by mysterious plantations of Scots and Corsican pine.

The varieties of imported rhododendron seemed endless. Many had grown into gnarled trees whose stems were stained and streaked in crimson and russet like marbled end-papers in some antique book. Others had bark like staghorn, and blue-green leaves lined with soft golden plush; or sage-coloured foliage and barbs of Indian red. All were beautifully spaced, and pruned into shapely bushes—of decorative value apart from their flowers.

At first I felt bewildered by the lay-out of the garden, with its series of steep-sided glens radiating from the house—one glen looking very like another—in which it was not difficult to lose oneself. The whole of the fifty-acre garden was sited on a peninsula, aptly described by its Gaelic name *Am Ploc Ard* (The High Lump), and bounded on the north, west, and south by the salt water of Loch Ewe.

Several of the glens had been fenced or hedged in and given names. 'America' and 'Japan' were obviously intended to house natives of those countries, although aliens had come creeping in as immigrants always do. 'The Peace Plot', planted at the end of the first world war, brought me to a standstill beside a great boulder with a carved inscription to the memory of Donald Grant, gardener to Aunt Mairi's father for sixty years in this place. 'Bamboozlem', the most sheltered of all the enclosures, certainly made me feel bewitched or bamboozled when I saw the white flower-heads of the climbing hydrangea (*petiolaris*) poking from a larch tree some fifty feet above the ground.

As I wandered on, impressions of soft sub-tropical vegetation and exotic perfume followed swiftly upon hardier ones of rocky slopes and salt-sprayed heather, with recurring glimpses of the Ardlair hills and the peaks of *Beinn Eighe*[1] to remind me that this was indeed Scotland's rugged north-west coast.

Several varieties of the eucalyptus, or blue gum tree, some of which had caught my eye on arrival, seemed to have been given the rôle of bugler—for they sounded decisive notes not only at the entrance to the policies but also in the heart of 'Bamboozlem,' and again near the mansion house to mark an abrupt cleavage between formalities of lawn and border and the steepest wooded brae whose rocky edge plunged to the sea below. The skewbald patterns on the ever-peeling boles of the gums gave an effect of light and shade whether the sun shone or not, and beneath their delicate blue-grey foliage long rolls of papery bark lay on the grass like a giant's cigars.

The splendid eucalyptus trunks were not obscured by creepers, but many other trees, in addition to the hydrangea-clad larch, were hosts to climbers such as clematis, honeysuckle, philesia, and blue-berried billardiera from Tasmania. Along the drive a closely trimmed hedge of rhododendron covered with small, bright nasturtium flowers looked unreal, until I discovered a number of plants of *Tropaeolum speciosum* rooted out of sight at the back and climbing through to blossom on the side away from the sea-winds. The sturdy rhodos gave firm support and shelter for the creeper's fragile growth, and their dark, glossy leaves made an excellent foil to the sharp red of its flowers.

The lay-out of the garden made the best use of natural contours—the only level area of any size (an old sea-beach below the drive) being the obvious site for vegetable and fruit growing. Here, in the shelter of a fifteen-foot wall, were also flowers for cutting: roses and sweet-peas, scabious and brilliant Kaffir lilies growing between beds of strawberries and asparagus. In this enclosure plants were regimented and paths short and straight, the whole effect being one of reels and strathspeys compared with the *Ceòl Mór* (Big Music) or pibroch of the wild garden outside.

The walks of Inverewe were a study in themselves: winding

[1] Pronounced 'Ben Ay'.

between trees and rocky banks, descending unexpectedly to a water-garden, and climbing to an open view-point with a seat facing the Minch and the long, low line of the Island of Lewis far away on the horizon. The smaller walks led the eye gently forward without betraying too soon the secrets of their plan, and their peat foundation under a thin carpet of mossy grass or pine-needles was soft and springy underfoot. Outside the walled garden there was only one broad walk—which led, through a plantation of the biggest rhododendrons, from the back of the house to a little seal-haunted bay called *Camas Glas* on the Atlantic side of the peninsula. All the other paths were narrow and unsociable, forcing visitors to walk singly and concentrate on the garden without the distraction of gossiping companions along-side.

Themes and rhythms, repetitions and developments: the garden as its plan unfolded made me think on that first evening of musical composition, and more particularly of the great fugues of Bach. I mentioned some of my thoughts at the tea-table, to which I was summoned by a horn. Aunt Mairi looked unimpressed, and said drily that I seemed to have done much daydreaming. Her old housekeeper, Sheena, joined in from her armchair in the corner. (As there were no visitors we had tea in the great kitchen.)

'It will be as well for her to have a good look round now, I'm thinking,' she announced firmly. 'It's little time she'll have for it once you put her to work.' In days to come I learnt that old Sheena always had the last word.

Our meal done, Aunt Mairi fetched an assortment of traps from the gun-room and went out to set them in the enclosure named 'Japan', where cyclamen and dog-tooth violet and tiny bulbs of *Narcissus nanus*, scattered under an old Japanese cherry tree, were being devoured by field-mice and voles. I started to help bait the traps with cheese, but she said with a meaning laugh that if I really wanted to begin work there was always bracken to pull.

So I went up the nearest brae towards a group of Austrian

pines where curled fronds grew strongly to a height of three or four feet and began to drag them out of the ground with my bare hands. This marked an epoch in my life on a par with cutting a first tooth, learning to read, or wearing the first long evening dress. (It was as painful as the first, required as much effort as the second, and tripped me up as frequently as the third.) I looked at the number of fronds growing in a square yard of soil, tried to work out how many yards there would be in fifty acres of garden, felt dizzy, and gave up the attempt. Then the midges arrived to create a diversion and settled on me in swarms. My hostess, having finished her traps, called in her small, rather high voice with a crack of laughter in it that I had better come in before the wee beasties drove me mad.

Thankfully I followed her down to the house, and lay soaking off the travel stains in a luxurious bath for some time before I got between the sheets, fragrant with the scent of bog-myrtle, of my soft bed.

2. Tigh-an-Uillt *and Inverewe House*

I AWOKE to a great commotion of gulls on the shore beneath my bedroom window. The tide was well out, and bunches of wet weed growing on the rocks below high-water mark glowed a vivid tawny colour in the brightness of the morning. A variety of sea-birds were squabbling over small tit-bits stranded in the mud, and among them a dozen tall herons stood like statues, apparently replete and enjoying their digestive processes in the warmth of the sun. A boat was glucking on the wavelets by the stone jetty, and a cormorant sat, with its black wings 'displayed' like a heraldic charge, on the mooring buoy.

On the southern shore of the loch Poolewe's closely knit rows of little white houses, clearly reflected in the dark salmon pool below the bridge, were sending wisps of rich blue smoke into the still air, while some departing motorists fussed in and out of the hotel, intent on an early start to their day. Presently the brown-and-white mail-bus cruised gently along the road on its daily trip from Laide to Achnasheen, and halted at the gates of Inverewe to pick up the contents of our letter-box. A note pinned there by

Aunt Mairi overnight asked Colin the driver to come up to the house for my luggage, so the vehicle turned in through the gates and creaked along to the front door. Big Colin took my heaviest cases from Janet as though they were sardine tins, and stowed them inside his bus among packets of letters, milk cans, a collie pup *en route* for a new master, and a small red-haired girl with a tattered school satchel. The locked leather mail pouch from the Inverewe private box hung in state on its own hook beside the driving seat.

Janet and Colin exchanged a few pleasantries, and then he swung his long legs into the space left for them amid the cargoes, and the bus went away down the road to a farm-gate beside a deer-house ornamented with clusters of antlers, which served as a miniature lodge in front of my next home. The gardener's wife, who had been hovering there for some moments, helped Colin take my baggage into the empty half of the cottage, and the mail went on its steady way to the village. By the time this little performance ended, my watch showed a quarter to nine: time, I decided, to prepare for breakfast. With difficulty I pulled myself away from the scene to attend to the routine of dressing. Soon I was seated opposite Aunt Mairi at a round table in the ample windows of the dining-room, from which we could see an even more fascinating prospect than the narrower one I had just quitted, including a magnificent saddle-peaked ben a few miles inland.

'That mountain,' I said, 'it never keeps still!' I meant that it changed colour, and by means of shifting cloud shadows revealed different contours, every time I raised my eyes to it. She understood perfectly.

'I have seen it change for over sixty years, and this morning it looks different again. A woman came here last week to visit the gardens, and as she stood at the front door she turned and pointed and asked the name of it. "*Beinn Airidh Charr,*"[1] I told her; "it used to belong to me."

' "What a lovely thing to own!" she said.

[1] Pronounced 'Ben Erry Keyarr'.

23

'That's what *I* thought.' (And there Aunt Mairi had changed the sore subject.)

I already knew that, in order to ensure survival of the unique but expensive gardens her father, the late Osgood MacKenzie, had created (and to which her own life had been devoted), she had lately entered into negotiations with The National Trust for Scotland. The Trust being unable to accept the property unless it was heavily endowed, much of the estate was in process of being sold to release necessary funds. The conversation I have mentioned was the only direct reference to the sale of her land Aunt Mairi made to me during the following months of almost daily contact: a token of her characteristic reticence about personal troubles.

Next minute her warm, generous hospitality came into view as she pressed me to stay with her for several more nights until I'd had time to arrange all my belongings in the cottage and find my way about.

'And don't forget to ask for anything you need,' were her parting words as I went off down the drive.

My cottage, which stood some fifty yards back from the road, was constructed of large, roughly dressed stones, and had the steep-pitched roof and gabled upper windows commonly seen in the crofting counties; but unlike most croft houses it had not been whitewashed outside. The natural colour of the building stone— a faded brownish pink—blended well with the old heather, lichened rocks, and trunks of fir trees on the hill behind.

I found the key and went in, followed almost at once by Lizbie, the gardener's wife, who had been listening next door for my arrival. Already the kind soul had lit the 'Rayburn' stove in the scullery, and the tank was full of hot water. The front door opened into a small porch, with hooks and stowage for oilskins, Wellington boots and fishing-rods, and thence to the living-room. This had a delightful old Highland grate for log- or peat-burning, consisting of a raised platform on the hearth, with an arched and vaulted chimney over it; the whole was coated in spotless whitening. I remarked to Lizbie that I'd seen white door-steps before, but a white *chimney* seemed even less practical, although cheerful to look at when newly done. Sounding a little puzzled, she said they were all like that; so, not wishing to hurt her feelings, I made no more criticisms.

A small dining-room which had evidently been the kitchen at one time led through to the back of the cottage, where a lean-to scullery and a bathroom made up the rest of the ground floor. Above were one bedroom about ten feet square, and a tiny attic with a skylight. There were candlesticks in the upper rooms and a couple of oil lamps on a shelf in the scullery, but Lizbie said with pride that very soon now the 'hydro' would be coming, and then we'd be able to have cookers and fires without carrying fuel to them, and other things like irons to plug in.

She showed me the wood lodge with its neat stack of pine logs, a barrel of kindling her husband, Colin, had split ready for me, and a bundle of dry old whins and heather—good for lighting or reviving a fire, she told me, and plenty more up the brae for the carrying.

I told her that what I liked best about the cottage was the sparkling water that ran down from the hill and passed close enough to my windows for the cheerful sound to be heard indoors in every room.

'Aye, and that's how the place got its name "*Tigh-an-Uillt*",'[1] said Lizbie, 'meaning "The House by the Burn" in Gaelic.' Sighing that she must away to her work, she flitted off, but in a few moments was back again with a beautiful present of brown eggs, six in a pudding basin.

'These'll do for your tea,' she said with a shy smile, and flew home as though ashamed of her gift.

When she had gone I ran an idle finger over my boxes, and then sat down on a huge old green sofa in the living-room to get the feel of the house. Yes, it was good and friendly—quite agreeable to have me as an occupier, and free from spiteful influences or sad hangovers from previous tenants. But I became all at once fully aware of the extreme remoteness of the place. Not that I was personally isolated or friendless, but the village a mile away was

[1] Pronounced 'Tie-an-ilt'.

a mere hamlet, and it in turn six or seven miles from the larger village of Gairloch, while to the north there were hardly any houses between us and Cape Wrath. Where and how, in such a small and scattered population, did I expect to find work? Yet, without some paid part-time job, life would be difficult.

I conned over my financial position. After paying for the journey north I had probably enough money saved to keep me for a year, or perhaps longer with great care. But that nest-egg had been laid aside for rainy days and not for bread and butter when I was fit and able to work. In any case, it would not last for ever. There were only two ways to deal with a financial crisis: one, to earn more, and two, to spend less. Until something profitable turned up, I must see how little I could manage on. First I had better make a list. It went like this:

Assets	Essential Needs
Free milk	Bread
Free eggs	Butter
Free vegetables	Oatmeal
Free firewood	Cheese
	Herrings
	Sugar, tea, coffee
	Paraffin and candles
	Soap and matches

I decided to do without marmalade or jam, cake and biscuits; but to stick to butter, as substitutes spoilt everything. I would abjure meat because of the expense: no great sacrifice for me, as I'd chosen to eat in a vegetarian café during the war. Then I added to the list of needs:

Newspapers
Stamps

The last item gave me a jolt. Stamps—what about the compulsory Health Insurance? I had overlooked the fact that for years the Government Department had taken charge of the card, and that my salary had been too healthy to notice the deductions.

Now I should be responsible for the whole, and without a salary to draw upon. Well, the contributions must come from my nest-egg for the present.

Feeling rather thoughtful, I decided to put the kettle on and make a pot of tea.

The day had not developed as brightly as it began, and presently a glum-looking cloud blew up and obscured the sun. Then rain came down, and my view of loch and village was screened off, while the light inside my cottage grew dimmer and dimmer. Sitting there alone beside the cooking-stove and listening to the rattle of tiles and drumming of rain on the roof of the lean-to, I began to feel as though I had indeed arrived in the uninhabited wastes of Greenland or the North Pole, where some of my Civil Service colleagues seemed to imagine I had gone.

The picture of their faces, could they see me now, floated momentarily before me—to be quickly erased by a subject of closer interest.

Drip, drip, drip-drip, drip.

That was not the sound of water outside where it belonged, but right at hand inside my kitchen. Yes, a pool had formed on the stone floor, and a depressed spider had just got all its feet wet. I gazed up anxiously at the roof-light and received a fat drop smack in one eye. The cupboard provided an enamel mixing-bowl which, put beneath the leak, raised the pitch of the tune: *ping, ping, ping-ping, ping.*

I relaxed and poured out a large cup of good rich tea. Two sips were on their way down when the original splashy sound began again. Looking round in anger, I saw that the upper edge of the skylight had now sprung a leak and was trying in quicker tempo to catch up on the first puddle:

Drip, drippety, drip-drip-drip, drippety, drip.

This time the washing-bowl went down on the floor, and up went the pitch again. Well, at least it sounds quite conversational, I thought, and after all I *had* been feeling a bit marooned. I was about to settle to the tea once more when it occurred to me that the attic also had a roof-light. I rushed upstairs and met a stream oozing steadily across the landing. Without bothering to find the source I sped down for the largest bucket and, after swabbing the floor, put it under the leak. That should last until bedtime, however hard it rains, I told myself comfortably.

By the time I got back to my tea the basins in the scullery were half full and spluttering over every time a stream descended from above. I poured the water down the drain, followed by my cold tea, and took another cupful. Aunt Mairi had instructed me to return at one for lunch, and I was surprised to see that I had now less than an hour left.

As the rain continued to fall lustily, it seemed wise to unpack oilskins and Wellington boots, so I unlocked the old canvas kit-bag labelled 'TRINCOMALI' in white painted letters, which had once carried my tropical clothes to Ceylon, and fished out an armful of wet-weather gear. The porch looked lived-in when these were hung up. There were also two articles of furniture: a barometer registering 'Stormy' and a ship's clock, ex the yacht *Fiona*, which had stopped at ten to three.

'Stands the ship's clock at ten to three, And is there honey here for tea?' I murmured, as I wound the clock and set it to 12.30. It duly ticked, but to my amazement the sound of winding went on after I had finished turning the key. *Creek, creek, creek, creek!* It was most eerie and made my spine tingle. This can't be another water-work, surely, I thought, and examined the cottage thoroughly without tracing the sound. Every few minutes a rather cheap alarum clock was wound by someone, but the whirring seemed to come from a different direction each time.

Deciding that it must originate outside the house, I opened the front door and went forth. There was a break in the storm, and a shaft of sunlight struck the loch and shone on wet rocks at the water's edge with dazzling brilliance.

Creek, creek, creek, creek, sounding close behind me, made me swing round. There was nothing to see. Then Lizbie opened her front door, and I called out to ask if she had been winding a lot of clocks. She laughed.

'No, that will be the corncrake you heard,' she said. 'The field

28

is just full of them, but never a one can you see. Sometimes their noise goes on all night and drives me mad, for I'm an awful bad sleeper.'

So that was it. I had been fooled by an invisible bird running through the cornstalks beyond the garden wall.

At lunch I told Aunt Mairi that although my unpacking made little progress, there hadn't been a dull moment.

'You weren't out in the storm?' she inquired.

'Well, not exactly; it came in to me,' I said. So Roderick Mor, the head man, was instructed to look at the skylights as soon as the weather improved.

During the afternoon, in a sudden burst of energy, I unpacked the rest of my possessions, lit the living-room fire, walked to the village, and back with a parcel of groceries, and had arranged these in the larder before the mail bus came in at a quarter to four. It stopped beside our deer lodge, and Lizbie's small daughter got out carrying two milk pails and a newspaper along with her satchel. She tapped on my door and thrust one of the cans into my hand.

'Here'sh your milk,' she said with a bright smile. 'I'll be fetching it from the farrum every day if you like.'

I said I liked very much, if it wasn't giving her too much trouble.

'No,' she said, 'I have to go for oursh anyway, and can easily fetch yoursh at the same time.'

I gave her thanks and a sweetie and she responded with another wide smile before leaving my door for her own.

The extreme softness of the local speech sometimes led to the *sh* sound at the end of words ending in *s*, and this habit was to me (a Londoner born) absurdly reminiscent of the Cockney 'Yersh' for 'Yes'—though the slow, pure English of Ross-shire is as unlike raucous Cockney as it could possibly be.

At tea-time I told Aunt Mairi that, as her farm had already begun supplying me with milk, with the small Flora to deliver it, I had decided to move in next day. No Highlander would ever be so lacking in courtesy as to quote the old saying that 'fish and guests smell at three days old', but there used to be a subtle version of it when, at the end of the traditional hospitality of forty-eight hours (which was offered to any stranger who came), the family piper would parade at breakfast on the second morning playing *Lochiel's Farewell to his Guests.* As she possessed no piper, it was up to me to play myself out, I said. In any case, much as I loved staying with her, it would be a mistake to grow too accustomed to the life of luxury afforded by the Big House and its ample larder. She looked at me sadly.

'I can't think how you will manage down there by yourself,' she said, 'or get enough to eat. And you're so thin. Well, you must have a good tea up here with me when we come in from the garden.' As her good teas probably provided more calories than my usual daily intake at home, I felt that the food problem had been solved. Henceforth I could live on one meal (of the Inverewe sort) per day, like a pet dog.

'You could often have a rabbit for your lunch, when Roddy Beg has snares set,' went on the quiet voice, 'and venison if we get a stag or a hind. Sometimes my guests get fish: I don't have much time for fishing now. "Mac" brings himself bought fish from Gairloch every week, and would get some for you. You can order meat from Aultbea, but it's expensive. Some people have it sent by post from Glasgow.'

Aunt Mairi, I knew, had been on her feet since eight o'clock in the morning, supervising her men, cooking in the kitchen, providing light occupations for old Sheena in her fireside chair, answering telephone calls, and (when Janet was upstairs) the doorbell also. In addition she had cut and packed two large hampers of flowers to go to an Edinburgh hotel by tomorrow's bus, and weeded a stretch of rockery. Yet as soon as our high tea was finished she insisted on showing me the house.

The present house of Inverewe (completed a few years before the second world war) stands on the site of the original mansion-house built in 1864 by Lady Mary MacKenzie of Gairloch for her son Osgood. As he says in his book *A Hundred Years in the Highlands:*[1]

[1] Published by Geoffrey Bles Ltd.

In the year 1862 my mother bought for me the two adjoining estates of Inverewe and Kernsary on the west coast of Ross-shire . . . and after taking about two years to settle where we should make our home, we finally pitched upon the neck of a barren peninsula as the site of the house. I had all my life (he was about twenty) longed to begin gardening and planting . . . so my mother undertook the whole trouble of house-building and I set myself to the rest of the work.

Fifty years later the house Lady Mary built was largely destroyed by fire, while the gardens made by her son on the unpromising site endure and flourish marvellously still, and have become world-famous.

Lady Mary did not live to see the conflagration; and her son and grand-daughter (Mairi) with her first husband were away from Inverewe at the time. Luckily the leaping flames were spotted from a warship anchored in Loch Ewe, and a party of sailors rowed ashore. Hampered by lack of water and appliances, they were unable to extinguish the fire; but they did manage to bring most of the antique furniture and other family treasures out to the surrounding terraces and lawns. These were soon moved to the shelter of the one-storey lodge beside the gates, and when Osgood returned he enlarged it to make the rather straggling bungalow which became the family home for a number of years.

Aunt Mairi's father died in 1924 and her first husband nine years later; neither of their children survived infancy. Then in 1935 she married Captain Ronald Sawyer, and very soon after they arrived at Inverewe there were plans to rebuild the Big House.

As she told me this we moved slowly from the square dining-room, with its wide bay and deerskin-covered window seats inviting one to linger and admire the changing colours of loch and hill. She pointed out a cupboard below the serving-hatch, warmed by pipes from the central-heating system, in which many a late breakfaster or unpunctual fisherman had found a hot meal waiting for him.

'And where did that idea come from?' I asked.

'I just thought of it,' she modestly replied. 'And I made the architect put all these rounded corners to skirting and cornices. So much easier to clean. I had all the walls downstairs panelled in oak, to avoid fussy wallpapers or other decorations, and the floors and staircase of polished wood—no staircarpets, and only my Persian rugs for floor covering. English oak was too expensive and scarce, so we had Austrian.'

I admired the pale honey-coloured wood, while the newest kitten, a creamy-ginger one, lay on its stomach on the lowest tread of the stairs to show how well he harmonized with it. Dining- and smoking-rooms both opened into a big lounge hall, from which the staircase with its wide treads and shallow risers mounted easily to the bedroom floor. Embrasures and window ledges all held copper pans full of rhododendrons and leaves of eucalyptus, whose fragrance mingled with that of the peats burning on the open hearths. This characteristic scent, permeating every cranny in the house, became one of my most enduring memories of Inverewe.

We stayed to look at Osgood MacKenzie's portrait in oils above the fireplace in the lounge hall, and it seemed as though the keen eyes, aquiline nose, and patriarchal beard, framed in Mac-Kenzie plaid and topped by crested bonnet, epitomized all that was finest in the Highland laird of the old school.

'My father and I always spoke the Gaelic to each other as well as to the men,' said Aunt Mairi. 'I spoke nothing else until I was seven. Then he said I must learn English, and I wept.'

Below her father's picture stood a modern photograph—that of her late husband, Ronald Sawyer.

'Did he speak Gaelic too?' I asked.

'Oh, no! I remember, soon after we were married, he was supervising some rockery work I wanted the gardeners to build.

'I came up behind them and heard one of the men say to another in Gaelic, "It will look hideous, of course, but he's English and I suppose we had better do as he says." Ronald was none the wiser!

'Well, now, you've seen the kitchen already,' she said. 'I

32

thought that the most important part, so planned it first and built the rest of the house round it. I was determined to have a big one, with plenty of storerooms and larders, for we meant to entertain a lot here. But almost as soon as it was finished the war started and upset everything.

'Ronald became the Regional Controller in Inverness and I stayed here to keep the gardens going as best I could. Ronald was terribly overworked, and just as the war ended he got very ill and died. Well, I had every happiness during those years with him: that's far more than many people have to look back upon.'

She settled herself into a large blue armchair in the smoking-room and applied bellows to a smouldering heap of logs on the hearth. Presently there was a soft knock on the door and red-haired Janet came in. She stared at us glumly.

'The Bands are on,' she said with reproach.

Aunt Mairi laughed and turned on her wireless set so that the kitchen loudspeaker could deliver the latest instalment of Scottish dance music.

When it was done Janet appeared again—with a parcel under one arm and the usual pleasant expression on her face

'Will I show you my dress for the dance?' she asked. We assented, and a charming conception in cyclamen-pink organza was withdrawn from its tissues.

'It's lovely! Where *did* you get it, Janet?' crooned her mistress.

'From Harvey and Nichols', said the girl, rosy with pleasure.

When the door had closed behind her, Aunt Mairi said, 'She has never been to London in her life, but she gets my catalogues and sends for things by post.'

Janet presently made a third entry, this time with a tray of cocoa and biscuits, and announced that she was away to her bed early—so as to be fresh for the late dance night at Gairloch tomorrow. I was not long in following her example; but Aunt Mairi said with a sigh that she must attend to a huge pile of correspondence. I roused as a clock somewhere in the house struck twelve, and heard her coming slowly upstairs to bed.

3. Inverewe Gardens

It is surprising how much personality a house develops if you live in it alone. At least, the personality may have been there all the time, but it retires into obscurity when human or even animal companions are present, and emerges directly they have gone.

Tigh-an-Uillt had a strong but kindly character, and seemed to reflect the spaciousness of mountains and sea around it. Except for the shelter it afforded from rain and wind there was very little difference in feeling between being outside and in. Small though the rooms were, I think one could have borne confinement by illness or injury within its walls for weeks without any sensation of cramp. Yet I have stayed in a forty-roomed palazzo in Italy, complete with grand marble staircase and painted ceilings, and felt like a caged canary. Evidently character, rather than size, counts in buildings as much as in people.

I soon found that amplitude of both time and space was to be the dominant novelty of my new life. No one ever seemed to hurry or worry about time, and there was so much room everywhere that nobody showed the slightest inclination to push and shove.

Somewhere in the fens of eastern England there is an inn bearing the following legend:

FIVE MILES FROM ANYWHERE—
THE NO HURRY.

Inverewe might have been labelled:

A HUNDRED MILES FROM ANYWHERE—
HURRY UNKNOWN.

Nor was there any noise. Even children at play raised their voices very little; adults conversed in what sounded to me like whispers until I grew accustomed to their soft, muted voices. There was only sparse motor traffic, and aeroplanes were such rare birds that all heads went up if one approached.

After my first morning's residence in the cottage I went along the shore to the Big House and walked round the gardens with their owner. We started in the walled garden, which Colin (my next-door neighbour) had presided over for many years. Small, lean, and merry-eyed, he gave me a charming smile and said it was a fine day. I assented, though privately considering it a rather poor one, with blustery wind and sharp showers. In time I learned that on the west coast any day on which you could stand upright against the wind and do without oilskins was described as 'fine'. The other sort were discarded as being unfit subjects for conversation.

Aunt Mairi presently pointed to a quantity of groundsel seedlings which flourished in one of the beds.

'I weeded the next one myself,' she said.

'Yes,' said Colin with severity, 'and it doesn't do to leave the pulled groundsel about. The seed spreads on the wind and covers the whole garden.'

'That's what I was thinking,' said Aunt Mairi, eyeing the

expanse still happily growing and blowing. No more was said, and we passed on.

'How naughty they are. . . .' She sighed (with an indulgent smile) when we were out of the gardener's sight. 'Imagine letting all that groundsel seed, and then scolding me for leaving a few heaps on the path for the boy to clear up! But he is a dear little man, and has been with us forty years.'

We wandered slowly along this path, sniffing at a bee-laden hedge of sweet-peas and snipping dead roses from the bushes. I remarked on the lusty growth of raspberry canes in a long bed beneath the water-side wall.

'Yes,' said Aunt Mairi, 'they are almost back to their old form now. Last year they were bad: yellow and poor from being mulched with seaweed that was too fresh. We get beautiful raspberries when they are properly fed.'

She told me that this part of the garden had been an old sea-beach, and when her father began his work he found it composed of three parts pebbles and one part rather nice black earth. The millions of pebbles had to be got rid of, so in deep-trenching it forks were mostly used, and every man had a girl or boy opposite him to handpick the pebbles—much as though they were gathering a heavy crop of potatoes.

The cost of the work was great, even in those days of low wages, as thousands of barrow-loads of stones had to be wheeled into the sea, and the place of the pebbles made up with endless cartloads of peaty stuff from old dykes, red soil carted from long distances, and a kind of blue clay marl from below the sea (full of decayed oyster-shells and crabs and other good things), hauled up at very low tides.

The terrace where Colin's vegetables now flourished had been cut out of the face of the steep brae which originally flanked the beach. It had been carved from solid gravel and covered with soil brought from afar. Beyond the terrace the cutting was fully twelve feet deep, and Osgood had built the retaining wall (on the seaward side of the drive) which now bore fan- and cordon-trained fruit trees.

When the cutting was first made, the men found a number of large holes or burrows going deep into the hillside. These must have been inhabited long ago by a colony of badgers, and no sooner was the light let into the galleries than up came a collection of raspberry seedlings. Evidently badgers, like bears, are keen on fruit and had made their dessert off wild raspberries, and digestion of these had not prevented the seeds from germinating eventually.

There were no signs of wild raspberries growing above ground at Inverewe at the time; but the sight of these seedlings encouraged Osgood MacKenzie to think that where wild rasps used to grow, tame ones could be cultivated with success. His expectations were fully justified.

Other things he planted could have had no precursors in that northern land. Australian club palms (*Cordyline*) which have grown to some twenty feet in height, and the queer scarlet bottle-brush like something from an Ideal Home exhibition; Kaffir lilies from Natal, wandflowers, agapanthus and Watsonias from the Cape, were but a few of the strangers that thrived and increased as fast as couch grass in their new climate of mist and rain and in a soil of peat.

We went through a wrought-iron gate in the west wall of the kitchen garden, and found there in a sheltered gully between wall and a high rocky bank a great clump of the giant forget-me-not (*Myosotidium nobile*), prospering far from its native home in the Chatham Islands off the east coast of New Zealand.

Aunt Mairi stood looking at them while telling me how, twenty years earlier, someone had given her two diminutive plants which for a long time had clung to life without making any growth. One day she read in *The Times* an article by a sailor who had recently landed in the Chatham Islands. He related how he had been amazed to see growing on the shore, amongst rotten seaweed and the carcases of sharks, plants with large vivid green leaves and huge heads of gentian blue forget-me-not flowers.

'I realized that this must be none other than *Myosotidium nobile*,' she said, 'and quickly put a good mulch of seaweed round my little starvelings. I had no dead sharks, but when the tide ebbed I collected pailfuls of herring fry off the shore and gave them an ample top dressing. Almost immediately the plants shot up, and when next season the first of these wonderful blooms appeared I was very glad indeed that I had read the article. Now they even seed themselves quite naturally, and I have replanted groups of them in the woodland gardens.'

Looking up the rocky bank I could see on the top a row of tall agave-like plants with spires of bloom on stalks as thick as broom handles. Aunt Mairi said it was the New Zealand flax plant (*Phormium tenax*) and had made visiting soldiers from New Zealand, who were stationed in Gairloch district during the 1939–45 war, very excited and home-sick. One said: 'That is what the Maoris call *Toe Toe*; and taking out his pocket knife he quickly shaped one of the huge leathery leaves into a dart and sent it skimming across the garden and out to sea. In New Zealand they make binder twine from the tough fibres of the plant, he said.

An unexpected response to this story came from the loch, whose waters at high tide were sucking audibly but out of sight behind the southern wall.

'*Oo-ooh!*' said a voice, and '*oo-ooh, oo-ooh!*' echoed a second and a third.

'Who in the world is that?' I asked, facing about with a jump; 'not another corncrake, surely?'

'Eider duck. I noticed a whole raft in front of the house this morning. They have babies with them too,' said my companion. 'Listen!'

The eiders sounded uncannily human, just like a collection of little old ladies expressing surprise and concern at some rather shocking incident. They shared with the corncrakes a ventriloquist's knack of throwing their voices to make them sound closer than they really were.

I ran down some rocky steps and through a small gate which led to the shore. The raft was perhaps twenty yards out; the drakes large and very striking in their harlequin plumage of black and white, the ducks a sober brown with black bars, and the little ones a dun-coloured row of midgets following the adults in single file.

At first they were silent, swimming parallel with the shore and eyeing me suspiciously, but presently one spoke softly, and I answered it with the best imitation I could make. Several of the birds responded, and they all came eagerly towards me, their beady eyes bright with curiosity. They very quickly realized that I was a fraud, and swung round and took themselves off; but not before I had had a good close-up view of them.

The eider differs from all other ducks in being completely a sea-bird. It does not even visit the freshwater lochs which so often lie a few yards inland from the sea on the west coast of Scotland. It suffers no privation in winter when marsh and lochs are frozen, for it rests and feeds in the open sea.

It does not migrate, and usually stays within a few miles of its breeding ground. It is common in small numbers in northern Scotland, but the really large colonies are found in Arctic regions, and in Iceland, Scandinavia, and Labrador. The duck lays from five to seven eggs in a nest on the ground lined with weed and moss, and plucks the famous 'eiderdown' from her breast to cover her eggs and keep them warm when she goes off in search of food.

Aunt Mairi said that a fisherman friend who had visited a big nesting site in Iceland, where the down was collected regularly for the trade, told her that when a nest was robbed of its down the duck would return and pluck herself again, but if the down were removed a second time she had no more to give, and would desert the nest.

While listening to this with lively interest, I suddenly remembered aloud that I had come to Inverewe to garden.

'There's no hurry for that,' she said. 'You must see everything first and learn your way about.'

'I've seen the groundsel,' I murmured; 'wouldn't you like me to clear it off at once?'

Aunt Mairi looked thoughtful. 'Perhaps not,' she replied slowly. 'Poor Colin is overworked and I wish I could afford another

39

man to help him. But he might not like you encroaching on his domain. I told the men you were coming to prevent me from getting over-tired, and they don't mind that. But they may not want you to help with their jobs. Most of them have been here for years and years and look upon Inverewe as their own. They are wonderfully loyal and I couldn't carry on here without them.'

I said I quite understood and would do exactly as she said. We moved on together as we talked, and a sudden bright spell of sunshine tempted us to sit down on a smooth boulder at the foot of the rockery below the main terrace on which the house stood. The pockets of this rock garden, which had been constructed from the stone of the original mansion, were full of treasures. Aunt Mairi said that her friend of the Aviemore alpine nursery sent her many to try out. Unfortunately the most charming had to bear the uncouth name of *Rhodohypoxis Baurii*; this she first saw growing in the Drakensberg mountains of Natal in lovely masses of cherry and white blossom, when touring Africa with her father.

A cabbage palm and a blue gum tree[1] cast some shade on us, and dropped more substantial things from time to time, for the grass beneath them was littered with rolls of eucalyptus bark and the shabby discarded 'palm' leaves. The tree I admired most was growing a little farther west: a fine Monterey pine (*Pinus insignis*) down on the shore.

This had, one imagined, taken root where it had been set, but managed to give the impression of having crept forward unobserved to watch over the motor launch with its dinghy and boathouse, and the weary old hulk permanently careened in mud near the landing jetty, its day done and work at an end. Aunt Mairi said that in California also the Monterey pine loves to have its 'toes' in salt water.

We climbed the steps, and I was looking up at the grove of big trees beyond the rockery on the western edge of the lawn—marvelling first at the height (98 feet) of the tallest eucalyptus, and then at the story of how the finest Douglas fir had arrived at

[1] The cabbage palm (*Cordyline australis*) was destroyed in a winter gale, 1956. The gum tree, although damaged, was still living in 1958.

Inverewe ninety years earlier *by letter post*, when a movement among the rhododendrons at the foot of the trees caught my attention.

Presently the delicately modelled head and large, sad eyes of a miniature deer came into view as it peeped at us from the shadow of a bush. I was fascinated by the creature's fine-spun beauty, and afraid to breathe lest it took fright. My companion did not share this rapture.

'A roe!' she exclaimed. 'Bother! They get round the wires fencing the policies and into the gardens at low tide, and chew up my best plants. I must go at once to tell Roderick (her head man and stalker) to fetch his gun.'

The thought that she might be responsible for the slaughter of so charming a creature hit me like a crack from a cudgel, and I ran forward to the roe's hiding-place in the hope of driving it away to safety. But bracken and bushes were dense beneath the trees, and I caught no glimpse of it. Nor, I afterwards learned, did the man with his gun.

I wandered off through the woodlands, in a paradise that had suddenly lost its glory and become soiled. Yet, as the first emotions of disgust with ourselves and pity for the threatened animal calmed down, I saw that none of the floral wonders of Inverewe could have survived if every wild creature bred in the surrounding hills had been allowed to subsist on them. Everything practicable had been done to bar them out, and the few who persisted in poaching must take the consequences. But reason was powerless to banish completely my feeling of shame at the prospect of killing so gentle and lovely a thing.

During these pangs I had gradually descended to a spot where the grassy walk opened out to a level grove of birches and thence to a sea-beach. Here on the edge of the shore stood a chicken-house, open to the warm sun (which had come forth again) and shut well away from wind by the high rocky cliff and the woods I had wandered through. A collection of Rhode Island hens were systematically turning over the rigs of weed left by the now ebbing tide, while their adolescent young pushed each other around in a sand-bath. From the peak of the hen-house a curious object was suspended, and I went close to see what it could be.

I found a fat, furry tail, about fifteen inches long, of a snuff-brown colour patterned with blurred rings of rusty black. This puzzled me extremely. It looked more like the brush of a half-Persian cat than anything else, but even the shock of realizing that roe-deer at Inverewe were regarded as vermin could not bring me to believe that the domestic puss was hunted as well.

Aunt Mairi, who had spied me from the cliff top, soon came down to the shore and put me wise. No purring hearth-rug pet this, but a fierce wild-cat off the hill, which had been wreaking havoc in the poultry yard. One night a trap was cunningly hidden by the men, and *Felis sylvestris* met his doom. The tail hung on the hen-house as a warning to others, but his huge body had been prudently put to other uses.

'I buried it beneath an anaemic young eucalyptus,' she said. 'Some time ago I did the same thing with another wild-cat carcase, making a grave in autumn under a *Buddleia asiatica* which had ceased to bloom and was three parts dead. The effect was electric, and the following year it bore a profusion of blooms and has never looked back since.'

Saying that she must now see what Roddy Donn was doing to the Cuddy Rock path, Aunt Mairi went away through the birch trees and past some great bastions of bamboo, over the burn that drained the water-garden, and up above *Camas Glas* to the most westerly point of the peninsula. Here the path grew very narrow and rough underfoot, and we found Roddy Donn at work widening and levelling it. He stood up as we approached and looked at his mistress for approval. She spoke to him in Gaelic and he replied in the same tongue.

'*Oo ay weshy cruer argus shell arler.*'

'*Argus shell arler, weshy cruer,*' is roughly how their remarks sounded to me.

We passed along the rocky tip of the land and climbed down to the water's edge, leaving Roddy to his task of burning the boughs he had trimmed away from the sides of the path.

'Roddy never reads anything except his Gaelic Bible—not even a newspaper,' said Aunt Mairi. 'One day I couldn't make him understand how I wanted something done, so I brought out a gardening paper with an illustration in it. Roddy stared at the picture for some time without a word, and presently another man joined us and peered over his shoulder at the book. 'The *writing* in it is the other way up, Roddy,' he said very gently. So the paper was turned round, but I don't think it made much difference to him. He is simply unused to seeing things in print.

'He is wonderfully wise about natural history, though, and the weather, and has a splendid memory. They say he knows every sheep in the parish of Gairloch by sight. When there are disputes about ownership of ewes which have strayed and escaped the branding, Roddy is always called in to arbitrate, and his decision is accepted by everyone concerned. He is the one who works most with me on the shrubberies, and has been here for over forty years.'

Cuddy Rock—so named because it used to be a good stance from which to hook the coalfish—had been one of her favourite hide-outs in childhood. She said her governess would often toil down from the house to fetch her in to do her lessons. Asked if she disliked her governess as much as we had hated our elderly one, she said no, this governess had been youngish and interested in gardening. In fact she had helped to plant Mairi's very first rhododendrons, on an island in the lochan opposite another home of the family—the house of Tournaig, a mile or two north of Inverewe.

'And how old were you when you started gardening?' I asked.

'Just ten. A long, long time ago; the island is now completely covered in rhodos.'

And with that we went back past Roddy Donn and his sweet-smelling fire to the even more delicious fragrance of the house, and to a lavish high tea I had not earned, but for which the sea and mountain air had me very well prepared.

4. *Weekdays and Sundays*

I HAD arrived at Inverewe on a Wednesday, and on Saturday did my first afternoon's work in the gardens. As it was a half day the men went off duty at noon, so Aunt Mairi and I had the whole fifty-acre enclosure to ourselves. So far as gardeners went, that is; for at that time visitors were admitted at any hour on weekdays, if they made a contribution to the Nurses' Fund.

We pottered happily down to the greenhouses, which were built inside the walled fruit and vegetable garden. I was amused to see that the handsome purple-pink passion flower which rioted in one of the houses had managed to squeeze one shoot through a crack in the glass and to scramble over the roof, where it bloomed just as well outside as in. We loitered round, sniffing carnations, looking to see how many peaches had set, pinching out tomatoes, pricking seedlings into pans, and watering anything that seemed in need.

Both of us cast frequent glances at the weather, at a pair of great northern divers who were busy in the loch immediately below us and made me think of waterlogged boats because they floated so low in the water, and at the Saturday afternoon traffic on the road. Aunt Mairi would say: 'There goes Colin away to the village'; or 'Who can that be, coming this way on a flashing new bicycle?'; or 'Mac' (the farmer) 'is very late with his cows this afternoon.' Most of the cars and vans she recognized at once, but when the odd unknown one hove in sight it was a matter for interesting speculation.

At about half past three the great moment of Poolewe's day came with the arrival of the mail bus in the village. It halted at the post-office, its cream and brown bulk showing up plainly although it must have been over half a mile away in a direct line across the loch. By road it was just one mile. There was a lengthy pause ('While the Inverewe mail is sorted,' said Aunt Mairi), and then the bus came on steadily round the shore, stopping at the farm to set down empty milk pails from Slatadale and Gairloch and collect supplies for Aultbea and Laide. As Flora was not in school on Saturday there was no need to stop at the cottage, and Inverewe came next.

Fetching the mail from a little green sentry-box outside the gates was usually Janet's job, but as she had gone to *Tigh-an-Uillt* to have tea with Colin and Lizbie (her father and stepmother), I met the bus instead. At first I thought the driver had grown since Thursday morning, but soon realized that this larger edition of 'Colin the Mail' must be his brother Arthur, of whom I had already heard. I took our mail bag from the box where he had just put it, and turned to wave goodbye, when Arthur appeared from behind the bus with a large parcel for us. At least, I supposed him to be Arthur, although he now seemed thinner and more like Colin. Then I saw the real Arthur bringing a wad of newspapers from the front of the bus, and it was plain that the brothers were on the job together.

The soft voice and courteous, gentle manner, fine features and physique which I had admired in Colin a few days earlier were now duplicated, and I found the combined charms of the two brothers quite overwhelming. They were bareheaded and dressed alike in neat blue suits, and had such natural dignity that one felt,

45

if they had suddenly been asked to take their seats in the House of Lords, they could have done so with as much ease and success as they handled the laden bus in all weathers on that narrow mountain road.

I said something of this to Aunt Mairi on my return to the greenhouse—adding that surely no other part of the world could produce such outstanding characters as the remote villages here in the north, and that these two men in particular were grand examples of their race. She at once fizzed up with merriment, and I grew huffy and shocked by her levity about a subject on which my feelings were deep. Quickly she pacified me by explaining that she also had a great liking and admiration for the men, but my description of them as *typical Highlanders* amused her because they happened to be two of the very few people on that coast who were not pure-bred. Their mother was a native of Somerset, and her story an interesting one as related by Aunt Mairi.

In her younger days some spirit of adventure had brought her north to the Island of Skye, where she took service as lady's maid to MacLeod of MacLeod's wife in the castle of Dunvegan. After a little while she left the castle and went to work in a small hotel on the coast of Ross-shire, a few miles beyond Inverewe. Here the future father of Colin and Arthur used to see her when delivering mail; for he was a postman and in those days had to go his rounds on foot. (Many a rest he would have had in the hotel kitchen, no doubt.) He could not speak one word of English, nor she of Gaelic; but notwithstanding this little handicap they became engaged and were married.

Everyone thought the southerner would be defeated by the hard toil on the croft, but in this they were proved wrong. She soon learned to cook girdle scones and gut herring as well as or better than her neighbours, and to help with the potatoes and the peat-cutting as though she had been born to it. She had three fine sons (the third became a policeman in Edinburgh) and one daughter, and was now enjoying a sprightly old age, none the worse for her life of hard work and plain living far from the fields and woods of Somerset. She was a native of Frome, of which place she often spoke with great affection, although she hadn't been back in nearly fifty years.

Not long after the mail had passed we heard the sound of a car pulling up at the gates, and then the slam of doors and several voices. Aunt Mairi was busy with seedlings, and saying that my hands were cleaner than hers, asked me to go and see what these people wanted. I found two men and three women, Londoners on tour, who had heard about the gardens in the Kinlochewe hotel and sought permission to explore them. I walked down to the Big House with the visitors, so as to put their donations into the Nurses' Box and their names in the book, and to tell old Sheena that I had admitted them.

On the way I answered questions about plants and trees and the gardens in general, as well as I was able. Presently one of the men addressed me as 'Mrs. Sawyer', and I was startled to find that my halting ignorance had been taken for expert knowledge. When I confessed to the real owner that I had been tempted for fun to let the misconception continue and to act as guide to the whole garden, murmuring names such as '*Impetigo rubra irritans*' when gaps in my botany had to be filled in, she exclaimed: 'I wish you had! Why didn't you?'

As I was wearing a MacLeod kilt at the time, the impersonation of a MacKenzie would have been piquant; although to the English visitors our clan tartans and old feuds doubtless meant nothing.

Aunt Mairi told me how, reversing the positions, she had sometimes been mistaken for a gardener, and even offered tips. One dear old lady hovered around watching her at work for some time before finding the nerve to address her. Then she blurted out unexpectedly, 'Excuse me, but are you the head gardener, or just one of the under ones?'

'Just one of the under ones,' said Aunt Mairi, sticking out her underlip in a thoroughly dejected manner and stooping again to her toil.

We had tea in the kitchen, and with a sly glance at her old

friend the housekeeper, my host said that Sheena had laid it in specially grand style for my benefit. I looked inquiring, so she explained that the jams had been put out in glass dishes. 'When I'm alone with her we dip into the pots.'

Sheena muttered something in Gaelic which was not translated to me. Then she said in English: 'Yon women from London walked all over the lawns making holes in the grass. Their shoes had little sharp heels on them like lace-bobbins.'

Aunt Mairi said we intended dosing the plantain and thistles in the lawns with poison after tea, and perhaps Sheena would like to walk round with a bag of soil and spoon it into the heel pits.

'No, I would not,' said Sheena. 'I'm going to sit at the window and watch you being eaten with the midges.'

We braved the swarms for half an hour, and were then driven in to join Sheena on the window seat, where we sat silently putting salve on our bumps and watching the hills turn orange, pink, and finally a theatrical violet-purple as the sun went down behind the Outer Hebrides.

Most of my work during the week that followed consisted of pulling up bracken, annual weeds, and thousands of self-sown wild rhododendron seedlings, all of which went on the bonfire. But I had to be careful and well informed, because here and there the 'good' rhodos had seeded also, and these were carefully cherished. Even if we did not use them ourselves to plant fresh areas of woodland, there were plenty of folk along the coast who would be glad to have them. Of course nobody wanted the *ponticums*, which grew wild outside the gardens as well as in.

During the war, when volunteer gangs of soldiers and sailors used to help with the work, there was a system in which the wanted seedlings were marked by bamboos, or by little white rags tied to their stems, to indicate to the unskilled labour that these were not to be pulled up. Here and there I found flapping remnants of the rag markers—looking rather like the Buddhist prayer-flags I had seen in Ceylon. Such aids were not supplied for me, but I soon learned to distinguish between the sheep and goats without trouble.

The flowering season of the parent bushes was drawing to a close; the many varieties at Inverewe have a spread-over blossom time of six or seven months, between December (*nobleanum*) and July (*Fabia*), and now at the end of June there were only a few bursts of rhododendron flowers gleaming among the trees.

I loved best to work alone deep in the wooded glens, where the mingled scents of warm, moist peaty soil, pine trees, eucalyptus and the salt sea breezes were trapped and concentrated. All sorts of small birds, quite unafraid, peeped and twittered at me while I weeded, and above me on the brae a turtle dove crooned in domestic bliss incessantly. The mixture of broad-leaved vegetation with the pines made a good environment for insect and bird life, and there was none of the sterile, sad emptiness one so often finds in plantations of conifers alone.

From several of the glens I could hear wavelets rickling on the stones of the shore, and always there were the cries of sea-birds to bring to mind the stormy Minch and the open Atlantic not many miles away. Sometimes I would feel myself, after a solitary spell amid the trees, on the verge of losing human identity and becoming part of the wild life around me, so that it required an effort to disentangle my threads and run down to the house when I heard the horn blown for tea.

Sunday in Wester Ross really is a day of rest, and Gairloch (stronghold of the Free Kirk, whose members are sometimes known as 'Wee Frees') must send nearly a hundred per cent of its physically fit population to church. Indeed, the Sunday population of the various churches—Episcopalian, Presbyterian and Free—*seems* in the aggregate to be larger than the weekday village one! But, except for essential journeys to and from the kirk, people do not usually go out on the sabbath. Few go to visit relations or for country walks or picnics as they do further south. That is, the natives are seldom seen on such expeditions; for the hotel visitors bring their own customs with them, and the local folk are on the whole very tolerant and charitable towards these.

At Inverewe the home farm cows had to be milked, of course, but as none of the consumers would fetch their pails the farmer brought the whole day's yield to the Big House, and we were able to make ample supplies of butter and cream from the gallons which arrived in the dairy on Sundays.

Many people in Poolewe were addicted to what they called 'a long lie' on Sunday morning, and their homes were clearly marked (and also the length of the lie) by the tardy appearance of smoke from their cottage chimneys. Some families went in a body to morning service at noon, while other divided up, mother and any daughters going in the morning only, and father and sons in the evening, with possibly a reversal the following week.

According to Aunt Mairi, it was customary in these households for the evening church attenders to stay in bed until the afternoon, and when they rose the morning party took to their beds. This was not due to laziness so much as a desire to escape the temptation to do things on the day of rest. If the weather was uninviting I sometimes followed the example, but if the sun shone I considered it would do no harm to go out and enjoy it.

At *Tigh-an-Uillt* I was careful to make the minimum of noise and to keep my radio turned down, for my neighbours might have been distressed to share a house with a sabbath-breaker. Lizbie was a staunch adherent of the old ways, and brought up her own child to strict sabbath rules. Her stepdaughter Janet, no doubt influenced by her experiences at Inverewe and the freer attitudes there of hostess and guests, saw no harm in Sunday walks and boldly promenaded, dressed in her best clothes, with any kindred spirits she could muster. It was a little sad to see Flora's face pressed against the closed parlour window as she watched the older girls enjoying the sunshine and fresh air.

Aunt Mairi was careful not to offend local feeling. She had a letter one day from the secretary of a large horticultural society in southern Scotland, saying that two coachloads of members of their Tomato Growers' Association would like to visit Inverewe on the last Sunday in August, and would she kindly allow them to see her gardens. She got me to type a letter in which she said that she would be delighted to welcome the Tomato Growers if they came on any other day of the week.

The secretary replied that the members were unable to make the long journey on weekdays, because they were all professional growers and couldn't leave their tomatoes except on Sundays. So I had to write back saying that while we much regretted being unable to allow parties into the gardens on the sabbath, any such excursion would cause distress to the Inverewe gardeners and could not be permitted.

During the war the Germans managed to break the sabbath— although fortunately they damaged nothing else. Sheena told me how, one fine Sunday afternoon, she had looked out of her bedroom window and noticed a column of smoke rising from the Cuddy Rock, which made her exclaim indignantly that someone had lit a bonfire—some trespassing picnic party landed by boat, perhaps. The fire was investigated, and turned out to be the result of incendiary bombs scattered by a hit-and-run plane which the residents hadn't even noticed. This was Inverewe's only attack of the war.

On my second Sunday Aunt Mairi, who had a rare spell of freedom from visitors, suggested a picnic on the sea-shore. Old Sheena helped to put a lunch basket ready, and waved us off before the church-goers appeared on our road. Saying that she would introduce me to her favourite beach, Aunt Mairi turned the car northwards as we left the drive gates. We skimmed up a hill bordered on each side by the wooded Inverewe policies, and at the top left the boundary fence behind and came to a bare windy moor covered in a jumble of boulders and the stumps and derelict aftermath of timber felling.

We slowed down to see the house of Tournaig, an uninspired building on a fine site, with Loch Tournaig before it, and beyond to the south-east the precipitous northern face of *Beinn Airidh Charr*. I was shown the island in a lochan on the opposite side of the road, where Aunt Mairi's first plantation of rhododendrons still flourished.

The property had been sold a year or two earlier, and was now used only as a holiday haunt by some people from England.

51

'The garden was so nice when we lived there,' said Aunt Mairi, 'but is now in a sad state. I hate to see it unkempt. Thank goodness Inverewe will not look like that when I go.'

The thought of her 'going' was happily a far-off occurrence which need not trouble us, I said cheerfully; and even when she murmured that I was mistaken it made little impression at the time. Afterwards I remembered the conversation with great sadness, but on that lovely day it was impossible to be gloomy and we both gave ourselves to the sun without further thought of shadows to come.

The sandy beach at the end of the rough turning we had taken faced northward across the wide stretch of Gruinard Bay to the Summer Isles and the Sutherland hills, whose strange isolated shapes floated clear and pale above a thin wisp of haze which blurred the outline of Achiltibuie's little fields and croft-houses on the opposite shore. The west of Scotland is said to have an island for every day of the year, but I should not be surprised if it had several, for Gruinard Bay alone must have in sight a score, if the smaller skerries are counted.

The Summer Isles, where Fraser Darling and his wife Bobbie reclaimed a derelict croft on *Tanera Móró* in the nineteen-forties, appeared to us like a clotted mass of rock lying low in a brilliant sea. With its streaks of turquoise, emerald, ultramarine and deep purple, I thought I had never seen such bright enamel-like colour in water before—not even in Italy or on the French Riviera. The fine white sand of the sea-bed probably has something to do with it, and also the purity of the atmosphere, but such diamond-cut splendour eludes explanation or description in words.

We ran the car off the track on to a gentle slope of grass where black-face ewes graze and a scatter of hens and ducks foraged busily. Three or four white houses, with slated roofs, and a derelict school were built along the upper edge of this 'village green', and a few feet below it lay the sandy shore. I spotted a familiar brown and cream shape in the shadow of the school wall: the Achnasheen mail having a Sunday rest from its weekday run through the mountains. Aunt Mairi told me that Arthur lived with his family in the adjoining house; but today there was no sign of inhabitants, and the shore, to which we soon made our way on foot, seemed deserted.

A little burn, swirling through the rocks on the last lap of its journey from the high boggy land between us and Inverewe, made us pause to pull off shoes and stockings before wading the chill water to our chosen pitch of firm sand beneath a flowery bank. There we lay for some time, side by side and flat on our backs, without speaking.

Wild bees were busy in the flowers of the machair behind us, and their steady buzzing mingled with the sharp *'bi glic, bi glic!'*[1] of the oyster-catchers down at the sea's edge. There were many gulls and terns about, and a stolid cormorant squatting on a smooth grey rock shaped like a seal. From a field of oats above the southern cliff came the familiar *creek, creek, creek* of corncrakes. The sea was so calm and transparent that it was hard to tell where dry sand ended and water began.

Presently we heard distant voices, and a family of holiday-makers arrived at the far end of the wide strand, followed by a Cairn terrier which, when its owners sat down, trotted off alone to investigate the shore. It was evidently quite young, and soon began to toss a dead crab it had found under tide-cast weed. Presently in play the pup rushed downwards into the sea and found itself splashing in water which deepened so quickly on the shelving beach that the little beast had to swim for it. It came out looking very surprised, but after a run and a shake appeared to consider that bathing was good sport, and paddled gaily into the water for another and longer swim.

We wished we had brought bathing gear so that we might follow, but Aunt Mairi said just to lie flat on the ground refreshed and rested her almost more, as though vibrations from the earth passed into her body and revitalized it. I thought of the un-ceasing daily activity of her life, and reflected that, although the word 'old' was unthinkable in connection with so much vigour,

[1] Gaelic for 'be wise!'.

53

she had in fact far exceeded the middle years with which people not in the secret usually credited her. That golden Sunday on the beach at Mellon remained the only occasion on which I saw her completely relaxed and idle for any length of time during daylight hours.

5. Fishing—for Work

A PAIR of visitors were sitting on the lawn at Inverewe when we returned. They had driven over from Gairloch in a jeep with the wife's sketching gear, and finding that we were out she had set to work in the trust that Aunt Mairi's approval wouldn't be withheld. We admired the drawings and took the couple in to tea with us, which they enjoyed to the full. Kirstie was an enthusiast, and talked with animation of their work and plans. Her husband had thrown up a good job after the war in order to be his own master, and with his Service gratuity bought land and constructed (largely with his own expert hands) a bungalow and a showroom and weaving-shed on the Strath at Gairloch. Here they were busy making and selling handwoven tweed and other woollen goods.

Kirstie had graduated from a London art college, and her husband was a trained craftsman from Glasgow. With a son and two young daughters, a breeding Cairn bitch, some goats, cats, and assorted poultry their small house and parcel of land were stretched at the seams, like their bank account; but they were a cheerful family, in love with their surroundings and the life they had chosen, and determined to make a go of their venture.

When Kirstie heard that I also had defied the good advice of family and friends and thrown over safety for the life at Inverewe, her fellow-feeling was at once aroused; both she and the more silent husband looked sympathetically in my direction.

'Well, now, we must see what can be done to get you a job!' said Kirstie briskly, with a gay good-bye to me. As they turned to go, Aunt Mairi remembered a length of tweed she had got in Inverness on the day I arrived, and summoned the guests to see it. The parcel was unwrapped and the pair bent over the cloth in silence.

'Do you like it?' asked Aunt Mairi. Kirstie smiled up at her with an expression of delighted approval, and then said: 'Well, no!'

Her frankness startled me, but Aunt Mairi placidly rolled the material in its paper with the comment that perhaps she ought not to wear so bright a blue now. After they had gone she said she thought Kirstie very nice, and so sincere—but did not find the husband easy to know. He seemed rather shy, and, 'When two shy people get together, the result isn't so good.'

I said that having married so forthcoming a wife he had probably no intention of coming out of the shell wherein he dwelt quite happily.

'How I wish I could stay in mine,' Aunt Mairi said, 'but I'm not *allowed* to.'

It occurred to me that when Inverewe was formally handed over to The National Trust for Scotland there might be even more publicity and less opportunity of becoming shell-bound than she realized; but for the present the gardens retained their private character and I kept my thoughts to myself.

Because we had eaten scones and cake with the visitors at four o'clock instead of our usual high tea, I was bidden to stay to supper. I asked if I could have a bath first, as I was suffering from sand between the toes—and went away to the bathroom I had used before. With a big soft bathsheet hanging on the heated rail

I prepared for a pleasant twenty minutes as I turned on both taps. The bath was about a third full when the cold supply stopped of its own accord, while the faucet gurgled and choked and spat a few drops at a time. Then it suddenly spewed out a live eel, which wriggled madly in the hot water as I tried to catch it. Then another little eel shot from the tap, and a third, and soon I was grabbing at half a dozen of them as they rushed to and fro.

There was only one thing to do—empty the bath and begin again, so I pulled out the plug and let the eels go down the drain with the water. I was laughing so much by this time that Aunt Mairi heard me from the landing and came to see what the joke was. The contrast between primitive water-supply and stream-lined equipment made her laugh as much as I when the cold tap fired another round of eels into the expensive bath.

I asked if a tea-coloured stain on the bottom had been caused by the peaty water off the hill, but she said no, that was a Wren officer's bath salts, she must have put too much in when she stayed at Inverewe during the war. Janet got very annoyed about it and scrubbed that bath over and over again, but the marks wouldn't come off.

I said it reminded me of the boarding-house where I lived when a student in London. A dusky visitor from India came to the house so well oiled (in the literal sense) that when he took a bath he left a dark brown scum behind. The little maid-of-all-work saw the stains and ran in a panic to the manageress, wailing, 'Oh, Mum, 'is colour's come off on the bath.'

Aunt Mairi said at supper time that she planned a visit to friends in Inverness for the following week-end, as she wanted to see her tailor. In spite of Kirstie's disapproval of the blue tweed it must be made into a suit, for a sudden and unwelcome increase in weight had widened her waist and made most of her clothes unwearable.

'Not long before you came,' said she, 'I was away on the coast in the village of Melvaig one day and spoke to a crofter's wife—someone I've known all my life but hadn't seen lately. She looked me up and down, and said, "What *annoys* me is, you've grown so stout!" I told her "It annoys *me* too!" quoted Aunt Mairi with feeling.

Kirstie had given me an open invitation to stay with them when opportunity allowed, so I now thought that if they could have me for a long week-end I might perhaps go as far as Gairloch in the car with Aunt Mairi and be picked up on her return journey. This was soon arranged by telephone, and although the children were at home for the holidays Kirstie said they would fit me in somehow, for the young were always glad of an excuse to sleep out in a tent, and I could have one of their bunks. It would certainly be a change from having a whole cottage to myself.

They gave me a bunk on the verandah where the son usually slept, for he had gone off to camp in Perthshire by the time I got over to Gairloch. There was a tarpaulin slung across the foot (where water sometimes came through in stormy weather) and I shared the verandah with a brooder full of cheeping chicks and dozens of silent cacti. The side of the verandah was all of glass and faced west, so that I had a splendid view of the Torridon hills and northern Skye from my bed; and on the road to Melvaig and *Rudha Reidh*[1] lighthouse, which passed between the bungalow and the shore, passers-by had an uninterrupted view of me.

The bunk was narrow but would have seemed wider if a tortoiseshell cat and two Cairn pups hadn't decided to share it with me. They were absolutely determined in a quiet, deadly, Highland sort of way, and wouldn't take 'no' for an answer however fiercely it was shouted. The mother of the puppies was called *Beurach*[2] because the weavers had her just when they were moving in, when everything was in a terrible muddle and confusion—which is what the Gaelic word means. The bitch wasn't at all muddled herself, but a very well-organized character. She had even organized the largest litter ever recorded for the Cairn breed in this country: nine in a bunch. This suited her owners well, because they could sell any number of her offspring at good prices. *Beurach* had also secured a wet-nurse for some of her surplus

[1] Pronounced 'Rue-ray'.
[2] Pronounced 'Boor-uck'.

pups, for on their birthday the middle-aged and excessively maternal cat who had shared my bunk had had her latest kittens removed, and adopted instead a couple of the newly born pups to wash, feed, and lavish her affection on—to the mutual satisfaction of all concerned, so far as we could judge.

The weavers were working sixteen hours a day on the production and sale of their goods, and their daughters—both practical and helpful lassies—deserved a holiday while home from school, so I took over some of the cooking and chores. In the middle of Monday morning the local schoolmaster and his wife joined us for coffee in the family meeting-place on the verandah —or what was left of it round the edges of the brooder, trays of cacti, and my bunk. Afterwards I noticed a conference going on at the gate while I cleared away the cups, but thought nothing of it.

Kirstie asked me at lunch if I could bake cakes and scones. I said yes, up to ordinary English standards, but perhaps not to hers. Her husband then stoked up the kitchen fire to heat the oven, Kirstie set out a supply of ingredients, and they left me to an afternoon of cake-making. Later on the results were inspected and passed. Then I was taken round to see our morning visitors at home. No reason for this second meeting in one day was offered, and as they were charming people I asked for none.

It was a complete surprise when the master said that he had heard I wanted a job, and would I care to teach cooking and domestic crafts. Thinking that some mistake had been made, I said that my certificates were for handicrafts, not housewifery; but this, it seemed, wasn't of prime importance. I *had* teaching qualifications and some experience, and I could cook. The mistress they had employed got married in the summer holidays and her letter of resignation went astray, so that the Education Department had not been able to engage a successor, and here they were with a new term soon starting and no one to teach the senior girls their domestic arts. There would be two days a week teaching cookery and housecraft in the Junior Secondary School, and one day visiting primary schools along the coast, to teach sewing.

I have never been particularly fond of needles outside sewing-machines, but with a wild hope that my guardian angel was listening, said I'd like the post if offered me.

The schoolmaster seemed pleased; Kirstie clapped her hands; I thought that now I should belong to the place and stand on my own feet and not be just a friend of the Big House: so we all parted in a good humour.

'I'll phone the office first thing tomorrow,' said the master, 'and perhaps the Organizer of Homecrafts will come out to see you.'

'There,' said Kirstie, 'I thought it would be a good plan to have some cakes ready! We'll give her a grand tea and tell her you made it. The job's already yours, I'm sure.'

She was right. Kirstie's plans did not gang agley, they worked out just as she had predicted. The Organizer came, was given tea, enjoyed the cakes and scones; Kirstie said her piece about my having baked them; and I was asked to undertake the cookery and sewing classes. The Organizer was sympathetic about my confessed lack of experience in teaching cookery, and promised to send me a detailed syllabus and to visit my classes as often as she could: and that was that. Only the formalities of medical examination and the signing of a contract remained to be completed.

I finished off the day by purchasing a suit-length of tweed from the weavers, of a splendid sulky blue like the *Quiraing* of Skye seen from my bunk at twilight. And then we all went to the cinema show given by the mobile outfit of the Highlands and Islands film guild. This came to the village hall twice every week with a good programme of thrillers, Westerns and comedies suitable for all ages. All ages certainly went—from ninety to nine weeks, for there were no baby-sitters in Gairloch.

When Aunt Mairi returned next day she found me in possession of a part-time job and a roll of the finest handwoven tweed. She did not leave empty-handed either, for the prettiest of *Beurach's* pups made a dead set at her, struggling to climb up her legs on to a lap it couldn't reach in a jump. She held out a helping hand and the pup sat on her knee staring into her face with eyes like gimlets. This mute appeal overcome Aunt Mairi in a very few minutes.

'It likes me!' she said. 'I don't really want a dog, but this one *does* seem to want to be mine.'

The weavers transacted some more business; and when we got home to Inverewe and went through to the kitchen with our purchases, Aunt Mairi's puppy stole the thunder of my new job and my tweed as a subject for Sheena's appraisal. She looked hard at the tiny grey face of the dog and said, 'It is just like a little old woman.' So *Cailleach*[1] (old woman) it was named, and the ginger kitten spat on it by way of baptism.

[1] Pronounced 'Kye-oh'.

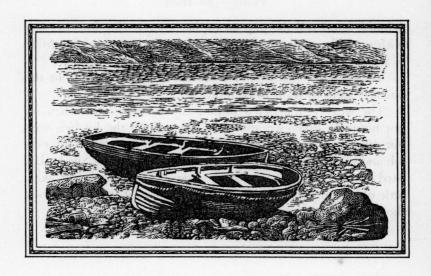

6. *A Day in the Hills*

WE MANAGED to get a surprising amount of work done during the next few days—considering that I used up as much time trying to persuade *Cailleach* (and her suspicious but fascinated attendant, the ginger kitten) not to give amateur assistance, as Aunt Mairi expended on turning me into a professional gardener.

On Saturday she said I had earned a break, and suggested taking me up to Kernsary and to Fionn Loch, where four of her men had spent the week on road repairs and the painting of boats and boathouses. It was one of those days with shining morning faces when no one sound in mind and body could choose to be indoors. Roddy Donn lowered my spirits a little when he called for the boathouse keys, and to Aunt Mairi's 'Good morning!' replied in a depth-plumbing voice, 'Too bright!' She told me not to worry, as he always said the same on sunny mornings, but she believed today's cloudless brilliance would hold. Lasting or not, it had made a perfect start—with a fresh, luminous colour on the hills that gave every stone a newly minted look.

With Aunt Mairi's rod ('in case I might get a few trout') and a picnic hamper stowed in the car, we drove off towards the village and turned up, before crossing the bridge, along a rough road on the north bank of the River Ewe. This swift stream has only about a mile to flow between Loch Maree and its outfall into the salt water of Loch Ewe; but although so short it stands high in reputation among fishermen.

Aunt Mairi told me how in 1852, at the age of ten, her father took thirty salmon from it in nine days of fishing—the heaviest being a twenty-eight-pounder—and so tired his young arms that he had to stop early in the afternoon and go home for a rest. His tutor had been an Urquhart, one of two brothers said to be the best hands who ever cast a fly into the Ewe. These men were grandsons of an earlier MacKenzie's head herdsman at Gairloch. 'A hundred years later we have yet another Urquhart at work at Inverewe,' said my companion.

Some time in the eighteen-forties, when Osgood MacKenzie's half-brother Francis, heir to Gairloch, was still a minor, his trustees bought the Kernsary estates for him from Lord Seaforth, so as to give the Gairloch estates both banks of the Ewe.

In 1862, when Lady Mary MacKenzie bought Inverewe for her son Osgood, his half-brother sold him most of the Kernsary land which marched with Inverewe, keeping only that portion of it which ran along the river for himself. Thus Aunt Mairi's father, and later she herself as his heir, acquired the Kernsary property, with its little shooting-box in a sheltered glen and beyond it several miles of the shore of Fionn Loch.

When this loch first came into the possession of the Mac-Kenzies there was no boat on it, and no access by road. The loch is six miles long and parallel to the famous Loch Maree, but lies five hundred feet higher up in the hills in a wild and lonely strath. A laborious task it must have been to drag the first heavy sea-boat over five miles of bog and a ridge eight hundred feet high, but they managed it and were rewarded by some first-class fishing. In later years many other boats were taken up, and finally Osgood had made the road on which we were motoring; nine miles of it were levelled and roughly surfaced by his men.

I marvelled at the difficulty of this work without modern appliances, but the Gairloch MacKenzies were no strangers to Highland road-making. During the potato famine of 1846-8, when crops in western Scotland and Ireland were smitten with blight, something had to be done for the support of the crofter people. Lady Mary, then already widowed, managed with some Government assistance and considerable private borrowing to undertake the employment of the people, so that they were able to buy imported food to replace their ruined crops.

At that time the road from Dingwall ended at Giant's Point at the upper end of Loch Maree, whence the Gairloch traffic had to be brought by water—often a hazardous voyage for small boats in the sudden storms that loch provides. Lady Mary, helped by her brother-in-law, Doctor John MacKenzie of Eileanach, organized the employment of all able-bodied men on the making of a road from Loch Maree to Gairloch, and Osgood well remembered, as a very small boy, having to cut the first turf. A great crowd assembled, many of them starving Skye men (for famine had hit the islands more hardly even than Ross-shire), and when after great efforts with his miniature spade the child threw up a clod of turf, he was applauded by rousing cheers.

For some years this work went on, and other roads were made from Gairloch to Melvaig and Poolewe to Cove, so that the young Osgood MacKenzie saw little of his busy mother. She would go off on horseback from Monday morning to Saturday night, supervising the road work, improving the croft houses and system of land tenure and even acting as doctor to the whole parish of about five thousand souls.

This indefatigable lady was no Highlander born, but a daughter of the English Quaker family of Hanbury; after hearing her story I had a shrewder idea why Aunt Mairi had said that Arthur and Colin (the mail drivers) were perhaps all the better for having an English mother!

When I cried that to a southerner it was nearly impossible to believe that any place in Britain with a population of five thousand could have been without a road almost within living memory, Aunt Mairi assured me that her father had often referred to the excitement caused in his boyhood by the arrival in Gairloch of the first wheeled vehicle—a carrier's cart. Before that all heavy goods were hauled on rough wooden sledges made of birch trunks, shaped and smoothed below to slide along the ground. The mails came in to Poolewe in a sailing vessel (rather intermittently) and were delivered by a postman on foot.

And here were we, skimming easily by car into one of the more remote glens in a matter of minutes. Our way presently parted from the River Ewe, now in a deeper bed between the bare rock face of Tollie and the wooded banks surrounding Inveran House. This plantation of birches, contorted and moss-grown, looked to me as ancient as some of the olive groves below my old home near Spezia in Italy, but Aunt Mairi said that although the roots were aged, the trunks were secondary growth from stumps left when her father sold the timber some forty years earlier.

'When a Highland laird needs money, away go his trees,' she said. Her remark gained import as we came out of the wood and in sight of the western end of Loch Maree, where a part of her land known as Fox Point was being stripped of its conifers. A primitive, rusty-looking railway line ran down the slope and over a plank bridge crossing a tributary of the Ewe to the edge of the pinewood, where felled timber was being loaded on to trucks. Further up the road we passed an encampment of caravans where the foresters lived, surrounded by a huge barrier of planking and sawdust heaps.

Soon we left this melancholy business behind, as our track snaked beween low hills. Hairpin bends and many potholes reduced our speed to a horse-walk. Boulders as big as byres lay around in the peat, among clumps of scrub willow, wild rose bushes, rowan trees and old heather stumps. Whirling designs of lichen were scattered all over the pinkish rocks in shades ranging from champagne to oatmeal stout. 'Crotal,' said Aunt Mairi; and I knew that with this lichen all the old brown hand-woven tweeds were dyed by their crofter weavers. She told me that the older the crotal, the deeper the dye, and that the richest-hued grew on rocks beside the sea, where salt spray regularly drenched it.

We came to a gate, the third since Inveran, but this one required a key. I had noticed that the Inveran gate was open; the one beyond the saw-mill unlocked but marked 'private'; and now we had a lock to fiddle with. Aunt Mairi explained that the first gate gave access to Inveran House and must therefore be open to everyone; the gate on the bridge was labelled 'private' to deter motorists from going beyond the turning-place; and the gate we had now reached was kept fastened to prevent all and sundry from driving up to the Kernsary house and Fionn loch. Any driver foolish enough to ignore the notice found himself up against an impassable barrier on a narrow road, with ditch and bog on either hand. As she had to maintain the entire length of road herself, it would not do to let everyone use it—nor to row her boats or fish in the Inverewe waters at will.

I opened the gate and locked it again behind the car, and as we rounded a bend a little low house came into view—perched on a green bank with wooded braes at the back of it, and a stream rushing past a few feet from the front porch. Glimpses of rugged hill appeared at the top of the glen, and down to our left Loch Kernsary reflected the sky. Some blackface sheep nibbled peacefully along the grassy banks of the burn, and a field of oats stood up, tall but yet unripe, inside a high deer-fence.

The windows of the lodge were dark and uncurtained and no smoke came from the chimney, but a thrush sang in the woods and there was no feeling of desolation about the place. I asked if we could go in, but Aunt Mairi said we hadn't time to loiter. I felt that her unnaturally curt manner hid some motive other than a desire to catch up with the men; and knowing that she and Captain Sawyer had spent many of their happiest days at Kernsary I thought perhaps it held too many memories to be entered since his death. Long afterwards, I learned that during the prolonged business of disposing of much of her estate she had at first been adamant about keeping the little house, but that its sale with the land had been made a condition of purchase. At the time of our visit she had probably been fighting a losing battle and could not bear to enter the much-loved haunt which might so soon be hers no longer.

After we left this green oasis the scenery changed to a narrow pass with the dark rock precipices of *Beinn Airidh Charr's* northern face high above us on the right, and a steep pine-clad brae to our left, which Aunt Mairi said owed its trees to her father's tireless planting. We came out of this pass on to a flat barren moor with numbers of small lochans dotted about, and fields of cotton-grass with its wisps of white floss mapping the bog land. In front of us the waters of the Fionn loch gleamed, surrounded by bare hills, and in the background the triangular peaks of *Beinn Eighe*.

We found the Inverewe men at the boathouse, their work just done, and as they had something to consult their mistress about at Kernsary, she took all four aboard (which loaded the car) and suggested that I might like to explore a little on foot and join her at about one o'clock for lunch. This I was pleased to do, and they drove away leaving me alone in the great silence of the hills. And silent it was—for here there were neither the song birds of the woods nor those of the sea-shore, and even the sheep had been left behind. Nothing stirred for some moments after the car had gone, until a very slight breeze rocked the water and it clinked the pebbles at my feet.

I sat on the stone jetty eating some buns which Sheena had supplied for elevenses, and feeling sorry for everyone shut up in houses and offices. Then I was startled by a peal of childish laughter, and stood up on the pier looking for the source of it; but there was nobody in sight. Ours had been the only car on the road, and I knew it was a very long and difficult tramp to the loch from either Kinlochewe or Dundonnell—quite beyond the capacity of a child. Deciding that I must have imagined the laughter, I returned to my seat.

Presently I heard more peals of merriment, sharp and clear as village bells on a still Sunday morning. This puzzled me sorely, and I scrambled along the shore for some distance to a rather higher piece of ground from which a broader view was possible.

67

But this brought no solution, for as far as I could see there was no sign of life beyond a pair of hoodie crows picking at a desiccated rabbit carcase. I knew that sound would carry far in such stillness and over water, and concluded that a picnic party must be in progress at some distance—although the children had seemed so close.

I sat quite still, with my ears cocked and eyes roving round the hills and along the innumerable boulders with which the opposite shore was strewn. Away to the far right was, I knew, the entrance to a narrow, hidden, rock-girt stretch of water known as the *Dubh Loch*, and sometimes compared to the weird Loch Coruisk in Skye. Perhaps the children had scrambled down among the rocks there. Then I realized that even in the silence no human voices could carry so far—and the mystery in any case would remain as to how children could reach the spot without transport.

No habitation now existed where they could possibly be staying; although round the shores of the loch were odd-shaped humps and hollows and piles of stone, with nettle patches and strips of greener grass—all relics of the shielings where once many crofter families spent the summer months, with their children helping to herd the beasts and having many a game at the water's edge, no doubt. I began to fancy that some change came over the scenery as I stared at it: a glazed look, followed by a sort of quivering movement, like a bad motion picture in a cinema; and I wondered if another shot would appear on the screen.

Then I told myself that silence and solitude were going to my head, and that it was time to make my way back to Kernsary and companionship. Just before I left the loch I heard the children again: two or three quite young ones evidently having good fun together. They at least seemed genuine flesh-and-blood youngsters, and no idle fancies or phantoms.

It took me over forty minutes to walk back to Aunt Mairi, who was sitting in the car beside the oatfield putting her fishing-rod together and fixing on a cast. She suggested that we should carry the picnic basket over to an old sheep-fank which she wanted to look at, as the wall would do to sit against on firm dry ground. We scrambled across boulders and bog, and it surprised me to find that the fank contained a little orchard. Captain Sawyer had planted the trees in the unused enclosure to provide handy supplies for the times when they stayed in the lodge, and some of them had borne particularly delicious fruit.

The gate in the wall, secure though it was, had not been able to keep a blackface ewe and a half-grown lamb out of the fank, and they crashed away through the trees in alarm at our entry, with loud bleating from the lamb. Saying that we must get them out somehow, Aunt Mairi stalked them left-handed while I dodged round to the right; but instead of diving back and out of the now open gateway, the ewe took to mountaineering, and had scaled the wall and disappeared before we got there. We managed to drive the frightened lamb through the gate, and then fetched faggots and a piece of loose wire to reinforce the slight dip in the wall where the exit (and no doubt entry) had been made. I had never before seen a sheep climb, but apparently mountain-bred blackfaces were as agile as goats. This ewe had recently been shorn, and unhampered by the usual trailing petticoats round thin black-stockinged legs (which give the breed such a Victorian look for most of the year), had felt exceptionally skittish.

While we were eating our sandwiches Aunt Mairi pointed out a large dark blob in the sky over *Beinn Airidh Charr*, which soared and glided without any perceptible wing movement; she said it was undoubtedly an eagle. Presently two smaller specks appeared over the hill and flew close to the bigger one and round about it in a menacing manner. Aunt Mairi thought they were probably hawks of some kind, although identification was difficult as we carried no glass: the size and flight of the first made her certain that it must be an eagle. The others looked like blue-bottles in comparison with the great bulk of their adversary. The pursuit and attacking motions went on for several minutes, until the eagle passed away from the Beinn and disappeared over the Fionn loch, when the smaller fry sheered off in the direction whence they had come. All the time the eagle had floated along with effortless dignity, apparently indifferent to the insults of the hawks.

I wondered what the attack signified, for it seemed unlikely that there were nestlings to defend so late in the summer; but we supposed that it might have been a territorial matter, and the hawks were warning off the eagle from their hunting grounds. Aunt Mairi told me that eagles were growing very common in Wester Ross. One day in the previous year she had seen a group of very large birds over *Beinn Eighe* which her stalker assured her were nine eagles. To her objection that eagles were not gregarious birds, he replied that it was perhaps two broods engaged in a combined flitting, owing to food shortage in their breeding place. Sheep-owners in the district complained of losing many lambs to the voracious eagles, and considered that this once rare bird was now causing too much destruction to be preserved.

I remembered a railway journey I had taken to the Kyle after the war, when a young man in the carriage had told me that in his spare time (he worked in a lumber camp) he would have fine sport in the hills in the early part of the year, looking for eagles' nests. Questioned as to what he did when he found one, he said 'Why, climb up to it if I can, and lift the eggs.' He added that he knew a man in London who paid a good price for them. When I pointed out that the eagle was protected by law (as I believed) and that he might be fined for robbing the nests, he looked thoughtful and begun to discuss the weather instead. Aunt Mairi said she thought the farmers would look upon his activities with relish, having regard to their loss of lambs.

She quoted from her father's book *A Hundred Years in the Highlands* a story of the white-tailed sea eagles which used to nest on an island in Fionn loch, evidently feeling secure so long as no boat was on it. After the first boat was taken up they moved to the precipice at the back of *Beinn Airidh Charr*, and as Osgood MacKenzie shared with other small boys a love of egg-collecting, he plagued his mother to let him make an expedition to the nest. They went up with ponies, accompanied by an expert rock-climber with his ropes and tackle; but after all their trouble they arrived too late—for someone else had just robbed the eyrie. However the man was traced, and agreed to part with the coveted prize in exchange for a pound note; and Osgood was able to ride home in triumph with a couple of enormous white eggs. Beyond the Fionn loch is a smaller one called in Gaelic *Loch an Iasgair*, (the Osprey's Loch), for in the Gaelic an osprey is known as *Ailein Iasgair*, or Allan the Fisherman. Unfortunately egg-collectors in the last century prevented that beautiful bird from breeding successfully, and there are none left there now.

After we had packed up our luncheon basket and taken it down to the car, Aunt Mairi drove a short distance along the road past the Kernsary lodge to a point near the loch, where she said she would try for a trout. I lay in the deep heather watching her cast and envying the skill with which she handled rod and line—although not a bite did her efforts bring.

'Roddy Donn was right, so far as fishing goes,' she said, dropping her voice to a perfect imitation of his warning drone; 'it *is* "too bright".'

She gave up after twenty minutes, and we drove home past the lumber camp—where stoves were now smoking merrily in the caravans, and a strong whiff of frying told that the cooks were busy—and along the banks of the Ewe again. Away to our right some men were working at the peats, adding to the stacks drying beside a stretch of bog. This is no longer the Highlander's chief fuel—for modern transport and the larger incomes now earned by most crofters have led to the use of much imported coal—but peat-cutting is still an important part of the West Highland summer, except in districts where the accessible bogs are worked out and useless. If the weather in May and June allows, the prudent man cuts a store and leaves it to dry; then in late summer or early autumn he carts it to his croft door, where it is stacked in neat bee-hive formation until wanted.

In Poolewe I noticed that the peat-reek was most noticeable in spring and autumn, due to the fact that, when days were mild enough to warrant only a small fire, the easily lit peats were used

—whereas in really cold weather a hotter and more lasting coal blaze was kept going all day.

Near Inverewe a perfect bronze spear-head was found in one of the bogs, with a deer's antler close by: giving a vivid picture of one of the earlier hunters at work. These were lying fairly near the surface, which suggested that the deepest layers must be of a very great age. Aunt Mairi said peat was so fine a preservative that the woodern shaft of the spear had remained almost intact beside the bronze head. Some valuable bronze vessels were also unearthed in a peat bog in the district. These were at a depth of only three feet, but the deepest bog explored at Inverewe was about fourteen feet thick. The average depth of the Ross-shire bogs—about seven feet—could not be compared to those in Lewis, where they have miles of bog going as deep as twenty-five feet.

It is not surprising that Lewismen now resident in Wester Ross say that mainland folk do not know what peat is. I heard a woman of Aultbea chide a Stornoway man because, she said, the men of the Outer Hebrides should think shame to let their womenfolk work down in the bogs. In Ross they are usually employed only on the stacking and carting, but in The Lews she had seen them throwing peats up from the bottom as they were cut. The Lewisman would have none of her criticism, saying his peats at home were so much better that a man *needed* his wife's help. A mere boy could manage alone in Ross-shire because the peat was poor, light stuff and the bogs so shallow. He added that they were sociable people in Lewis, too, and the work went more merrily with the men and women together—and plenty of Gaelic songs accompanying their labours.

When Aunt Mairi and I got home to Inverewe, Sheena heard my story of the invisible children playing by the Fionn loch with a look of apprehension. Asked what she made of it, she said something in Gaelic which was translated as 'You must have been hearing the fairies!' We both made gentle fun of Sheena and her wee folk, but the old one looked at me very searchingly and would not be drawn into the merriment.

A Day in the Hills

On Monday I heard that the story had spread through the village and up as far as Kinlochewe by the Highland 'underground telegraph', and that it was thought certain no other party had been up at the loch on Saturday. Even Aunt Mairi now seemed to believe in Sheena's theory, and said she would henceforth avoid going up there by herself. I argued that the voices were happy and pleasant, and said I had had no mental shivers or sense of anything uncanny or fey;[1] but she shook her head at me. Fairies were not to be trusted, it seemed.

A visitor who listened to the story thought I had spent a few moments outside time, and had listened to the voices of children who once lived in the now ruined shielings.

I myself considered it more probable that some strange bird had bamboozled me, for had I not already experienced much bewilderment in connection with the cries of the corncrake and eider duck? The only flaw in my solution seems to be that no one has ever heard a bird-call which sounds like the high-pitched laughter of young children. Neither our green woodpecker nor wryneck nor even the Australian kookaburra make sounds which by any stretch of the truth could be said to resemble it.

Of two things I am certain: I was absolutely sober, and thoroughly wide awake all the time.

[1] From a Gaelic word meaning 'doomed'.

7. *Housekeeping in the Highlands*

THE burn which ran so swiftly past my step looked as pure as an icicle, and so did the piped supply indoors, but remembrance of all those little eels in the bath at Inverewe unnerved me every time I filled a kettle for tea. If eels could get into the water, so might other less visible and perhaps more noxious things. I knew the Big House and the cottage tapped the same reservoir, but had my burn a share in it? I wasn't sure—and was pondering whether it would be a good idea to dip a bucket of water from the pool beside my wood-lodge, when a party of domestic ducks arrived there. After this it seemed safer to stick to the tap. Then Lizbie appeared on the front path carrying a bedroom jug. She unlocked the deer-house and drew a gallon of clear sparkling water from a spring in the corner—which, she assured me, had no connection with either burn or tank, and was always clean and very cold.

Having the matter of drinking-water settled, I inquired about bread. Hitherto I had, except for one loaf purchased in Gairloch, been supplied from the Inverewe bins; but I now wished to become self-supporting. Lizbie told me it was delivered to the village shop by a van from Inverness, which made the trip through the hills twice a week.

'On Tuesdays and Fridays,' she said, 'so you'd better go to-night if you're wanting any.'

The shop hours were elastic, and she thought 'Swift' would not shut before eight o'clock on a bread day, so away I went: to find shopping in full swing, but no bread left. A little put out, I said I hadn't expected a shortage. The regal woman behind the counter looked thoughtful. 'There's not a shortage of bread,' she said very gravely, 'it's just that there's so many people wanting it.' Silenced, I took a packet of rye biscuit instead.

There were two shops: Swift's, which had something of every-thing and was dimly lit, crowded, mysterious and old-fashioned, and its opposite neighbour and rival (to which was joined a small hut housing the post-office), where a modern provision store complete with refrigerator took me by surprise.

Modern or not, it had no bread.

The first business had been run by its fragile-looking owner for thirty or forty years, and it seemed as though the same things had been kept in their customary places for most of that time. Otherwise, how could the old man play his intricate sort of Pel-man game so faultlessly, I thought. His imposing wife, who assisted him at busy periods, would sell goods from the front line of the shelves, but if those in the middle or inner layers were asked for she summoned her husband at once.

When I added to the rye biscuit my desire for an enamelled milk saucepan, she handed me over to him. The slender white-aproned figure came towards me smiling, with a far-away look in his mild blue eyes. 'Let me see now. An enamel saucepan. I am sure I have one. Behind the ladies' black shoes are the toilet rolls (he removed shoe boxes and Broncos, placing them in a row on the counter between a side of bacon and a paraffin can) and at the back are the gravy-strainers and large tea-pots (out they came) and—yes, I *knew* I had a milk saucepan.'

He brought it reverently and put it down in front of me, lifting the lid with a gesture as though displaying some rare

Etruscan vase or T'ang figure. I bought the utensil, in spite of its being larger and heavier and more expensive than I wanted, because it seemed impossible to refuse such an adroitly excavated treasure. In any case, it was the only one and I needed it.

It took Swift several minutes to add the price of both purchases together and deduct the result from the note I gave him, but the change when he spread it slowly on the counter was correct, and one felt that he could always be relied on to get things right in his own time. His wife came forward to say that she was sorry about the bread, and would I be wanting any on Friday. She agreed to keep some for me, and when asked if it should be 'plain' or 'pan', I replied 'pan' in order not to betray ignorance, although I had no idea what it meant.

Then I noticed that the other counter bore some copies of *The Glasgow Herald* and *Bulletin*. These were bespoken, but Mrs. Swift offered to place an order for me. A shepherd who had recently come into the shop spoke in Gaelic to nobody in particular, and was answered by Swift in the same tongue, while his wife fetched a large black waterproof bag stuffed with loaves and handed it over to their customer. I thought I heard the word *'Bulletin'* amid the Gaelic (all Gaelic speakers must needs use English for such modern inventions as newspapers and electric gadgets), and it transpired that the shepherd's mother had gone to Inverness that day, and so her unwanted copy of the paper could be mine. I put down my pence and turned to thank the man—who smiled shyly at a kettle hanging from the rafters and made no further remark.

His two black-and-white sheepdogs seated at the entrance parted like ebbing waves to allow me passage to the road, and silently flowed back across the steps after I had descended. Somehow they achieved this without looking at me—with the same shy manner as their master. I like to speak to animals; but felt that to their aloofness it would be an unwelcome intrusion, and departed as silent as they.

Across the street in the post-office I bought a book of stamps and then, seeing some bicycles propped against the side of the little hut, asked the bright young girl behind the wire-netting if she knew anyone in the place with a second-hand one to sell, for it seemed to me that I should save much time and trouble by pedalling round the loch to get my 'messages' (as I was learning to call shopping) instead of tramping the mile each way every time. The lass called through a communicating door to the grocery department, and another girl, an elder sister by her looks, came in to join the conversation.

It appeared that neither of them had any knowledge of a bicycle for sale, but both were certain that their mother would willingly lend me hers. They were so kind and pressing that I accepted the offer of a temporary loan until I could buy one, and we parted with smiles and a promise that the bike would be waiting for me at the post-office by six o'clock next day.

On my way out I saw a handbill advertising performances by the Highlands and Islands mobile film unit in Poolewe on Wednesday evening, so I said that I would make a night of it and go to that as well as fetch my mount. The girls stopped smiling and looked at one another, and for a bad moment I thought they disapproved of such things. Then the elder said apologetically that her mother's bicycle had no lights on it. It was just an old one that she used to ride occasionally.

'But the tyres are quite good, and the brakes work,' added the younger girl quickly. I said it wouldn't matter a bit about lights, as I could well push it home to *Tigh-an-Uillt* after the films; and then their smiles came out again. So that I should know where to go, they took me out of the post-office and round to the back of the shop and showed me a long green hut lower down the bank, just above the dark water of the salmon pool at the river's mouth.

'The recreation hut,' they said with pride. 'It costs a shilling to see the films.'

Next evening I took my empty milk pail along to the farm as usual and hung it on its hook in the wall outside the yard gate. There were a number of hooks, and on them pails of various sizes, all with wire handles and close-fitting lids and names painted in red or white enamel on the lids. Each bore a surname except that of Arthur the mail driver, and he just had ARTHUR on his pail because there was no one else of that name on the coast. He must have got it from his English mother. No doubt if his brother Colin wanted a pail he would have had his full name on it, for there were many Colins; but he had his own cow at home and needed no milk from our farm.

As soon as I had taken possession of the borrowed cycle and leant it against the recreation hut, Janet appeared on her gleaming new one and put it alongside. Mine was certainly aged (though serviceable), and couldn't be compared with hers; but she didn't seem at all puffed up about it. We sat together on the wooden chairs provided, and all the school children went to the front, and the old people clustered at one side where the stove was—for although it was summertime there came a chill off the sealoch percolating through cracks in the walls and floor as night fell. The stove was called a 'Tortoise', and had an iron pipe going up through the roof; when the wind blew it crackled and spat and made a red glow like footlights—but on the left of the stage only.

Everyone seemed to enjoy the show, from cartoon to news, and this was expressed by the stamping of feet on the wooden floor. When a picture of the Royal Family came on to the screen I thought the whole building would slip off its concrete foundation into the salmon-pool below, since it shook so much with the warmth of the applause.

Janet with her lamps lit cycled home to Inverewe afterwards, while I followed on foot pushing my unlit bicycle. I paused on the bridge and listened to the fuss of the river as it boiled through the rocks below me, and I sniffed greedily at the fresh, cold air off the mountains. A line of orange-coloured squares of light in windows along the village street only made the dim shapes of the surrounding hills seem darker and more vast.

Soon I left the sound of the river behind, and then, when the hut had emptied and the audience dispersed to their homes, everything fell suddenly very quiet. The silence was so intense that one had to listen to it carefully (but in an unbelieving frame of mind), and then listen again more intently to make sure that the world could be as silent as that. As I walked back round the shore of the loch, placing my feet accurately on the grassy verge so as to make no intruding clatter, the loud '*Kraak, kraak!*' of a night-fishing heron made me jump. Presently another answered, more faintly, from the Inverewe peninsula, and then one on the near side spoke again. As my eyes became accustomed to the darkness, I detected round shapes on the sand which were rocks or bundles of weed, and in between the slender, long-necked, static figures of the herons.

I had counted thirteen of them by the time I reached the white-walled house and byres of the Home farm, about two-thirds of the way between the village and *Tigh-an-Uillt*. A collie in the yard barked at my approach, scaring an oyster-catcher from the rocks to my left. It flew out to sea with a high, sharp '*Bi glic, bi glic!*' call like the tinkling of Japanese glasses in the nursery when I was a child. Then I heard the familiar gurgling of the burn to tell me I was home; and pausing by the deer-house I looked across the narrow inlet of the sea-loch to Inverewe, and saw Aunt Mairi's reading-lamp liven the uncurtained windows of the smoking-room—while all the rest were dead. The white house gleamed against the dark mass of pinewoods on *Ploc Ard* like a child playing ghosts in a sheet at bed-time. Behind the braes and out over the open sea there were faint traces of sunset after-glow still.

Without a moon, the stars shone in a clear sky all the more brilliantly, and I was loath to leave them; but, sleepy with gardening and film-gazing, I soon had my bicycle stowed in the wood-lodge and a bundle of heather gathered up to cheer the sitting-room fire which I had smoored with damp peats before leaving the house. It smelt very good to me when the front door was opened, and a few puffs of the bellows under a pile of dry heather made a healthy blaze in a minute. I felt glad to be in a country where summer evening fires were customary and not looked upon as extravagant luxuries.

I enjoyed a pot of tea, made from the black kettle beside the
fire, and a read of a good book; then the late news on my radio;
and took a candle upstairs to bed, thinking that Highland cottage
life was fine. There was no need to lock the door or close downstairs windows, for no burglars or other unpleasant characters
were ever met with. Neither the Aultbea nor the Gairloch con-
stables had ever made an arrest in the district. The worst night
terrors were fox and wild-cat, but as I had no fowls to tempt such
marauders I was able to slide into sleep without a worry in my
head.

      ·   ·   ·

It was old Sheena who put me wise about the Scottish names
for the different kinds of bread, 'pan' being what English bakers
call 'tin' loaves—rectangular and crusted all over—whereas
'plain' ones (which I've never seen south of the Border) are
roughly the same shape, but being cooked together on one tray
stick to each other and have to be pulled apart when done. This
leaves them with soft and crustless sides, and indeed when I tried
one I fancied the whole loaf to be softer and more doughy than
the other kind. They are a little cheaper, and in Poolewe most
customers took away six or eight of them every bread day in
huge black bags like the one the shepherd fetched from Swift's.

To Aunt Mairi I commented that Swift was a very English
name for a Highland shopkeeper, and this seemed to amuse her,
for she asked with a chuckle if I had addressed the old man or
his wife by it. I couldn't remember doing so, and she then told
me it was just the local nickname for the dear old clansman, because he had never been known to bestir himself to a quick
movement. His stately wife did not share it, but was known, for
very obvious reasons, as 'The Queen'. Owing to the duplication
of clan names and also of forenames, these inventions were of
practical use in the small community, and the people were adepts
at coining new ones—'Even for a newcomer like you,' she added.
When she had been cajoled into telling me that I was known

as 'The Motor-Bike' I felt puzzled, for my newly borrowed bike
had no engine, and I hadn't even ridden it yet. She explained that
this had nothing to do with it. My nickname had been derived
from the speed with which I *walked* round the loch, and she supposed it would be used in the village for years—even if I never
footed the road again. These names, once bestowed, were retained
for life, and sometimes into the third and fourth generation: as I
discovered later when I started teaching.

Many of the names were simple adjectives, like '*Beg*' (little,
small) or '*Mhór*' (big), and those of colour, '*An Ruadh*' (red),
'*Buidhe*' (yellow, golden), and '*Dubh*' (dark, black-haired). The
Gairloch MacKenzies, Osgood's ancestors, had their share of
these—for his grandfather had been known as 'The Buck-toothed
Laird', his grandmother as 'The Auburn Lady', and the second
baronet as 'The Lame Laird'. A much earlier MacKenzie was
called '*Eachainn Ruadh*' (Red Hector). Aunt Mairi mentioned a
man of Loch Broom whose name always amused her father. He
tells in his memoirs how this man, Iain Bait or *Bàthadh* (drowned),
had once fallen into the Ullapool river when it was in spate, and
screamed '*Bàthadh, bàthadh*, O God save me!' Presently, feeling
some rock beneath his feet, he shouted 'Oh! Perhaps Thou need
not trouble.'

One of the most unfortunate hereditary nicknames in the
district—'Tally' (pronounced 'Tarly')—was said to have been
bestowed on a shopkeeper who was over-fond of the bawbees. A
third-generation descendant, also owner of a store, is known by
the same epithet although he does not deserve it; but by now he
is probably quite accustomed to the libellous word, and proud of
its historical interest. How sorry I am to have no little motor- bikes
to inherit my nickname!

Altogether, names were taking up much of my attention.
Memorizing the proper names of all the varieties of plant and
tree at Inverewe was in itself a big task for one not learned in
botany; and then there were Gaelic names of hills and rivers, the
people's nicknames, and in addition the unfamiliar uses of English
words—such as '*messages*' for errands, '*pan*' loaves, and '*policies*'

for enclosed grounds; and when Swift was cutting up his meat, I heard a woman ask for a '*jiggot*'. Aunt Mairi said the two last sprang from the Auld Alliance, which had left a legacy of French usage in Scotland.

'Never mind the French! I'm thinking it is time you were teaching her some Scottish cooking,' said old Sheena—for our conversation had been going on in the kitchen, as so often happened. Except when visitors were entertained at Inverewe, Aunt Mairi's indoor life (what there was of it) was spent mainly in the kitchen—or else at her writing-desk, when talk was not required. In response to Sheena's suggestion, she said that many Highland dishes would be better demonstrated by Sheena herself; as no one could match her ways with oatcake or black pudding, or cook a herring so well. However, on that day I practised with some scone mixture on the girdle—which is a heavy circle of sheet-iron with an arched handle; on this, small pieces of dough will rise and cook well. For hundreds of years most of the crofters had no ovens, and all their baking had to be done on a girdle over an open peat fire.

Afterwards we made a batter and I tried my hand at drop scones—small, thick pancakes made by dropping spoonfuls of mixture on a hot girdle or frypan, or even the plate of an electric cooker. The blobs have to be deftly turned over when they have reached the right firmness and are a pale golden hue on the under side. These are not eaten hot like English pancakes, but left to cool and used at tea-time with butter and jam.

I said I had cut down the use of my kitchen stove to twice a week, mainly for baths, as the oven had rusted into holes and would not bake; so that a girdle would be just the thing for me. Aunt Mairi at once went into one of her storerooms and brought me a spare girdle, a size lighter than hers, which I considered a very pleasant and practical old tool to have in the cottage. On her return to the kitchen, she said to Sheena: 'I've thought of something you can cook for our tea—salt herring! There are some left in the barrel and they want eating.'

Sheena looked shocked, and nodding in my direction said:

'She'll not eat salt herring! The people from the south never like them.'

'Just you let me try!' I said. She shook her head doubtfully, but I was permitted to have my way.

The first mouthful of salt herring was hard to swallow (I had never tasted anything quite so briny before), but I was made to wrap the next in a wad of floury potato and wash the sandwich down with strong tea—which we drank from breakfast cups. I soon became accustomed to it and thoroughly enjoyed the experience.

Encouraged by this, Sheena showed me how to manage a Highland breakfast on one oil stove. Needing it to heat my teakettle (I lit no fire during the day), I hadn't known how to cook my porridge. The solution was beautifully simple—one didn't cook the oats at all. 'There's nothing like a good *brose*,' said my tutor, 'and all you have to do to make that is to put a handful of meal in a bowl with salt and a lump of butter, pour on boiling water slowly, give it a good stir, and eat it with cream before it cools.'

She told me that the gardeners and most of the local men preferred it to porridge, because they believed it went on swelling inside them, taking longer to digest and so keeping them satisfied until it was time for the next meal. 'And their women don't get sticky pots to wash,' ended Sheena.

8. *The Wild and the Free*

I FELT quite eager for the next morning to come, so that Sheena's breakfast recipe could be tried out; but before going to bed had it in mind to collect some more old heather and whin off the hill, as my stock in the wood-lodge was done. The day's squalls of wind and rain eased off at sundown, and the evening grew clear and bright; so, hatless and coatless—but wearing Wellington boots against the damp underfoot, I set off, carrying an old sack for my kindling. The way led through a five-barred gate on the other side of the cottage and up a sloping field to a second gate, above which lay the wild hill-side. Beyond the upper gate our burn emerged from a wood, and beside it Colin and Lizbie had their chicken-house: a contraption made of rough stone walls with a faded old green boat upturned on top for a roof.

Next to this was a substantial bothy into which I peered, and found the whole interior stacked with fragrant wooden planks. I remembered Aunt Mairi telling me that when she sold the standing timber on Fox Point she bargained for a supply of sawn pine for estate repairs, and that she had stored it for seasoning in the

84

old laundry; so this must be it. I stood for a moment in the dim light of the bothy (whose small windows were more or less obscured by the wood-piles) and sniffed vigorously at the warm, resinous scent. I was picturing the rocky shores of Loch Maree, and imagining the lives of the trees from which these boards had been made, when a loud '*baa-aa*' at my back interrupted the brief reverie.

I turned to meet a half-grown blackface sheep which stood in the doorway looking anxiously up at me. I had met bottle-fed lambs before, and thought I recognized the expression of one who desired human companionship and the food we usually provided. Having nothing edible to give, I patted and spoke to it kindly (while working myself through the door), and then moved out of the presence backwards in case it felt like rewarding my un-generous behaviour with a butt in the behind. Even a half-grown sheep can put considerable force into such punches, as I knew from practical and painful experience. Luckily this one essayed no rude tricks as long as my eye was on it, nor did it attempt to follow.

I waded the burn above the laundry, at a ford where it widened and became shallow enough to wet only a third of my boots, and then the wood was all about me. Underfoot dead leaves and blown branches lay thick and untrodden, and great dollops of sphagnum moss grew on the dark, peaty soil. The trees were a mixed lot, with birch and pine predominating; and towards the centre of the wood they had clustered so tightly together for protection from the winter gales that there was little daylight beneath their interlocked boughs.

A rocky bluff to my left had a crumbling edge from which a shower of boulders had spilled, some to rest on shelves half-way down, or jammed between the face of the brae and leaning birch trees which sprouted from it; others formed a natural rockery at the foot where ferns and wild flowers companioned lichens and toadstools in great variety of subtle colour. I remembered how Aunt Mairi told me she had once entertained the dress designer Norman Hartnell, who was delighted by the colours on the hill and made sketch notes for future use; and I wondered how many Court and ball dresses now reflected the lichens and heathers of Inverewe—unknown to their wearers.

Further up the slope the trees were more thinly spaced, with many bushes of wild rhododendrons between, and ground cover of bracken. There had been no signs of bird or other animate life in the wood, so that a flicker of movement ahead on my right made me pause and watch closely. I caught the briefest and most tantalizing glimpse of a red-brown animal peeping at me from a thick tangle of branches and pine-needles before it turned and vanished.

My cumbersome boots squelched heavily into the leaf and peat mould as I plunged along after it, but it was a hopeless chase—my way being uphill and leading beyond the brae to a deep glen, thickly wooded, in which all but an elephant could find adequate cover. I came to the top and threw myself down, breathless, in a bed of heather beneath a hoary old rock. The living trees in the glen below me seemed as still and lifeless as the sawn planks in the laundry.

What a disappointment—to have so fleeting a sight of a creature which, from its tawny colour and yellowish neckerchief, I believed to be a pine marten! I had read in Osgood MacKenzie's book that the animal had become extinct on the estate during his lifetime; but it had been reported recently over the Sutherland border by Fraser Darling, and we were not far from Sutherland. Could the pine marten be returning to Wester Ross?

On the way home, trudging more soberly with a full sack over my shoulder, I had another and much clearer view of wild life without any trouble at all. In fact, so clear and easy that I did not at first imagine that the large snuff-coloured cat I saw strolling up a grassy bank behind *Tigh-an-Uillt* could be anything but a tame tabby. Idly I wondered who it belonged to, for I thought I knew all the pets and farm mousers in our small community by sight.

Then it stopped and turned its face to stare at me, and the flattened look of its head and ears, more or less in one horizontal line; the hostile eyes; and above all, exceptionally stubby tail, gave me a thrill. It was the spitting image of the stuffed wild cat I had seen in Donnie Tarly's shop in Gairloch. I gazed at the cat and the cat glared at me, but 'spitting' image was not a good simile because it made neither sound nor gesture. After a prolonged stare it turned its head and trotted away, apparently intent on businesss like any old mousing tom.

Until then it had somehow never occurred to me that one might see (and be seen by) a genuine wild cat in daylight and within a hundred yards of a road and home, but there was no doubt about this beast. It seemed extraordinary that so comfort-loving a creature—for such I had always thought it—could actually live out on these wild hills among rocks and heather, in wind and rain and sometimes snow. Of course I must have known in theory that this happened; but seeing the animal in the flesh made all the difference.

I was brimming over with excitement when I reached the gate into our cottage garden and saw Lizbie taking in some logs. Quite forgetting that wild cats were predatory, I told her what I had just seen. Her eyes blazed. 'Wild cat! I must tell my man to set a trap at once!' she exclaimed with fury. When I complained that all wild creatures were butchered here, she looked at me in astonishment.

'They're *awful* things!' she said. 'Why, yon cat would lift all my best hens in a night if it got the chance.'

I felt the power of her argument, of course. The poultry were a very valuable and essential supply of food for her family, and couldn't possibly be sacrificed to keep useless beasts alive. Yet, as the domestic hen is the only bird about which I can develop no enthusiasm, and the sight of wild cat prowling independent and free on some of the last acres of Britain left to him delighted me, I could not help an unneighbourly wish that I had kept my mouth shut.

At bedtime I made a vow to keep any future knowledge of wild cat to myself. Next day I enjoyed my first dish of *brose*, and have continued to breakfast off that good dish ever since;

but the strength of the vow has not been put to the test, because I have never seen a live wild cat again.

Before many nights had passed, the one I betrayed lost its life in a trap so that Lizbie's fowls might cluck on in safety. Obviously they can have no place within range of human beings and their feathered flocks. Slowly I was learning that by going to live in an outpost where civilization impinged on the wild country, one was inevitably drawn into clashes which took heavy toll of the very wild life one had come so far to seek.

Nothing could be done about it, and vain regrets are wasteful and not to be indulged in; but nevertheless my conscience was troubled and all I could think about was a fervent hope that the creature died quickly. Colin kept silence, but he was a gentle man and wouldn't fail, I knew, to visit his traps and end the suffering of any victim the moment it was light enough to see.

No doubt it was to him an unpleasing but necessary task, much as catching the larder mouse is to many town-dwellers. Perhaps I haven't very good trapping blood, even where mice are concerned, for my MacLeod grandmother in her later years used to feed the wee creatures in her dining-room with snippets of cheese secreted in a pocket for the purpose, while her disapproving but indulgent maids—knowing all but saying nothing —caught the growing population in the kitchen.

Neither side ever breathed a word to the other about mice, but I, as a privileged child visitor, was taken into confidence by both my dear grandmother Theresa and her long-suffering servants. Being strictly enjoined 'not to tell' by both parties, I have faithfully kept my word until this day.

At Inverewe there remained to tell the glimpse of what I fancied to be a pine marten, and at first I wondered whether that incident should be kept to myself: but the creature seemed so wary and had been seen so much further from the houses that I considered it to be in small danger of getting into a trap. Aunt Mairi was very interested in my description of the yellow-throated climber, and passed the story round among her men. A few days later news came that the Inveran keeper had recently seen a pine marten on the banks of the River Ewe, a mile or two south of the wood where mine had vanished: so it seemed probable that I had not been mistaken.

I voiced a hope that martens were not likely prey for the keeper's gun or trap. Aunt Mairi sounded doubtful, saying they were wicked little things and supposed to take game birds and even lambs when they felt in the mood. She recalled also a passage in her father's book describing how a fine tree of *magnum bonum* plums in the old *Tigh Dige* garden at Gairloch was being robbed of fruit in the eighteen-fifties. The angry gardener put several folds of herring net over his precious tree and caught a big pine marten.

After Osgood's uncle (Doctor John MacKenzie) had fetched his gun and shot the marten, it was skinned; and when they opened it up the stomach was found to be tightly packed with the great yellow plums. These it had cleverly stoned, piling the evidence in a neat row of heaps along the top of the wall against which the tree was trained.

'So the Inveran gardeners may not be content to leave a mischievous marten around,' said Aunt Mairi.

I said I'd far rather go without any fruit than have one of these animals destroyed; and she looked at me reflectively and replied, 'I believe *you would*.'

9. One- and Two-teacher Schools

THE time for me to start work as a travelling teacher drew near —for necessary medical examinations had been passed, a contract signed, and the autumn term had begun. The children were sorted into their groups and given a day or two to shake down, and then the normal routine of the time-table took shape.

It surprised me to be given a chest X-ray, as I had already taken medical tests for the London Civil Service without encountering this. It seemed just one more sign of the thoroughness with which things were done in Scotland; but later on I learned that it had arisen owing to the incidence of chest disease in the north-west, where a higher percentage of the population still suffer from the scourge than is now the case in the south.

The Headmaster of the largest school on my list had been asked to apportion my time, after consultation with the other schools, and he sent me instructions to report at the smallest and most distant one on the morning of my first day and to visit another in the afternoon. Transport was to be provided by the

Education Department. A car would call for me at half past eight on the day named.

I was going to be busy, for of course I had come to Ross-shire to help Aunt Mairi in exchange for the furnished cottage; and although I should now be in a better position to pay for it in cash instead of labour, that would not be a satisfactory substitute from her point of view—as it was my hands and to some extent companionship she had need of beyond all else. In any case my happiest and most rewarding hours were spent in the gardens with her, and I could not have borne to forfeit them.

It was therefore arranged that I should put in two whole days each week at Inverewe, and Saturday afternoons. This left me with one morning for shopping, and my evenings for chores around the cottage. With five midday meals 'on the job' I should not have much cooking to do at home, and on my three teaching days the evenings would be long ones—because lessons finished at four. Everything had panned out so well for me that I could now afford to smile at the gloomy prophecies of friends and family and the people in the Government office I had abandoned.

The evening before my new work began, the Headmaster rang me up at Inverewe to wish me luck. 'The first school is very small and *very* remote,' he said, 'so you won't expect anything grand, will you?' He added that the mistress in charge was the only teacher there—except for myself, and that he hoped I should get on with her. It may have been imagination, but I thought there was a faint hint of emphasis on the word 'hope', so I anxiously inquired if she was easy to deal with.

'Oh, yes, yes indeed!' he assured me. 'She is a most capable and experienced teacher and doesn't stand any nonsense, but I'm sure you will find her very nice when she gets to know you.'

I hadn't expected to be embraced or to walk on red carpet, so this sounded satisfactory.

That night I set my alarum clock for half past six, and next morning was out of bed and downstairs before the bell had finished tinkling; but, early though it was, the family next door were before me. I found it cheerful to hear their voices rising and falling in musical cadences of the Gaelic on the other side of a thin partition dividing my lean-to scullery from their own. Before the week was up, their small daughter would have become a pupil of mine; and as I well knew by this time that her mother had talent as a baker, I hoped Flora wouldn't discover too many gaps in my knowledge of Scottish cookery. But my first day's work did not include that subject, so the worry could wait until the morrow.

Arriving at the gate in good time to meet my hired car, I found Flora already there waiting for the mail bus, which came along a moment later and took her as far as the village—where she boarded the school coach for Gairloch. Arthur was driving the mail and gave me a particularly friendly smile. I was now one of their teachers, and felt immensely proud of it. In Scotland a high value has always been set on education, and all who take part in the teaching or running of schools share to some extent in the respect accorded to it by parents and children alike.

Away went the bus, waved on by me from the roadside and Lizbie from the cottage window, and then all was quiet again. I moved across the road to a boulder, and sat watching a cloud blow in from the open sea, shedding a veil of rain over the opposite shore as it approached. It had seemed very small in the distance, but looked black and forbidding as it came overhead, and I quickly put on the oilskins and hood I carried. The squall hit our end of the loch with a sharp rattle like gravel on a tin roof, and the rain blew cold and stinging against my face. Although August had not quite ended, there was an autumn feel to the day.

I moved up towards the gates of Inverewe and into the slight shelter provided by a hedge of escallonia and rhododendron bushes beside the road. There was still no sign of my car. I expected it to come from the north—the direction in which I was going—as I knew the driver lived along that road. When someone went out of the Gate Lodge and shovelled fuel into the furnace with a steady rhythm, I thought with longing of the stuffy heat inside the boiler-house, envying Aunt Mairi's marmalade kitten his favourite hide-out at that moment.

The rain now settled into a steady downpour, and I had just decided to return home when a car came up behind me from the direction of Poolewe and stopped at the deer-house. When I reached it the woman driver ushered me into the seat beside her, and introduced the three adult passengers who sat wedged into the back among various knobbly sacks containing (I think) potatoes, together with a large and smelly drum of paraffin and some car batteries.

The driver apologized for keeping me waiting and explained that the people had been fetching their goods from Poolewe, whither she had gone for petrol, and wished to travel in my direction—so of course she had taken them. It all sounded most artless, but I had a shrewd idea that circumstances had been assisted. In country where public vehicles run but once a day in either direction, all transport is a precious commodity; and I soon learned that spare seats in school coaches or taxis were of much service to the adult population.

It seemed a sensible and practical system, and made no difference to the Authority responsible for the cost of school transport; nor were the pupils or staff inconvenienced. And, after all, the whole community helped to pay for State education and everything connected with it.

So off we went northwards, with our loaded car (aged, but of good stock) pounding up the hills at a steady forty miles an hour without fuss. The unofficial passengers and luggage had all been dropped before we reached my village, which consisted of a very small post-office and telephone kiosk overlooking the great sweep of Gruinard Bay; one or two cottages and byres; and a modest chapel. Of school there was no trace—until, having turned the car down by the shore, we drove a few hundred yards back up the hill, and my driver stopped by a farm gate and indicated that my way lay through it. She apologized for taking me no further, but the track to the school was too rough to be good for the car, 'with tyres the terrible price they are'.

The wind and rain were roaring in off the sea with great force as I battled my way down the rocky lane, and through a stone arch at the bottom, to a grey building with gaunt windows, and an ancient-looking bell suspended above the door. Below the first entrance was a second door and some smaller windows with plants in them, which suggested that the school and teacher's dwelling were one and the same building. The small, stony play-ground in front consisted of a few islands in a sea of rain-water; and the general appearance was hardly inviting.

I couldn't distinguish any sound of life, but this was not sur-prising with the gale and rain drumming and lashing at every-thing like twin furies. Wondering if those within could possibly hear me, I thumped on the door with my fist, and waited. Nothing happened; so I tried the handle, but although the latch worked, the wood seemed to have swollen and jammed. While I struggled to force it open, someone came and tugged at the inner handle—with the result that I all but fell on top of her when the door gave way.

The mistress was a sturdy, dark-haired woman of middle years, dressed in a tweed skirt and hand-knitted woollies, who looked at me unsmilingly with keen grey eyes in which 'no non-sense' was plainly written. As I introduced myself I saw, from the tail of my eye, the hired car climb the last few yards of road on the distant skyline and disappear over the top.

'I don't ever have visiting teachers in the morning,' said the mistress firmly. 'I can't do with you at all just now! There's my Bible class and then the Gaelic lesson—we have those always in the morning. Everbody knows that quite well, and they had no business sending you.'

'How tiresome!' I said, shivering in my very wet shoes. 'I was told to come here this morning and to *Bualnaluib* after dinner.'

'You'll need to get that changed, then; you can go there this morning and come back later,' she replied.

'The trouble is,' I said wanly, 'the hired car has already left and won't be back until a quarter to one.'

There was an awkward silence, during which I began to picture myself cowering under a rock or in a byre for the next three and a half hours. 'It is ridiculous sending a visitor here in the morning! They know I can't do with you,' repeated the teacher. Then, suddenly aware that I was exceedingly wet, she thawed—and saying that I might as well go inside now that I *had* come, ushered me through into the schoolroom.

In this bare apartment, with rain beating through the leaky windows and forming pools on the board floor, were fifteen happy-looking children aged from five to eleven. The smallest were seated on a form in front, and behind them nine bigger ones in two rows of battered desks. Facing the unblinking stare of those fifteen pairs of eyes, I said brightly, 'Good morning, boys and girls.'

'Stand up!' said their mistress, and the flock obeyed instantly and repeated in unison, 'Good morning, miss.'

They remained standing while some prayers were said, and were just settling down while the teacher got out her Bible, when another visitor appeared. She seemed surprised and pleased to see him; and shaking him warmly by the hand, led him towards me and introduced us. He was a minister who travelled round the district encouraging the speaking and singing of Gaelic, and organizing broadcast programmes in that tongue. I gathered that some of the children in this school had made recordings for a recent radio feature with great success.

Saying that she would take the Bible class later, the mistress shut the Book and began to put the older children through their paces in Gaelic reading, while the little ones handled lumps of plasticine. Presently a nine-year-old boy was called out to the front to sing, unaccompanied, an old Gaelic song—which he did without trace of shyness in a clear, true voice.

'Beautiful, beautiful!' exclaimed the minister, wiping raindrops from his cheerful rosy face; 'we must have that one in the next children's programme.'

Next a girl sang; then there was some more reading; and he questioned the readers to make sure they understood what they had been saying. He congratulated the teacher on the proficiency of her pupils, and then, declining her offer of refreshment, said he must move on as he had other schools to visit.

The scholars were dismissed for their mid-morning break, and their mistress, now smiling and pleased, took me down to her house for some tea and biscuits. I gathered that the teaching of Gaelic and membership of *An Comunn Gaidhealach* (the Gaelic League) were a very important feature of her life, and noticed a copy of '*Gairm*' (the Gaelic magazine) on the table.

I asked if she had taught long in this school, and was told that she had spent nearly all her working life in it. 'Perhaps I should have been more ambitious,' she sighed, 'but somehow I stayed on and on here, and it is now too late to change.' As she spoke we watched from the window of her sitting-room a great storm cloud trailing over the nearest hill—which she called *Sàil Mhor* (The Big Heel); and then came a clear patch of blue sky and a sharp beam of sunlight focussed on the rounded crest of the peak.

I thought she could hardly have found a lovelier place to spend her life in, and she said: 'It is beautiful, and after all, it is my home. I was born up there by Dundonnell. My grandfather was evicted last century from a croft in *Strathnasheallag*.' She pointed to a vase of white heather on her mantelpiece. 'That's where I got the heather—in a glen known to our family for generations.'

She had spoken calmly and without trace of bitterness, but the word 'evicted' made me catch my breath. I had read terrible tales of the Highland evictions (just as I had seen pictures of wild cat at home), but meeting a member of an evicted family was an even greater shock than seeing the wild cat behind my cottage. There seemed nothing to say; and fortunately she did not appear to expect any comment. Whatever suffering her people had undergone at the time, they had the tough fibre to weather troubles and thrive, for the present generation had all worked their way through first-class education (my hostess was an M.A.) to positions of responsibility.

Any momentary feeling of depression I may have had on the school doorstep that morning was now wiped out, while admiration and affection for the schoolmistress developed fast. With the scantiest equipment she taught four or five different age-groups together in one room, and during her years of service had sent many a well-grounded pupil forward to the Grammar School in

Dingwall—and some ultimately to a university. As one expects from genuinely able people, she was most reticent and modest about her work.

She confessed to having a problem with the bigger boys, who required more scope for handicrafts—a subject she did not feel very competent to teach them. When she heard that I had been trained for this work her delight was obvious, and it was soon agreed that while she taught sewing and embroidery to my class of girls I should switch to basketry and leatherwork with the boys. She swept aside my doubts as to the attitude of the Education Committee to our private re-arrangement, saying that consent could safely be taken for granted. They wished to give her what help they could where it was most needed. We parted very happily, with my new programme and materials well in hand for the following week's lessons.

The boys hovered round beaming with pleasure, and gave me a grand send-off when the taxi arrived at the road gate. The first school certainly had a gap I could fill.

As we drove across the watershed dividing the Gruinard country from Loch Ewe, I looked back at the village and thought with amusement and relief of the transformation that had taken place in my feelings since the moment earlier that morning when, shivering and dripping at the school entrance, I had watched the car disappear over the same ridge.

The weather had also changed to match my happier mood. With one of those unpredictable switches so common on the west coast, heavy bundles of cloud had rolled back inland and could be seen fretting the tops of the *Beinn Eighe* range and looping in folds on *Beinn Airidh Charr*. Overhead and out to sea a bland blue sky dotted with white rabbit-scuts replaced the storm. The loch below us had turned a dazzling gentian violet streaked with jade green, and only some glints of foam on the wave crests showed where the now dying gale had lashed the water.

Soon we came down alongside the loch, past the hotel and village shop, and in sight of a rusty pier and mooring buoys— mostly relics of a naval boom-defence system left over from the recent war. A coasting steamer lay at the pier unloading coal, with a rabble of gulls whirling overhead as the ship's cook threw out a can of galley rubbish.

It was difficult to imagine this great empty sea-loch full of naval vessels and cargo boats, but so it had been during the latter part of the war, when convoys carrying supplies through the perilous northern waters to Russian ports had assembled here. I had heard at the time that the battleship *Nelson* (in which an old friend of our days in Ceylon was serving) had met with a torpedo attack somewhere off Scotland, though little dreamed that I should one day teach in a remote school within sight of the sea where his ship had been crippled. Yet here I was, with the driver telling me all about it.

The second school looked much like the first, except for being a size larger, with a detached house for the Headmaster. A fringe of yellow flag irises beside the burn bordering the school demesne provided the only spot of brightness on the land. The rocky play-ground was full of children, many of whom gathered round in silence as I got out. A cheerful red-headed boy, less shy than the others, came forward and ushered me into the presence of his headmaster. This tall Lewisman (a war-time captain in the Highland Division) somehow gave the impression of wearing the kilt even though he was in fact dressed in a tweed suit.

As it was lunchtime he took me straight through to the school dining-room, which was crammed to bursting with tables and benches set out for the meal. The master and his assistant mistress stood at a side table doling out stew and vegetables as the children filed past with their plates at the ready. Although this drill went forward at a smart pace, and there was very little room to move, even the smallest children (and the most awkward boys) managed to steer through successfully without spilling any of the food with which they were so lavishly supplied.

The master apologized in his deep, slightly melancholy voice for the rough meal, but I was able to assure him with truth that the expensive boarding schools I had known were not half as well fed, even if they had grander rooms and flowers on the table.

Here, the good Scotch blackface mutton had never seen the inside of a refrigerator, nor the root vegetables a tin or dehydrating factory, and the baked sponge pudding was as light as it could be, and most appetizing.

Appetites were not wanting either, and I have seldom seen children put away so much food in so short a time. Even so, many came again for second helpings. After grace had been said, we three members of the staff adjourned to the kitchen, where the cook made us a pot of tea. She was a bonny lass, not long out of her Domestic Science College, and glad to have work in this place where her father was a minister. While we were seated on kitchen stools enjoying our tea, the back door opened and in he came—so his daughter poured out another cup.

He looked most interested when we were introduced, saying, 'You come from the south—from Dingwall, is it?'

When told that I had come very much further than that, and was by birth a Londoner, his brows went up and his eyes grew round.

'You don't speak with an English accent at all!' he cried. 'But from London? Well, well, now. Oh, that's a terrible place, London! I was only there once in all my life. I stayed at a place called Clap Ham. Do you know Clap Ham? I shall not forget it. I was in a hotel there, and I had a letter to post. They told me to go down the road until I reached the main street, and then to cross over and I would find the post-office a little way down on the other side.

'So I went along the road the hotel was in, but when I reached the main street I could not get across it to the post at all. The traffic—I never saw anything like that in my life—it went by like a great shoal of herring, on and on and *on*. I stood on the pavement and waited for it to stop for me, but it never did, and after half an hour I turned round and went back to the hotel, and my letter was not posted that day.'

After this horrifying story we refreshed ourselves with another round of tea, and then the speaker looked at me anxiously, evidently wondering if he had wounded my civic pride.

'Of course,' he said, 'if you were born in London you would get used to the traffic, and I expect you will be very fond of the place.'

'I am *not at all* fond of living in it; there are too many people whose names are unknown to me, and not a wild hill to be seen,' I replied. I told how Aunt Mairi sometimes feared I might be dull at Inverewe with her, and secretly longing for a spell of theatres and concerts and a tour of the big London shops.

'I tell Mrs. Sawyer there was just one sight of that city which thrilled me,' I said; 'can any of you guess what it was?'

'Buckingham Palace, with the Royal Family on the balcony?' asked the minister's daughter. 'I'd like fine to see them myself!'

'It was not that,' I said; 'for one thing, I never have seen them on the balcony.'

The mistress suggested Chelsea Flower Show (because of my interest in gardening), the Headmaster the Changing of the Guard, and the minister, Saint Paul's Cathedral, but I shook my head. 'No! The only view of London I shall *never* forget was the glimpse I got from a taxi on my way to Euston station to catch the night train to Inverness,' I said.

Everyone enjoyed the little joke, and the minister, no longer wondering if he had dropped a brick, relaxed into his usual placid humour. I remembered seeing him before, soon after my arrival at Inverewe. One misty night I had gone for a walk at dusk, and thinking it too wet for the hill, started off along the road to Tournaig. I had not gone many yards when a small green car pulled up and the minister, who was driving, offered me a lift. I said I was only going down to Tournaig, but he made me jump in.

As we drove off, he said he hadn't known that the new owners of Aunt Mairi's old home had come up so soon, and I told him they had not yet arrived, nor was I on my way to visit them. 'Just out for an evening walk,' I explained.

'A walk!—all the way back from Tournaig to Inverewe in the mist! Oh, dear me, that won't do at all!' And with that, he spun the car round and took me home to the gates I had just left, frustrating my attempts at exercise but warming my heart with his kindliness.

In the school kitchen he rose to go before I had time to remind him of this earlier encounter, but he turned to me with a charming smile to hope that we should meet again in the future.

The Headmaster and the mistress then took me through to one of the two classrooms and on the way showed me a cupboard where sewing materials overlay a bundle of the cane used in basketry and a selection of paint brushes, crayons, and rolls of drawing paper.

I inquired who took the art lessons, and my companions looked doubtful. 'We do what we can,' said the master, 'but all that is rather beyond us. This cane is just a nuisance, for nobody knows what to do with it.'

'What a pity,' I said, 'we could do with it at Laide. I am teaching handicrafts to the boys there.'

This made them very excited. 'If you can teach the Laide boys, why not ours?' Before many minutes had passed, the happenings of the morning were repeated, and I found myself handing back the sewing girls to the mistress (who was good at needlework), while I took charge of a class of boys and basketry. They were very keen and showed a natural aptitude for it—which was not a surprise when one remembered how in the old days every crofter was a fisherman and made his own creels and lobster-pots.

The red-headed lad who had escorted me on my arrival looked a healthy, well-grown boy and it was a shock when the master said that Sandy would not be able to manage canework with his delicate little hands. Until then I had not noticed that they were as small and undeveloped as those of a child of four. But Sandy loved to draw; so he was soon happily settled with paper and crayons, and made me a good picture of the pier and the coal boat.

The moment the class was over and the boys beginning to carry their work and tools out to the cupboard, they were mobbed by the younger ones—all seething with curiosity, and jealous because they were not to have a lesson from me. Then I remembered

to tell the master that my friend at Laide would prefer me to go
there in the afternoons. As the mornings were longer, it seemed
that I could fit in drawing or handicraft lessons here for all three
groups—'If you can be bothered with the little ones?' he said. I
told him it would bother me far more to leave them out and see
their disconsolate looks.

'I suppose I had better tell the Education Committee what you
are doing,' he said, 'but they cannot object. It just means a supple-
mentary order for some material, as we shall not have enough
for all you are going to teach.'

'Meantime, I'll bring some of my own tools and things,' I
said, gathering up my coat and bag as a 'scout' dashed in to say
that my car was waiting.

Aunt Mairi was pleased to hear that my first day had turned
out well, and she enjoyed the minister's description of London.
She said she couldn't imagine him there alone, for he was one of
the most absent-minded men on the coast, and kept Arthur or
Colin busy running after him with forgotten parcels and umbrella
every time he went to Inverness.

She said he once absent-mindedly terrified a village girl by
almost marrying her to the wrong man. The maiden, suddenly
realizing that he was addressing the best man instead of the groom,
bawled out in a voice made raucous with fright, 'It's not him—
it's him!'—pointing to each man in turn. Unperturbed, the
minister said serenely, 'Well, well, now, there's no harm done—
we'll just begin again.' Patting the trembling bride on the
shoulder, he reversed the positions of the two men and went
through the service a second time. So all was well, and she walked
out of the church happily married to the man of her choice, but
would probably not forget the bad moment when she thought
the minister had given her the wrong partner for ever.

Osgood MacKenzie used to tell Aunt Mairi that his grandfather, Sir Hector, the fourth baronet, known to his people as
'*An Tighearna Storach*' ('The Buck-toothed Laird'), went, like our
minister friend, but once to London in his life. As he was in his
thirties at the time and was born around 1758, this must have

been in the last decade of the eighteenth century—when we had George the Third on the throne of England, and France was in a turmoil.

Sir Hector's memory of London sounds strangely up-to-date one hundred and seventy years after; for he complained on returning to Gairloch that money went nowhere in the Capital, and said he had been obliged to dip continually into his pouch. For some hours after his homecoming he could be seen, dressed in his best blue swallow-tail coat with gilt buttons, buff waistcoat, black breeches and grey silk stockings, with an array of plaited ruffles below the mutton-chop whiskers adorning his chin, showing the fascinated tenants (gathered in welcome) how the skin had been worn from his right forefinger and thumb by constantly forking out coins.

10. *Queer Characters and Goings-on*

ONE character I had noticed in the Gairloch district was to me a fascinating though somewhat unprofitable study. By the general cut of his jib he looked a typical seaman, with his blue uniform, peaked cap, and nautical roll; but he lived and worked ashore, and was seen either dashing hither and thither on a noisy motor-bike, or else standing about in lonely spots with the incongruous machine propped against a rock.

I couldn't get the hang of him at all—and when told that he was 'The Exciseman' felt little the wiser. Customs and Excise officials, I vaguely supposed, had to deal with dutiable goods; but as there were only a few coal boats and, at certain seasons, the herring-fleet in Gairloch (and at Aultbea what remained of a naval base), I could not imagine who went in for clandestine trade. The inhospitable coastline provided little scope for small-boat landings. Anyhow, it was difficult to see where, on these bare hills, smugglers could hide goods in any quantity—or, if there were suitable caves, transport much in the way of booty over the trackless heather. And what other taxable things could there be?

The Exciseman always looked rosy and good-humoured, and spoke civilly to everyone, but at first nobody would enlarge on their replies to my inquiries. He was just 'The Exciseman', and, having told me that, they changed the subject.

Then came a fine Saturday when my friends the weavers took me for a picnic on the sandy shore to the south-west of Gairloch. Here on a grassy promontory overlooking the bay we all inspected a vitrified fort, where the very early inhabitants had surrounded themselves with a rampart of rocks and then piled bonfires round the outside of their walls, bringing the stones to so fierce a heat that they melted and fused into a solid block.

Long after the others had tired of this and wandered away to the sea, I stayed on the hillock examining the vitrified remains. Next, continuing to indulge my antiquarian instincts, I moved on to a small enclosed burial ground beside the shore, in order to see how many of the old MacKenzie tombstones were still legible. Some of them looked very ancient, but probably exposure to the wild storms off the Minch had accelerated their decay.

When I reached the entrance I came upon the Exciseman leaning against a tree beside the rusty iron gates. These were locked, and I could not get in, so I bid the man 'Good afternoon' (to which he replied politely), and rejoined my friends.

They were amused when I said I wished he wasn't always hanging about staring at nothing in particular and giving me the creeps.

'What does the man do for a living?' I asked.

'Just that,' said the weaver. 'He spends his life watching, in the hope of catching somebody at it. He hasn't a dog's chance, of course; these folk are far too clever and too clannish to give anything away.'

'But what are they supposed to be caught at?' I persisted.

'Why, distilling unlicensed whisky, of course. It's the Highlander's traditional sport.'

'I can't believe they make whisky out in the bleak places where I've seen him,' I said sceptically, 'or in a graveyard!'

'That's all you know about it, and just as well,' was the reply.

Another friend now joined in the discussion. 'There was a good story going round a year or two back, which I happened to hear,' she said.

'Two men, father and son, had kept a still hidden undetected in a wonderful cave for many years—so long, in fact, that it got worn out and useless. The tragedy was that they couldn't possibly afford a new one. Nor, of course, had they the money for legitimate brands, and it seemed as though they would be forced to go without their daily dram—a bitter sacrifice for men whose work took them out on the hill in all weathers. Such men really need their ration of whisky; though it is a pity they have to drink the crude, terrible stuff of their own making, while so much of the finest Scotch goes away to America.

'One day the son came to his father in great excitement. "Exciseman is getting annoyed," he said. "He's offering a reward of twenty-five pounds to anyone who will give information leading to the discovery and seizure of a still in this area."

' "Oh, the man will never find ours!" said the father; "but why, boy, are you looking so pleased? You would never give away anyone's still to Exciseman, I hope."

' "I was thinking of that," said his son gravely, much to the older man's disgust. "I'm sure it is the best thing to do. If the still is done, he may as well take it. Twenty-five pounds is a lot of money, and will do us more good than *it* will do him."

'The crofter stood staring at his son, while a slow gleam of understanding crept into his eyes. "*Our* still. . . . I see. Perhaps there is something in what you are saying, Donald. But you would not be letting Exciseman find the place it is in?"

' "No, that will not be necessary; we can just take it up to the *Easan Dorcha*[1] one night, or some other place that no one uses, and then show Exciseman the way to it. Of course we must make some pretence at hiding it well, so that the man will not feel foolish at having passed it by so often; but that will be quite simple."

---

[1] Pronounced 'Aissan Dorrka'.

'The more they thought about it, the better the plan seemed —so on the first suitable night they moved the still with its unwieldy copper "worms" away from their real hiding-place to another cranny in the rock, and made a good show of disguising it. Then they went to the Exciseman and said they had stumbled upon a still while going after some straying sheep.

'The official needed no encouragement. He was on to the trail at once, and hustled them away to the hill at a faster pace than they were accustomed to use. Fortunately he had not previously been aware of the *Easan Dorcha* cave, so the story sounded convincing. He did know that Donald and his father were poor men, and also that they had but recently taken to sheep on that particular hill. They might not, therefore, be familiar with the owner of the apparatus they had discovered, and consequently the more willing to give its whereabouts away and earn the needed money.

'He was right in one respect: the two men accepted the reward with great alacrity—but no one suffered any loss as a result of their betrayal. Instead, the owners gained heavily, for they went into Inverness and got themselves parts to make a new still for only twenty pounds; which left them a fiver on hand to celebrate the occasion, and a real night they made of it.

'As for the Exciseman, nobody knew if he ever suspected that he had been duped, but on paper at any rate his honour was vindicated—for had he not captured an illicit whisky-making plant? No one troubled to investigate the age or usefulness of the contraption for which he had bestowed the Government's twenty-five pounds on Donald and his father.'

When I repeated all this to Aunt Mairi, I said it put me in mind of favourite fiction in my early school years—one of those enthralling yarns in *Chums* or the *Boy's Own Paper* which so often distracted my thoughts from French verbs or the Holy Roman Empire. (Although I went to a conventional girls' school, I couldn't stomach girls' books.)

It appeared that the Western Highlands were rich in such tales, dealing not only with illicit whisky manufacture but the much more romantic business (as it seemed to her) of smuggling in the old days. There really *was* a beautiful, fast schooner called *The Rover's Bride*, owned by one James MacDonald (nicknamed 'The Rover') who used to run many a cargo of contraband liquor into Gairloch, among other places, on the coast. Some time in the eighteen-twenties he gave a passage from Gairloch to Skye to Aunt Mairi's great-uncle, John MacKenzie of Eileanach, when he was a medical student on vacation from Edinburgh University.

The schooner was laden with what the lad supposed to be casks of salt for the herring curing, but the jovial James said, 'Tubs of brandy from Bordeaux, John—and there's not a cruiser afloat that can put salt on the *Bride*'s tail if there's a puff of wind.'

In those days everyone on the coast drank smuggled whisky, brandy, sherry, and port as a matter of course, and nobody looked upon it as a crime. James MacDonald maintained his position as a Highland gentleman of the Clanranald family, and at the same time lived outside the law, spending much of his life at sea engaged in smuggling for the adventure of it.

At one time he had leased the anchorage of Tanera (of the Summer Isles in Gruinard Bay), with the quay which was repaired and used more than a hundred years later by Dr. Fraser Darling—as described in his book *Island Farm*. Visitors to the district still hear tales about James MacDonald. Once *The Rover's Bride* was in the Tanera anchorage, stuffed with contraband, when a Revenue cutter appeared. Instantly MacDonald weighed anchor and sailed away north with the Revenue officials in pursuit. They made Cape Wrath, and then MacDonald set course for the Orkneys. The cutter was slowly gaining on him, but he was not troubled; for if only he could reach the islands before the other boat drew level he was sure he would give it the slip.

He was familiar with a difficult passage between two of the islands where he fancied the skipper of the other vessel might not care to risk his ship. This proved to be the case, and with every stitch of sail set *The Rover's Bride* went safely through those dangerous narrows to freedom, while the cheated Revenue men had to turn back in disgust empty-handed.

On another occasion the schooner was chased into Gairloch, but by the time the Revenue men were able to land, the smugglers (helped by innumerable willing hands) had unloaded the ship and successfully hidden every cask of brandy and claret where the officials could not discover them. It so happened that Sir Hector MacKenzie, who had been away at his Conon property, arrived unexpectedly just then in Gairloch without sending the customary notice. The people did not welcome him with their usual zest, and he sensed that something was amiss. This was explained when he found himself unable to enter his own house by the proper entrance—as the entire cargo of the schooner had been stowed inside *Tigh Dige*, and the only means of access was now by means of a ladder through an upper window. The Revenue men, of course, had not dreamed of visiting the *laird's* home in search of the missing casks!

When Doctor John MacKenzie came of age his father paid a considerable sum of money for what was called the 'superiority' of a district at Fortrose to make his son a Justice of the Peace, and one of the thirty or forty 'electors' of the county. After the young man had fined some smugglers in accordance with the law, he began to have qualms of conscience which told him that he was as bad as (or worse than) they—for he drank nothing but 'mountain dew', or liquor smuggled from France.

So he then decided to give up all connection with illicit alcohol, and for this rectitude was taken to task by no less a person than the Dean of Ross and Argyll, who said he himself looked back regretfully to the good old days when his father used to distil every Saturday what was required the following week.

The Dean agreed with a well-known grocer of those days in Inverness—who, although he held only an off-licence, used to supply his customers regularly in the back parlour of the shop. When censured for his law-breaking he asserted indignantly, 'But I never approved of that law!' The Dean and he were of one mind: that the licensing laws were bad and should be broken.

I commented that laws in general seemed to encounter many a rough passage on this coast still. I overheard one of my teacher colleagues complaining that State employees had their income tax removed before any pay was handed over, while others paid none at all. She cited a crofter known to her who had gradually increased his flock of sheep—aided by what the Gaelic speakers called 'sub-side-ease',[1] and also the high prices of wool and mutton—until on his own admission he had last year netted close on a thousand pounds. Told by her that he would have to pay quite a lot of tax on that sum, he refuted the suggestion on the grounds that next year his profits might be much less, and therefore the money was not *regular* income and couldn't be taxed. Nothing would convince him of the absurdity of his argument, and so far as she knew he had succeeded in keeping his earnings from the tax-collector's ken.

Aunt Mairi agreed that the people were adepts at going their own way, and said that in the last war the rationing officials had had a hard row to hoe. She remembered an Inspector coming out all the way from Inverness to one of the villages and giving the shopkeeper a lecture for sending in 5,000 points coupons fewer than were due for the goods sold.

'Well, well, now,' said the culprit with an air of startled innocence, 'I do not know what I can have done with the coupons at all, at all.' This was not exactly untrue, as he had done nothing with them—not even bothering to collect the necessary pieces of paper from his customers' ration books! As his was the only shop for some miles, and the people must be fed, the authorities could not dock him of his supplies; so he got away with his methods for the rest of the war.

In the same way, communities with only one petrol pump could not sell the coloured fuel supplied for farm and other essential vehicles (as was done in larger places), so the priority coupons were used indiscriminately for private cars as well; and nobody was detected in this illegal practice.

'And of course they all had plenty of unrationed meat,' said Aunt Mairi. 'It would be interesting to know just how many sheep died—as was said—from "broken legs" during those years.

[1] Subsidies.

We do not hear any more of this alarmingly high mortality rate now that rationing has ended!'

I said I supposed there was poaching of venison and salmon in plenty, too, but to this she replied that she thought not. 'Here we only *call* it poaching when those horrible gangs come out in motors from the towns and take game or fish in large quantities at night for the trade, and luckily we are too far from centres of population to be much troubled with gangsters.'

Her quaintest poaching story concerned a very small inn at which she had stopped, having taken longer over a car journey than expected and feeling in need of a meal of some sort. She said anything would do, with a preference for a poached egg. The shy fifteen-year-old serving girl hesitated, and then replied sweetly, 'I'm awful sorry we've no eggs, but I could give you some poached salmon.'

Sometimes, of course, poaching was inadvertent, as when a young man staying at Inverewe came back in triumph one evening with his first salmon—a twenty-pounder. Aunt Mairi followed the story of the catch with great interest and enthusiasm —until she got him to describe exactly the reach of the Ewe and discovered that it was not caught on her beat! A hasty telephone conversation with the factor of the estate concerned followed and as she could not deprive her guest of his prize, she perforce offered to pay ten pounds for it instead.

Sometimes appearances are very deceptive. On my next visit to *Bualnaluib* school I was told another 'poaching' saga which ended happily for the alleged miscreants. Two small boys, aged ten and eleven, arrived in the village carrying a ten-pound salmon between them. They were questioned by the factor, and stoutly maintained that they had got it out of the little burn running through the playground. This sounded such an unlikely defence that they were in great danger of being disbelieved; until a visitor to the hotel came forward and confirmed that he had watched the whole procedure from the hill, and the catch had certainly taken place just where the children said.

When I walked over to look at the stream it seemed to me

more like a sewer than a salmon river—for someone had cast an old cracked lavatory pan and cistern into a pool, where they rested careened among the yellow irises, immovably jammed against a rock. The question that came into my mind was, *could* this salmon have been spawned in so paltry a burn, and returned to its birthplace as is popularly supposed, or was it a case of the fish that took the wrong turning? *The Observer* for May 19th 1957 reported that a salmon marked in Ross-shire in 1955 turned up off the south coast of Greenland eleven months later. If these fish regularly travel such enormous distances and return to their place of birth (this one would have completed a journey of 3,400 miles in that case), one might reasonably expect an occasional error at the end of so exhausting a trip. But as yet most of our notions about salmon are based largely on conjecture, and still await proof.

The last piece of poaching I heard about from Aunt Mairi concerned the heaviest 'fish' of the lot. When, on Christmas Eve 1950, the Stone of Destiny (or Stone of Scone) was lifted from Westminster Abbey in the heart of London by a trio of young Scottish Nationalists, the rumour spread in Wester Ross that it had been transported up to our coast and hidden in one of the numerous caves on the north-westerly tip of the shore of Loch Ewe. Probably the fact that the parents of the girl in the plot lived nearby at Inverasdale had something to do with the theory, but it gained much credence and for a week or so newspaper reporters were thick on the ground.

In the middle of this furore the English owner of a neighbouring estate arrived one morning and tried to persuade Aunt Mairi to join him and his guests in a grand search for the missing relic. She showed little inclination to share his enthusiasm, and said flatly that she was far too busy gardening to go on a wild-goose chase.

The excited visitor, having (as a very close friend) the freedom of the house, then dashed through to the kitchen to see what old Sheena thought about the business. As usual, she had the final word. 'I'm thinking,' she said with an enigmatic stare at his monocled eye, 'that there's an awful lot of people with *very little to do.*'

11. *Junior Secondary and Puppy Schools*

OUR day at the Junior Secondary School began with the singing of 'Jesus Loves Me' to a rather out-of-tune piano, after which the three groups dispersed to their classrooms. Ordinary classes were held in the old building of what had been the original primary school, and a dour, hard-bitten place it was—with a rough board floor, open coal grates and useful brown paintwork. From their rows of antique desks the pupils could not possibly see aught but clouds through the high-silled windows.

Extra classes such as cookery, needlework, carpentry, and weaving were held in the modern one-storey building which had been erected when the school acquired 'junior secondary' status. This long white hutment, known as 'the canteen', served as the dining-room at midday. At one end was the kitchen in which my cookery classes were to be held. During the morning this was the domain of the school cook and her assistant; after they had served the meal and washed up, it became mine for the afternoon.

I received a friendly warning that our cook had a mind of her own and no inhibitions about speaking it. If the boys hung around in the hope of tit-bits, or in any way annoyed her, they were apt to get a slap across the mouth with a wet dish-clout and be sent quickly about their business. Before classes began I heard her quell one strapping crofter lad of fifteen with a clout accompanied by the words 'Cheeky brat!' So I wondered how on earth I should cope with a class of adolescent girls in her spotless kitchen and keep on good terms with the cook.

It seemed best to remember Malcolm, third Chief of the Macleods, who seized a fierce bull by the horns and overthrew it single-handed—thus giving the clan its crest of a bull's head *cabossed*. (Not that the cook was a bull, but it might sound impolite to call her a cow.)

I went straight up to her and said: 'I'm sorry to say that I have to teach the older girls cookery in *your* kitchen. Children of that age are notoriously messy, and I am not even a trained Domestic Science teacher. But I shall do my very best to make them leave everything exactly as they found it, and if you discover the smallest thing amiss next morning, I hope you will come to me about it at once.'

She gave me a grim glance and replied, 'I *will* so!'

My first class that morning consisted of eight little girls of about nine summers, who came shyly to me (in the dining end of the canteen) for a sewing lesson. A box of material had been put ready for me on one of the tables, surrounded by needles and cottons, thimbles, scissors, and a finished sample of the work they were to do. This article was called a 'lap-bag', and was worn throughout a girl's school days at sewing classes. When the lesson ended, each pupil had to pack her work into the large pockets of her apron and tie it into a neat parcel with the waist strings. It proved to be a very practical method of keeping all the little pieces of more complicated patterns together tidily and unsoiled.

Unfortunately, the unbleached calico supplied for the bags was the toughest kind of material the children ever dealt with in sewing classes, and had to be managed in their first year by the least experienced fingers. Many a struggle my pupils fought to prod their needles through it, and many a broken point I retrieved and disposed of in a safe place.

As soon as everyone had settled down to work, the brightest member of the class—a lively character of eight and a half—shook her long brown ringlets and with a heavy sigh exclaimed, 'Eh, dearie me, my back is that sore!' I asked what she had been doing to make it hurt, and she replied even more gustily, 'Picking stones!' It seemed that wee Jessie and her six elder sisters were set to work in the evenings ridding the fields on their father's croft of the rock fragments with which it was strewn. As Jessie put it, 'Directly we clear a part of it and move away to another part, the stones grow again and the first part we cleared looks just as bad as ever.'

She had a musical little voice and her enunciation was sweet and clear, so that apart from the interest of hearing about her life on the croft I was tempted to encourage her to talk for the pleasure of listening to her; but as she found it necessary to turn her large brown eyes in my direction, while her fingers drooped and ceased work, I was obliged to recall her thoughts to the needle. Before doing so, I asked how long she had spent in the field the evening before; and she said, 'Until it was dark.' She seemed surprised at being asked that question—I supposed because everything on the croft went on until the light failed, after which they all retired to bed.

Jessie and her companions had not yet realized that the Hydro-electric men, who were busily running supply lines all over the district, would be the means of altering so many simple old customs of that sort. Once people have the power to switch on a light almost as good as day, the temptation to cease rising and going to bed with the sun grows strong. Even so, not every crofter makes much use of the new light. One old man, livng alone in a croft already connected to the electricity supply, was visited by a meter-reader who expressed great surprise at the small number of units consumed—about six in three months.

'Why, Sandy,' he said, 'there must be something far wrong with your meter! Or haven't you been using the light?'

This occurred in early spring, before the days grew long, when even the poorest and most economical habitually used more than that.

Sandy took his pipe from his mouth and said slowly: 'Yess, I have used it. Indeed, it iss very use-ful to put on while I am finding the matches to light my lamp.'

·   ·   ·   ·   ·

Our sewing class ended at a quarter to eleven, and after the embryo lap-bags had been stowed and their cardboard container taken across the playground to its cupboard in the old building, the canteen opened for morning break and children of all ages came hurtling in. The cook and her friend slid open the hatch and passed out beakers of milk as fast as hands could grip them. Most of the children brought a 'piece' or biscuits from home to eat, but others (the rich ones) dashed off to Donnie Tarly's shop to buy chocolate biscuits or sweeties.

The two full-time mistresses came over to the kitchen, where I joined them for tea and a biscuit provided by the school. We had no minister to visit us here—but instead a large and jolly man burst in with a great hamper of meat for next day's dinner. He needed no persuasion to share our tea and gossip, and perching precariously on a stool made the kitchen echo to his rumbustious laughter. He owned a small lock-up shop in the village, but as he had no assistant to mind it and was usually out collecting carcases, delivering joints, or working on his croft, the shop hours were few and erratic. I asked how I could get some liver for my Sunday dinner, and he slapped his fist down on the table and roared that he would deliver it to the school on Friday—and it could go into the refrigerator until I was ready to take it. The cook pretended to be furious at this free-handed use of her equipment, and drove him from the kitchen with the aid of her famous dish-clout and a torrent of abuse, accompanied by loud laughter from the victim.

'Donnie's a blether!' said his attacker after he had gone. Then, in a high good humour, she showed me a little annexe where the utensils and stores for my cookery classes were kept separately from the canteen equipment. Discovering that I had almost no experience of coal ovens, she proceeded to instruct me in the use of hers, and ended by promising to bank up the grate ready for my afternoon's lesson before she went home. My spirits rose, for all this had been unexpectedly helpful. I prayed that the cookery girls would not undo the good work.

After break the Headmaster came over to say that it would not be possible to let me have another class of girls before dinner, but there was some work in connection with National Savings which he would like me to take over from him; and that I could go along to the post-office with cash in hand to buy the children's certificates, and order cookery stores at the grocer's shop on the way. The school had an account at MacKenzie's, and he would probably deliver the goods before two o'clock for me.

I totted up the columns in the savings register, sorted out the books of those who had subscribed enough to pay for another certificate, counted the cash, and set off clutching a canvas bag heavy with coins. The post-office was at the far end of the village, but as the road ran alongside the sea's edge nearly all the way the walk was a pleasure. There was a stiff breeze blowing in off the Minch, and big rollers crashing on the stones made my ears ring. Out to sea white wave-caps seethed, collided, broke, and cast spume shorewards in feathery trails. The sun glittered in the spray and on wet cliffs and uncovered rocks on the strand, on a couple of fishing boats plunging home to Gairloch harbour at the opposite end of the straggling village, and on a group of birds wheeling over the centre of the bay. Presently one of them dived, dropping suddenly like a stone into the water and throwing up a fountain several feet high.

As I passed the weavers' white bungalow and workshop half way along the strath, I saw them at their front door watching the diving display. 'Aren't the gannets marvellous!' Kirstie shouted above the tumult of the sea. 'This is real gannet weather!' I waved agreement and went on round the curve of the shore, keeping my eyes fixed on the unique demonstration of combined diving and flying operations given by the great white birds.

Their technique consists of a circling flight above the water (the elevation varies) in search of a herring shoal. When fish are sighted the gannet sharply checks its flight, partly folds the wings, and dives in a vertical drop with an impetus that can carry it several feet beneath the surface. The exact force is skilfully adjusted to the depth at which the shoal is judged to be swimming. The fountains of water thrown aloft by the diving birds can be seen miles away.

The gannet, or *Solan goose*, is much bigger than any gull, and can be easily identified by the greater length of its neck and the intense whiteness of the plumage, with black wing-tips. In any case the method of fishing is quite unlike those employed by the gull family. Gannets are useful to fishermen as 'look-outs' and markers of shoals. About twenty of them were busy in Gair Loch that day, and a better display I have never seen. The business they had in hand was strictly practical; but the abandon with which they plunged into the sea, and the flashing fountains they sent up, combined with the windy glitter of the morning, gave an impression memorable for its physical energy and sheer *joie-de-vivre*.

I was the sole customer in the little post-office, and received some useful instruction about National Savings rules and regulations from the efficient young postmistress. Then, lighter by seven pounds, fifteen shillings' worth of coinage, I walked back as far as MacIntyre's haberdashery and household goods shop. The owner, who had been standing outside, followed me in to inquire what I wished to buy—and I noticed that, polite though his manner was, his eyes were irresistibly drawn towards the open door.

'I was just out watching the gannets,' he explained with an apologetic smile; and we were at once on the most friendly bird-watching terms. The binding I needed to finish the many seams of an unlined tweed jacket was available only in single cards of each shade: so after a fruitless search for duplicates he sold me one grey, one brown, and one fawn. This seemed to worry him— until I said it would make the sewing less tedious to finish off the tailoring in a variety of colours. That cheered him up, and he returned happily to his gannets.

Next I called in at Osgood MacKenzie's grocery store to order cookery materials for my class. It used to be the custom for clansmen to name an eldest son after their Chief—or one of *his* sons—and when the latter bore Highland forenames this passed without comment. But as Aunt Mairi's father had been christened 'Osgood' after an English grandparent (of the Hanbury family of Holfield Grange in Essex), his name attracted attention in the remote Highland shop. Customers soon saw that this shop was not of the traditional village type—was, in fact, so up-to-date and spruce that it might well have belonged to one of London's Home Counties, where the proprietor's name originated.

Mr. MacKenzie himself took my order and promised to bring the purchases along to the school in good time for my class that afternoon. As there was still time to spare I turned in at the weavers' gate on my homeward journey. Kirstie reminded me that she would be coming along after lunch to take a weaving class in the canteen: so we should be sharing that building for the afternoon. 'Don't forget, at twenty to four most children will down tools and tear off to the hall,' she said, 'for today is what they call a "fillum" day.' Seeing my puzzled frown, she explained that educational films were provided every other week for the scholars. This had created some dissension at first, for many of the parents thought that films were sinful and had never ventured to see one themselves. When the much-respected Education Authority showed films to the children, these quiet folk were bewildered. Education was Good and films were Bad, and how could the two be reconciled?

One of the local ministers settled the matter for *his* congregation by preaching against the innovation—and as a result a petition was organized in protest, with a rider that if the shows were not withdrawn altogether, the children of the signatories should be excluded. The film shows went on, but children of the dissenters were given other things to do.

One of the petitioners had a daughter in the school at the time who was duly barred from the fun on film days—much to her disappointment. Some months later her younger brother reached school age, and when the next film day came round the Headmaster warned the boy's teacher that he must be kept away from the show. She dutifully took him along to join his sister, and all appeared to be in order. Next morning the Headmaster was astonished to have an early visit from the father of the children, who complained that his boy had missed the free films—which wouldn't do at all. He was reminded with some emphasis that he had signed the protest against film exhibitions, and that one of the points made was that children of petitioners must be excluded from these shows. 'Yes, yes,' said the aggrieved parent with an impatient gesture, *'but wee Alec was not in school when I signed the paper!'* The difficulty of pleasing parents is one of the occupational hazards of a headmaster or -mistress; but this incident we thought unique as an example of failure.

Kirstie said one never knew what might come under the ban of the Free Kirk, or how a prohibition would work. This brought her to the subject of evening classes in handicrafts for adults—which some people were keen to have during the winter months. The Education Committe would pay an instructor and provide a room if a minimum of ten students could be enrolled. She herself did not feel able to undertake the extra work, but thought I might do it. 'It would be worth trying,' she mused, 'even if you *were* preached against.' 'Surely,' I protested, 'no one could see evil in a cane basket or a lampshade!' But Kirstie was not prepared to say.

Had not the Women's Rural Institutes (Scottish equivalent of the English 'Women's Institutes') recently come under fire in the West Highlands? 'There was a meeting in Skye,' she said, 'when the laird's wife had a speaker up from Headquarters to introduce the W.R.I. to a community which had no branch. Most of the local women attended and were enrolled as members.

The organizer and speaker both went away home well satisfied
that the movement had got off to a flying start in the village.
Then came the sabbath, and a minister who began his address
with these words: "On Saturday the Devil came to Skye; and the
Devil's tail was curled round; and the curl took the form of the
letters W, R, I. . . ."

After that the members dropped off like salted snails, and the
Rural Institute soon petered out altogether in the village. 'So you
never *can* tell what will happen up here,' said Kirstie.

I said it was inconceivable to me that anyone could seriously
imagine that gatherings convened to discuss problems of health
and hygiene, and to learn making, and mending, could possibly
be harmful. Kirstie said it wasn't so much that the meetings were
considered harmful in themselves, but the fear that people would
be distracted by too many outside interests from reading their
Bibles and keeping to the straight path. And one couldn't dispute
that these strict rules of life *had* produced some very fine characters.

Had not I myself remarked on the joy of being able to leave
doors unlocked in safety, and parcels by the roadside for the
passing mail to pick up in its own time? How often I had quoted
Arthur's remark to a passenger in that same mail, when the old
man said humbly, 'I'm awful sorry, Arthur, I've no money for
my fare'—and the latter replied gently, 'That's quite all right,
Angus, you can pay me next week.' Where in the 'enlightened'
centres of 'civilization' could such trust and trustworthiness be
confidently taken for granted in every member of a community?

We agreed that if the proof of the preaching was in the
behaviour of the flock, there was indeed much to be commended;
but I still thought the goodness of these folk would not be under-
mined by a few more entertainments and amenities. The practical
offshoot of this discussion was my undertaking to instruct a
handicraft session every Tuesday evening if required, and with
that settled I hurried back in time for school dinner.

Luckily I found the cookery syllabus easier to understand
than the maze of religious theories. It began with breakfast dishes,

and worked through a day's meals, so that by the end of the school year a pupil should be able to cook two or three menus for each. My class was very quiet and well behaved, except for one outsize girl who managed to knock over two kitchen stools and upset a bowl of fat on the table, but her accidents sprang from excess zeal and superabundant health rather than wickedness. We prepared a substantial breakfast of porridge, bacon and egg and fried bread, coffee, tea, and some rather piebald toast; and then half the class polished china and cutlery, made mustard and set the table, while the rest served up the meal. Then the girls sat down and solemnly ate their way through the food, and said it was very good.

During the sitting I heard a friend ask the lively one if she remembered 'the name of yon wicked woman the minister telled about on Sunday', to which without hesitation the reply came: 'Jessie Bell'. Thus was Jezebel artlessly given Scottish nationality.

I began to understand how the buxom lass had achieved her weight when she carefully collected what remained of the feast to eat on the homeward journey. Somehow or other I managed to jerk the replete and somnolent class into the necessary activities of washing up and tidying the kitchen—getting it back into its usual immaculate order before a cry of 'fillum!' outside drew the girls away in a rush to the hall.

Kirstie had already invited me to stay for a long week-end while Aunt Mairi was from home, and I helped her to put away the weaving-looms (with their gay tartan warps just made by her class) before walking home with her along the strath. Both daughters of the house were now back at boarding-school, so I had their room and a choice of two berths, one above the other. I chose the lower one, not dreaming that *Beurach's* remaining pup might have used it for purposes other than sleep. Not until I put my hand in with a hot-water bottle—when the feel of a damp patch told me all too plainly what it had been used for.

The weavers were furious, and the pup, summoned for reproof and punishment from a snug basket, cowered away from the storm in a narrow space beneath the bunks where none of us could reach her.

This puppy had originally been destined for the kennels of a well-known Cairn breeder; but owing to an outbreak of hard-pad in her new home could not be delivered, and was now nearly three months old and untrained. The little thing had a permanently bewildered expression and seemed unusually nervous, so I offered to take it in hand and have a shot at training it if the owners would leave it entirely to me during my stay.

I took the little beast aside and explained to her that some things weren't done, gradually gaining her confidence and accustoming her to my voice and touch. With tiny grey head tilted and solemn eyes fixed on mine, she seemed uncertain of my meaning—but quite wishful to please. As with young children, the safest way to keep an immature creature on its best behaviour is to foresee and prevent the other kind. I kept a sharp eye on her perpetually, and made many journeys to the garden. The reward came when, on the evening of the second day, she asked of her own accord to be let out. When the performance was over I gave her the most extravagant praise—which she enjoyed so much that her endeavours to earn more saved her from further disgrace.

Her trust in me was now such that she crept into the small of my back when I lounged in an armchair. Several times people who dropped in for long, chatty visits were startled by the sight of a crushed-looking body left behind on the seat when I rose to say good-bye.

Big moments in life have a way of ganging up on us without warning, and some of mine hatched when a large and noisy family of children came to ask if the weavers (who were out) had a puppy to sell. They grabbed at my charge, who snapped in terror and wedged herself between my ankles for protection. I said quickly that this was the last of the litter and already booked. After they had gone I confessed to the returned weavers that, although I well knew the original sale had been cancelled, it seemed criminal to let the frightened thing go to unruly youngsters who obviously had no idea how to treat a pup. There was a pause.

'Well, it seems destined to be *your* dog,' they said; 'you had better take it away with you!' This was a novel and a serious proposition: but I had no heart to refuse the offer.

When we returned to Inverewe Aunt Mairi seemed none too pleased to have a second puppy around the place, but she softened after I said that companionship would make life happier for *Cailleach*. Then the latter did her best to disprove this by biting her sister in the leg. For once Aunt Mairi's calm deserted her, as she hurried from the room saying, 'Stop them—*do* stop them!' She could not bear dog fights. I lifted *Cailleach* off with my foot, and the anguished *Busdubh*[1] climbed up me as though I were a ladder and perched on my shoulder, with a cold muzzle pressed into my ear, while she sobbed about the harsh ways of bigger sisters. I gently detached her and staunched the wound, and quite soon she cheered up enough to make further advances to *Cailleach* —which were received more graciously.

I now know that all dogs—even puppies (related or not), if of the same sex—are best introduced out-of-doors; preferably on territory belonging to neither of them. And of course both must be free of any leash. Inverewe House had become *Cailleach*'s preserve, and honour demanded that no other bitch should be allowed in it without at least a demonstration of who was mistress. Had they met first outside, *Cailleach* might have accepted my pup and herself invited it inside quite peaceably. This technique has often worked since then when *Busdubh* and I have visited other houses where a bitch reigned.

If it hadn't been for a late garden excursion with my new companion I might have missed a wonderful display of the Northern Lights. Aunt Mairi had to be fetched out too, and with her arm through mine we stood together enjoying the brilliant ever-changing beams of coloured light as they flickered up from horizon to zenith and died back again towards the earth. The erratic mazy motion of these shafts of electric blue, emerald, flame, and saffron luminescence put me so much in mind of a gorgeous Russian ballet that when Aunt Mairi told me the

[1] Pronounced 'Boost-doo' (Black Muzzle).

Aurora is known in Gaelic as 'The Merry Dancers' it seemed a perfect title.

This fantastic ballet danced by beams of light upon the stage of the sky is one in which the same figure is never repeated. Nobody seems able to forecast when displays will occur or how long they will last, and local people gave me every sort of conflicting information about the best kind of weather and time of year to see them. Reflected in Hebridean seas, and silhouetting the islands and peaks of Ross-shire's mountainous coast, they are an unforgettable sight. According to experts, the brilliance of these displays is largely determined by the amount of sunspot activity. They occur when electrically charged particles emitted by the sun enter the earth's magnetic field and ionize the atmospheric gases, causing the atoms to discharge light rays which change from moment to moment and range through the spectrum colours. They are associated with severe magnetic storms.

In dark intervals between the acts I told Aunt Mairi about my first day in the secondary school, and the re-naming of Jezebel. It seemed that the girl's family had a bent for misquotation, because her mother, put out by her daughter's failure to pass the 'qually' (qualifying examination, equivalent to the English 'eleven plus') for entry to a grammar school, had tried to persuade the head of the 'Junior Secondary', to which the girl was sent instead, to get her through the examination at a second attempt. For this purpose she paid him a visit, wearing her best hat and smile, and said, 'Now, just think, if you could succeed with Robina where Mr. K . . . [head of the previous school] failed, wouldn't that give you *a fine bee in your bonnet?*'

It is a pity that so many parents are fascinated by what my English pupils call the 'snob-value' of grammar school education —to the point of trying to force unsuitable candidates into years of bookwork which their brains were not built to deal with. In Wester Ross there are excellent alternatives; for not only are there good junior secondary day-schools with a practical bias, but at Balmacara and Duncraig, near Kyle of Lochalsh, the County Education Committee runs residential schools where selected boy pupils are given first-class instruction in farming, and girls in cooking, dairying, weaving, and other useful arts.

Aunt Mairi approved of these, so far as she could commend any mass education. She used to say that she was old-fashioned in her views and thought people had mostly been far happier, a good deal wiser, and worked much better before 'all these grand lessons made girls despise domestic chores, and so many boys want more money and excitement than they can get working on a croft'.

12. *A Sort of Battles*

THE weather, as advancing autumn coloured the bracken on the hill, was often unsuitable for outdoor work on my Inverewe days, but there were plenty of other jobs to do.

Aunt Mairi went in for seed-saving in a big way, and many heads of *Watsonia*, *Libertia formosa*, *Primula*, and *Myosotidium nobile* I collected, and later rubbed out for her when dry. Sheena and I would sit like witches on either side of a great African basket, shaking the rattling pods in a syncopated rhythm—so intent on our task that we felt completely withdrawn from our surroundings, and not a murmur passed between us. When all the pods of a variety had been dealt with, we picked out husks and other débris, and then the precious seeds were poured into a labelled tin and stored on a shelf in the garden-room beside the front door.

We raised a number of plants from them ourselves, but what Aunt Mairi loved was to give or send little envelopes full to any visitor or correspondent who inquired about how to obtain and grow the flowers they had seen at Inverewe. A variety of primula that excited them during my first summer had itself come through her letter-box in an envelope. The sender had admired the many different kinds which flowered along a small burn in our policies, and happened to meet Aunt Mairi there. Rather diffidently he told her that he had raised a beautiful flame-coloured primula, and asked if she would care to try it. He lived in a suburb of Glasgow and nothing in his address or appearance suggested the out-of-the-ordinary, so Aunt Mairi had forgotten all about the incident when a little packet of seeds arrived a week later.

These were duly raised in one of the greenhouses, and when they reached maturity and flowered they were indeed a most astonishing clear flame colour. They thrived and increased with great rapidity in the moist peat soil, and soon we had a double row bordering the entrance to 'Bamboozlem', where in autumn an edging of deepest blue *Gentiana asclepiadea* succeeded them as a showpiece.

Aunt Mairi meant to write to the sender of the primula seed to tell him how much they were admired, but by the time they flowered she had mislaid his address, and I am not sure if she ever found it. It is possible that even if she *had* written, the recipient would have been little the wiser, as her writing at times looked like *Ogam* or some other archaic script.

Bobbie Fraser Darling told me that when living at Dundonnell she received one day a letter from Aunt Mairi which seemed to convey some sort of invitation (she could decipher 'I hope you can come'); but though she puzzled over it dozens of times, she could not discover what she was invited to, or when. This put her into such a state of worry that she telephoned Aunt Mairi, hoping that some light would be thrown on the matter in the course of general conversation—for she could not summon up courage to say that the writing was illegible.

Aunt Mairi asked the usual polite questions, and after Bobbie had followed suit, she tried desperately to keep the conversation going, but it dragged and dwindled and still nothing helpful had come out. Probably Aunt Mairi was also waiting—to hear what had made Bobbie ring her up—and wondering why she was so slow in coming to the point. Finally someone arrived to see Aunt Mairi, and poor Bobbie had to hang up her receiver without getting any nearer to a solution.

She need not have been so considerate, for Aunt Mairi was accustomed to hearing critical remarks about her handwriting. She told me that her great dread on board ship or at Christmas parties was any sort of paper game.

'What *is* the use,' she said plaintively, 'of dragging me in to play those awful games where you have to write things down for other people to read, when hardly anyone can read my writing? And if they could, the spelling is so queer that they wouldn't know what I meant, or be able to mark my entry!'

She generally rounded off such remarks with a little *coda* about how she had spoken only the Gaelic until she was seven, and that as Gaelic spelling was much freer—just like English in the days of the first Elizabeth—it was more difficult for her to conform to modern English standards than it would be for a non-Gaelic starter. Often she added with a laugh that her writing had grown purposely 'difficult' in order to disguise the spelling. 'The typewriter is no use at all,' she said, 'it shows everything up so plainly!' Some of her earlier letters to me are typed, including the one from which I took the opening sentences of this book, but for the most part they were hand-written.

I told her that the most up-to-date methods in education rated correct spelling very low in the scale of accomplishments. I also said (with truth) that I had never failed to read her letters: but did not betray how long this feat sometimes took. Forty-eight hours was, I think, the record.

My mother once called to me from her evening bath, after we had both tussled with a letter at intervals during the afternoon, saying, 'I believe I've got that bit about "cheese gyrating overhead all day".' It is meant to be "geese migrating"....'

'Of course!' I said. 'This *is* the time of year when they come down from the far north!' I could see in my mind's eye the neat V-shaped formations following each other high overhead, and

I

imagine the '*honk honk!*' of stragglers pleading for time to catch up with their comrades.

Soon after my arrival at Inverewe, Aunt Mairi handed her typewriter over to me and made me type business letters, inventories, lists of plants, articles she wrote about her gardens, and anything else that 'needed to be right', as she put it. On wet days and in the lengthening autumn evenings it became a regular custom for me to turn secretary. Many of our most delightful, appreciative, and observant visitors came from the United States, and I recollect some lively correspondence with members of The Garden Club of America.

In addition to the everyday typing, I gradually browsed through bundles of papers relating to the estate right back to the early days when Osgood MacKenzie planted trees and waited twenty years for the growth of sufficient shelter to begin planting his rare and delicate treasures. All such interesting matter I filed and labelled for easy reference. There were notes on the behaviour of plants, trees, and shrubs obtained from many parts of the world by Aunt Mairi and her father on their travels, and also accounts of moneys spent on garden equipment and estate labour. This last was unbelievably small—something like one shilling a day being paid to the men who made the road up to the Fionn Loch.

In addition to secretarial duties there were handyman jobs to be done, and I shortened or lengthened curtains, mended Persian rugs, made plant and seed labels, and once re-coloured (with a paint-brush and little pots of Drummer dye) the faded flowers in a favourite pre-war set of loose covers, used in summer to clothe sofas and armchairs in what estate agents call the 'lounge hall'. This took nearly a fortnight; but Aunt Mairi's pleasure in the result made the labour well worth while. She said she had sent for patterns to all the best London firms, and found nothing she liked half as well as the old chintz.

Sometimes I was sent out to gather flowers, and shall not easily forget one very stormy day when I battled round with a hand-cart—first to the walled garden for Kaffir lilies and dahlias, and then up to 'Bamboozlem', where I cut a great load of the blue hydrangeas for which our gardens were justly celebrated. Many of the flower heads were as large as old-style soup plates, and it was sad to see the lower ones beaten into the sodden peat, and some even blown right off their parent bushes and bowling about the walks like blue balloons. The tones were wonderfully varied, ranging from palest azure to rich ultramarine, and there were also some imperial purple heads borne on nearly *black* stems. The glory of the Inverewe hydrangeas does not end with the flowering season—for the slowly fading blossoms turn all sorts of metallic steely grey, verdigris green, and aged parchment tints and are a lovely sight in the winter woods, even in their decay.

We used to make arrangements of dried hydrangeas and the huge candelabra seed-pods of the Himalayan lily for winter decoration; but without any of the gilding or silvering recommended in women's magazines. We both thought the natural effects autumn and winter had bestowed were far more subtle and interesting than anything we could add out of a paint-pot.

By the time I had collected a truck-load of flowers on that stormy day, I was more than a little wet. Aunt Mairi received the armloads of blossom in the gun-room, appraised the quantity, and said she could do with twice as many; and as I was already wet, I might as well go out again and get wetter. When the second load had been cut I was as damp inside my waterproof as out, for arms uplifted to gather tall sprays allow the rain to run down inside one's sleeves; and what my posture could not do to help the water in was managed by the gale. At times my skirts swirled up shoulder high, so that I must have resembled an inside-out umbrella. I did not wear slacks at Inverewe. Neither Aunt Mairi nor her men would have approved.

On returning to the house at a quarter to one I was instructed to remove all my clothes for Janet to dry in the furnace-room, and to appear for lunch in a set of Aunt Mairi's garments. As no visitors were expected the effect need not be studied. The skirt she lent me was unsuitable—not so much on account of its MacKenzie plaid, but because the waist measure happened to be larger than my widest bulge. This detail had not occurred to her, and not wishing to draw attention to such contrast in our measurements by asking for a belt, I made a reef with binder twine and covered the knots with an ample pullover.

All went well during the meal; but early in the afternoon I was happily sifting seeds when the same neighbour who had been so excited about the Stone of Scone arrived, with his charming wife and daughter and some lady guests from their house party. I jumped up to welcome them, forgetful of my temporary garb: the feckless twine snapped undone, and the borrowed tartan fell in a heap to the floor before I had a chance to clutch it. Luckily the copper bowls of rain-washed hydrangeas, and other flower arrangements resulting from our morning's work, attracted more attention than my dishevelled appearance.

I felt very little embarrassment at appearing disguised as a Displaced Person before these London visitors in their trim suits by Hardy Amies or Creed; for having battled with wind and rain to produce the goods for Aunt Mairi's lovely decorations, my scars seemed honourable enough. When we were again alone—and she exclaimed, 'Poor you!'—I replied that the mishap hadn't troubled me much; but I thought her tartan, having *just* managed to endure me inside it in private, must have lost nerve when the people came—and given me the slip in consequence. Old clan feuds melted away in our little gusts of laughter; and then, more soberly, we hoped that modern strife on a larger scale might one day draw to as harmless a close.

We both hated battles of any sort. I understood her contention that, for the sake of peace and quiet in the kitchen, it seemed worth while supervising all the cooking herself—despite the extra work, and in face of criticism from friends. When professional cooks were employed she could never depend on this happy state of things in the home she loved so well. Nevertheless, she was not in favour of peace at any price, and gave me much moral support when a struggle came my way in connection with the school bus.

My contract stated clearly that, as a travelling teacher, transport would be provided, and that when visiting Gairloch my journeys were to be made in the school coach. On my second morning I duly boarded the luxurious new vehicle, and away we went. Six or seven boys and girls had come in it from Aultbea and Laide, and the rest got in it at the Poolewe post-office. An estate car met us there with children from the outlying villages along the southern shore of Loch Ewe; we filled all but five seats when the complement was aboard. The youngsters sang old Gaelic songs most of the way, and were much more lively than my silent fellow-travellers in the taxi on the first day's trip.

I thought the big, upstanding driver looked at me strangely when I got out of his bus in Poolewe on the last journey of that week, but I had shopping to do and soon forgot all about him. Next morning I was hard at work on my Saturday cleaning when the same elderly taxi that took me to the outlying schools drew up at my cottage gate, and the coach driver (who owned both vehicles) marched up to my front door. Saying that he wished a word with me, he invited himself in and demanded one and sixpence per day for my fare to Gairloch. I had no intention of paying this—and told him so with some determination.

The man's shock of red hair, never over-disciplined, seemed to bristle more fierily than usual as he advanced towards me with a blaze of temper in his rather small blue eyes.

'Do you think I can afford to run my coach for nothing?' he inquired, bending as he spoke to thrust a menacing chin close to my face.

'Of course not!' I said, standing firm but wishing I inhabited one of those rooms with a stout Victorian table in the middle to keep him at a safe distance. 'Nobody supposes that! The Education Committe surely pays for all school trips at a price contracted with you.'

'The Committe pays for twenty-six children, but not for a teacher,' he snarled—with emphasis on the last four words.

'In that case,' I said mildly, 'you must demand a new price now that my fare has to be covered. It would be terrible to think you were not paid, but you must get the money from the Committee; it has nothing to do with me. I am very busy, so I will say good-bye now.'

The sparks had all misfired and he couldn't raise any more just then, so with a gloomy expression he went silently away.

Not long after this meeting, I read in an English author's account of David Livingstone's fabulous African journeys on foot, and the superhuman achievements of the Scottish Presbyterian missionaries who followed him, the words: '*Scotland produces very determined men.*' I soon discovered that my driver was one of those.

On the Friday following our interview in my cottage, I shepherded the children from the school bus as usual on arrival in Gairloch, and turned to pick up my shopping basket before leaving myself, when the driver sprang from his seat and barred the door like a cork in a bottle's neck.

'I'm getting tired of lifting you without payment,' he said. 'I wrote a letter to the Committee and they have sent no reply. And now there's the other teacher gone to live with her mother in Aultbea, and wanting me to lift her as well. I told her she would need to pay me; but she said *you* did not, and so why should *she*?'

I had to think quickly. 'I fear she is mistaken,' I told him. 'As a *visiting* teacher, I get free transport; but as she is teaching in Gairloch all the time, she is expected either to live in the place or to find her own way there.'

'She is not paying unless you do,' he repeated stubbornly.

'And I am not, for the reason I have given you,' I said.

'I'm not lifting *any* teachers unless they pay for their seats!' His irate countenance, suffused with a magenta flush, accorded ill with his fiery hair. He continued to glare at me without stirring from the door, and I wondered what my waiting pupils would be up to in the school.

'This is what to do; now listen!' I leaned towards him in a confidential manner. 'I'll be waiting for you at the Inverewe gates next week as usual, but you drive past without stopping.

134

Then the Headmaster will complain to the Committee by telephone, saying that you won't bring his visiting teacher because
they are not paying you to do so, and something will be fixed
sharp enough.'

While he sat himself down to ponder this proposal, I slipped
away to my duties. I had already made brief mention of the argument to the Headmaster—who thought it just a temporary
awkwardness on the part of the driver, and not to be taken
seriously.

Aunt Mairi was rather annoyed about it; and her guest of the
week-end thought the fellow should be given a hiding for be-
having so roughly to a lady. I said I was getting bored by the battle
but had much sympathy for the man's point of view. He had the
fixed notion in his head that I was a Smart Alice from London
trying to put a fast one over on the 'simple' Highlander. Naturally
enough, he wasn't going to sit down meekly under such treatment. I admired his spirit.

'I wonder what will happen next!' said Aunt Mairi. 'I shall be
watching from my window to see whether he stops for you or
not.'

'If he doesn't, I shall get an extra day's gardening with you,'
I chuckled, '*and* be paid for it by the Education Committee—for
it will not be my fault if I am absent from my work.' But, as the
Headmaster had predicted, the coach stopped for me after all. The
contract for the school transport was a good one, and possibly
the driver's very sensible wife had told him not to jeopardize it.

Next time I visited the up-country schools, the taxi did not
arrive at four o'clock to take me home. I sat by the roadside for
half an hour, luckily in fair weather, and then went back to the
school house to borrow the teacher's telephone. A young voice at
the other end said that father and mother were away 'at the wedding in Poolewe'.

'Oh, my!' said the teacher. 'They'll all be in the hotel by now,
and no doubt the man has forgotten about you. I would have
driven you back myself, but my car is in the garage being sorted.'

'I'll telephone the hotel, and ask them to fish him out,' I said;

and, having delivered the message, sat down for another half-hour's wait. At last the familiar car came shooting over the hill, and stopped with a sudden application of brakes quite unlike the careful handling it usually received from its owner.

'Well, now, I thought you had left me here for the night!' I said pleasantly. He muttered a rather shamefaced apology as I got in beside him. Presently his courage—possibly fortified by the wedding breakfast—flared up again.

'I'm still not getting paid for your coach fare,' he began defiantly.

'But you're still taking me to Gairloch in it,' I said. 'I've told you not to stop for me, if you want quick action taken by the authorities. . . .

'Of course,' I added, 'you get all these taxi hires at present for driving me about. I don't know how profitable they are—but if I were not here, or if I bought a car, or said I should prefer to avoid unpleasantness by taking MacKenzie's taxi instead, you would miss the hires. . . .'

'There's no *unpleasantness*!' he said in shocked tones, taking a blind bend at speed and coming too close to the cliff edge for my comfort.

'I'm sure there is no *need* for any,' I replied, shutting my eyes to avoid sight of the dizzy drop below the unfenced road.

I felt rather gone at the knees when he deposited me safely at Inverewe, and drove himself back to the wedding reception; but as I heard no more about paying fares it was probably worth the strain.

A beaming smile greeted me next time I boarded the school bus, and as I got out in Gairloch the driver said (with an air of imparting a most valuable and novel piece of information) that he had seen the Transport Officer—who told him I was a *travelling* teacher, and therefore exempt from payment of fares; but that he might make any arrangement he pleased with the other mistress.

I forbore to say 'I told you so', and we became the best of friends. Aunt Mairi seemed horrified by what I hoped was an amusing description of my 'nuptial' journey; but I assured her that the man was an excellent driver, in whom I had complete faith. After all, had he not brought me home in safety even when he was in the middle of a Highland wedding? (Most people would be incapable of handling a car at all just then.) But for the fact that I knew him to be a thoroughly reliable chauffeur, I should hardly have risked an argument in the car on that occasion.

Afterwards I found him not only efficient but also most obliging and friendly, and the change in his manner was so marked and so sudden that I felt a little bewildered by it. Then some mention of Aunt Mairi put me on the track of a solution. For, with his sweetest smile (he was a handsome fellow), he turned to me and said that Mrs. Sawyer was a wonderful person. 'Yes, indeed, a very wonderful person!' he repeated.

There was a slight pause after I had expressed hearty agreement with this opinion, and then he added: *'She never lets you get the better of her!'*

From this, I assumed that the respect I now received from him was due to my refusal to let *him* get the better of *me*. I had won my spurs in battle.

13. *Further Education*

WHEN my classes in handicrafts for adults began, I wondered
whether this venture would involve me in another kind of war-
fare—this time with the local ministers of religion. Not a happy
thought, but I decided to hope for the best.

We were allowed to use two of the schoolrooms, and the
Headmaster made up the open-grate fires after school hours, so
that cheerful warmth greeted us at seven o'clock when the class
assembled. Much later, I discovered that our choice of meeting-
place had contributed to the success of the project in ways I had
not apprehended at the time.

The Headmaster, fearing that so small and scattered a community might not provide the statutory number of ten students,
obtained a special dispensation to form a class with as few as
eight people. We need not have worried: for on the first night
sixteen turned up and paid the fee for enrolment.

This pioneer band (it was the first craft class for adults ever
to be held in Gairloch) included the school cook, who was set on
weaving seats for wooden stools out of hanks of twisted sea-grass.

Although this modern version of the traditional rush-seating was not on my syllabus, I readily agreed to teach her. I could do no less for one who had borne so kindly with my cookery classes in her kitchen. She responded by making it her task to fetch large tubs of water for the basket-makers. In fact, her forthright manner protected the most golden heart. She reminded me of the man in the parable who said, 'I go not'—but went.

Another member of the class said she wanted to make a set of lampshades 'for the new electricity', and nothing else interested her. So lampshades went down on the schedule of things to be taught. This individualism went on until, instead of taking a class in basketry and leatherwork, I found myself committed to demonstrate six or seven different occupations at once—and all to beginners.

Within an hour I had filled a small notebook with orders for the variety of materials needed by my pupils, with careful descriptions of colour-schemes. Somebody wanted to weave a hearthrug, and this project brought everyone into a discussion of the most suitable size and pattern for the would-be weaver's sitting-room. With the exception of myself, they were all familiar with the room and eager to advise; and the Schoolmaster undertook to have a loom fashioned by his carpentry class.

A hard-bitten ruler and some blackboard chalk were used to set out shapes and sizes on the floor in front of the fire. Eventually this problem was settled and I returned to the lampshade-maker, who was poring over a double-page spread of diagrams in one of my catalogues. Here were depicted some two dozen wire frames, ranging from huge shapes resembling bird-cages, coolie hats, umbrellas and jelly-moulds to smaller types like tea-cosies, goldfish bowls, flower-pots and storm lanterns.

'They are all lovely!' said the pupil. 'I don't know which to choose.'

Tactfully I tried to steer her towards the simpler designs, for (in addition to aesthetic reasons) I knew it would mean giving a lesson to her alone if she embarked on the cutting of parchment to fit the convolutions of the larger and more fantastic shapes on which her eye was inclined to linger.

The frames settled, we spoke at some length about colour schemes. Lime green parchment with maroon bindings were selected for one room, peach and blue for another. When I pointed out that in order to make sure of getting materials by post in time for next week's class it would be wise to quote a second choice, they all said happily that it did not matter; they would accept the nearest the shop had in stock. It seemed that the long discussions had been enjoyed for their own sake, but my pupils were not fussy about the result. Living a hundred miles from a town teaches people to make the best of whatever is sent.

I had already bought some skins of leather, and three of the younger members wanted to make purses from these. The whole class watched with interest while I planned the shapes and cut out leather with a razor knife on a ground-glass slab.

While we were packing away equipment and tidying the rooms, I heard the Doctor's sister remark that with the Bible readings and the craft class she was 'set up for the winter'. We seemed to have made an excellent start all round.

MacKenzie's taxi from Poolewe came to fetch me home soon after half past ten, and we made the seven-mile journey through lonely hills without seeing the lights of any other vehicle. On this night-drive past windswept Loch Tollie there was no Aunt Mairi to say softly, as we came down to the banks of the River Ewe, 'That is the spot where *Allan MacLeod* was shortened by the head!' Having a brother of the same name, I never failed to blench at this customary quip of hers—even though I understood that the unfortunate Allan in question had suffered five hundred years earlier.

Before many moons had seen my Tuesday night trips home from the Further Education classes, his namesake (my brother) had been awarded the C.B.E. for his services to the Admiralty; and it so happened that no less a person than Flora MacLeod of MacLeod, twenty-eighth Chief of the clan, attended the same ceremony as he at Buckingham Palace—there to be invested by the Queen with the insignia of a Dame Commander of the Order.

Notwithstanding attempts to annihilate them, the Clan

MacLeod continues to flourish. All over the world members of it gather to meet the much-travelled Chief wherever she goes. These were heartening thoughts with which to ward off the grim spectres evoked by Loch Tollie on a dark winter night.

.   .   .

It is not always appreciated that the strong MacLeod contingent at the Battle of Worcester in 1651 (led by Norman of Bernera and Rory of Talisker during the minority of the Chief) was almost wiped out by Cromwell's troops, and that in consequence it was agreed after the Restoration that the clan should not receive calls to battle until it had fully recovered strength.

Memory of this near-annihilation caused Norman, the twenty-second Chief, to refrain from bringing out his clansmen in support of Prince Charles Edward in 1745—believing as he did that there could be no reasonable hope of success. After the failure of the rising, the old clan system was broken up by the actions of a government which feared its strength and solidarity. Unfortunately the clan *spirit* also suffered—damaged, sad to say, by the behaviour of certain chiefs who abused their newly acquired powers of ownership.

Before this time a chief merely administered territory belonging to the clan as a whole. Now, he was given absolute possession and power over the land, like any English squire. Some of them discovered that sheep and deer forests were more profitable than human tenants, and in their greed for money they mercilessly ejected the occupants—even though many of these people bore the Chief's own name.

In this ugly chapter of Highland history the MacLeods of Dunvegan were among the notable exceptions (including the Frasers of Lovat) who played no part in the evictions. Dame Flora meets clansmen all over the world, not because an earlier chief turned them out of Skye, but owing to the adventurous spirit which led their forbears to new countries of their own free will.

It is true that there have been other hard taskmasters, such as poverty and famine, for the people of Skye to battle with. As mentioned in chapter six, the potato famine of 1846-8 was more severe on the islands than the mainland. When Lady Mary MacKenzie of Gairloch and her brother-in-law planned the road-making operations to provide paid occupation for the hungry crofters and enable them to buy food, hundreds of Skye men came into Wester Ross in the hope of finding work. At that time the fortunes of the Dunvegan MacLeods had reached such a low level that they could do little to help their people. The Chief himself resorted to the expedient of taking a salaried position in London.

The present Chief—in an honorary capacity—works as vigorously for the folk of Skye and Inverness as any breadwinner, although she has passed three score years and ten. Every summer she entertains gatherings of clansmen at Dunvegan Castle, and every winter sets out to meet more kinsmen in other parts of the world. No longer required to do battle for clan territory or the person of their Chief, the MacLeods are now fighting (with dollars and sterling) for the preservation of the venerable castle.

When Inverewe was handed over to the National Trust for Scotland, Dame Flora told me that the MacLeods intended to retain responsibility for Dunvegan and never to let it pass to strange hands, however competent such a body as the Trust might be. No one—least of all the Trust officials and supporters—will fail to wish them success.

Among the many treasures exhibited in the castle, an 'Amen' toasting-glass shows that individual members of the clan played a part in support of Bonny Prince Charlie. The glass is in fragments, but an inscription can be deciphered. The last verse runs:

> God save the King I pray,
> God bless the King I pray,
> God save the King.
> Send him victorious
> Happy and glorious
> Soon to reign over us
> God save the King.   Amen.

These 'Amen' toasting-glasses are rare; and this example is unique in bearing also an inscription round the base, which says:

Donald MacLeod of Gualtergil in the Isle of Skye.
The faithful PALINURUS. Act. 69. Anno 1747.

Palinurus was the steersman of Aeneas, and the allusion is to Donald MacLeod's services in ferrying Prince Charles Edward from refuge to refuge in the Islands, and in arranging passage for the gay and gallant Flora MacDonald. Donald received also a snuff-box as a memento of his adventures with the Prince. The *Guide to Dunvegan Castle* records the following quaint conversation between Donald and a friend who asked why he had no snuff in it.

'Sneeshin' in that box! No, the deil a pickle sneeshin' shall ever go into it till the King be restored, and then (I trust in God) I'll go to London, and there will I put sneeshin' in the box and go to the Prince and say "Sir, will you take a sneeshin' out o' my box?" '

The famous *Bratach Sith* or Fairy Flag of the Clan MacLeod, believed to spread a protective influence round clansmen in time of danger, hangs in a frame on the walls of the drawing-room in the castle; and here also may be seen the Dunvegan Cup—an Irish mazer of bog oak mounted in richly chased silverwork and semi-precious stones, made in 1493 for a daughter of King Neil—and a huge ox-horn banded with Celtic silverwork, known as 'Rory Mor's horn'. From this every heir is expected to quaff nearly half a gallon of claret at a single draught on his coming of age.

Many other precious and interesting relics are housed within the walls of this ancient fortress; but perhaps the most absorbing of all are the 7,000 documents preserved in the muniment room at the top of the 'Fairy Tower', which provide a unique record of clan history and social conditions in the West Highlands for at least 500 years. If choice were permitted, I can think of few pleasanter or more fascinating occupations than to spend one's days in this sixteenth-century look-out, browsing through

143

the faded manuscripts to extract significant items and build up an authentic picture of five centuries of human life and endeavour in that remote place.

Content with my favourite 'water music'—provided by a falling torrent known as 'Rory Mor's Nurse', and the splash of Hebridean seas on the rocky shore of Loch Dunvegan—I should readily take the advice bestowed by Doctor Johnson on the Lady MacLeod who entertained him. This was given her at breakfast in the castle on September 18th 1773.

'Never leave Rory Mor's cascade!' thundered the Doctor, in response to his hostess's expressed desire to build a more convenient home in a less remote place.

'Madam,' went on her distinguished guest, 'if you once quit this rock, this centre of gravity, there is no knowing where you may settle. No, no; keep to the rock! It is the very jewel of the estate. It looks as though it had been let down from heaven by the four corners to be the residence of a chief.'

And the MacLeods have remained on their rock to this day; an unbroken recorded occupation by the family for nearly seven centuries.

Utterly different, but no less arduous than that of Dame Flora, Aunt Mairi's life-work was closely channelled into the care of her lands (and in particular the gardens) of Inverewe. 'I have to be head gardener myself,' she often explained to visitors, 'for my men have never been trained anywhere but here.'

These men, devoted though they were to her and to the place, yet had individual interests and responsibilities outside Inverewe —for they were mostly crofters with holdings and flocks of sheep to manage. It was the common practice for them to tell Aunt Mairi that they needed a week off for shearing, or dipping, or whatever their work at home might be, and for her to acquiesce however inconvenient their absence proved from her point of view. The rest of their time was given to her in very loyal service, and occasionally on duties for which they felt ill-equipped. During my first autumn at Inverewe Roddy Donn's devotion to Aunt Mairi was put to a severe test.

Lord Aberconway, owner of the famous Welsh gardens of Bodnant, wrote asking if his head gardener (a Mr. Puddle) might visit Inverewe and be shown round. Of course Aunt Mairi promptly issued an invitation to the man through his employer—who had himself been entertained not long before. She intended to take this highly skilled gardener round the policies herself; but he happened to come when some pressing engagement elsewhere prevented her from doing it, so she asked Roddy to deputize for her.

Poor Roddy Donn was dismayed. 'The man will be expecting me to know all the long names of plants!' he said. Aunt Mairi soothed him by saying she would explain that her gardeners were Gaelic speakers—and therefore not familiar with English or Latin words. Roddy, looking apprehensive but determined, finally agreed to carry out the task for her sake.

The day came, and Aunt Mairi saw the two men off on their tour of inspection before leaving for her own appointment. On her return she went in search of Roddy and asked how things had gone. He gave her a delighted smile and said: 'That was a nice man! A very nice man indeed! *You would never have guessed that he knew anything about plants at all.*' (A wonderful testimonial to the tact of Mr. Puddle, and also to the swift appraisal of his courtesy by the less learned Highland gardener.)

I was constantly thrilled and humbled by such demonstrations of perception and fine feeling, which caused me to exclaim that I was being given much more Further Education than I could possibly bestow. These people, so thoughtful and subtle in their ideas, made me delve into the inwardness of things—helped, no doubt, by the great sweeping lines of the hills; the expanse of the sea; the silence and freedom from bustle and distraction.

Here is a quotation[1] culled from the columns of a well-known London newspaper. It is headed 'Depressed Area'.

[1] Peter Simple: *Daily Telegraph*, July 1957.

Rocky bracken-covered hillsides, clear streams, winding lanes edged with foxglove; high mountains . . . dreaming in the distance; hardly anything to be seen anywhere that is not beautiful. This part of ——, I was told on a recent visit, is a Depressed Area.

The hill-farming is hard. Total agriculture, which is turning rural England into a faceless plant and animal breeding station for immediate cash profit, has had to stop short of this difficult craggy country.

So the wild flowers still bloom in wasteful beauty, unsprayed, on the hillsides and along the roads, making no money for anybody.

Depressed area it may be, but the people do not seem depressed about it. They go about their work among these superb surroundings as they have always done, with a friendliness, politeness, even vivacity and gaiety no longer easily found in England.

In the evening, in the pub, you will not find everybody talking about what they saw on TV the previous night. Amazing as it may seem, they can still speak of what really interests them. They have not yet entirely succumbed to the publicity-man's world where flesh and blood has been turned to plastic and cardboard.

Thanks to the shield of their precious language and still living traditions, they are protected for a little while longer from the relentless advance of the Great Moron.

I shall be told that all this is obscurantism and black superstition and worse, that the sooner people stop speaking —— and learn to speak bastard American the better for them. Yes, we know that bad money drives out good. But it is not our moral duty to hasten the process.

The blanks were filled by the words 'North Wales' and 'Welsh', but the whole quotation is equally valid if we substitute 'North-west Scotland' and 'Gaelic'.

It is certainly not our moral duty to hasten the ascendency of bad money or any other bad thing. But negatives are not enough. There is a more positive duty—that of trying to arrest the evil process. Yet how can the money-crazed be convinced of their craziness?

During my first months at Inverewe I was the recipient of many letters from friends in London and other cities, asking me how I was managing to endure existence so far from the centres of civilization. When I replied that I had re-discovered civilized (and civilizing) conditions of life, they thought *me* crazy—and said as much.

Once I knew a woman in a mental home who thought she was Victoria, the Queen-Empress. Unless her visitors pretended to think so too, and behaved with suitable respect and ceremony, she decided that they were mad. So it seems that, having pitched on what we consider a sane mode of life, we all doubt the reason of those who question our choice or choose differently themselves.

My recipe for testing the worth of any particular mode is simply the cook's method of tasting the pudding. If a way of life makes people happy, healthy, kind, contented, thoughtful, and interested in their daily work and everything around them, it seems good. But tired, strained faces, boredom with daily routine, discontent and craving for distraction all bring bad tastes to my palate.

May the remote places continue to breed such people as the young crofter of Inverasdale on Loch Ewe, who was interviewed by a slightly condescending B.B.C. man. The conversation went like this:

'Were you born up here?'

'Yes.'

'Have you been anywhere else?'

'Yes, I have been to Inverness, and once to Oban for the Mod.'

'Have you ever been to London?'

'No, I have not.'

'But you would *like* to go to London?'

'No.'

He was hastily removed from the microphone in favour of another victim, and could not overhear the applause his polite but uncompromising attitude had gained from at least one group of listeners.

So, while half my days were spent in teaching, I listened and learnt much as well. Everything had to be repeated to Aunt Mairi, who loved to hear accounts of all I had gleaned during my hours away from her. Sometimes I made written notes to aid my memory—jottings which I still possess. There were many pauses during our gardening work when we simply sat and talked. I did all I could to make a habit of these little breaks—knowing that Aunt Mairi had been on her feet since early morning, trudging round her fifty-acre gardens to encourage the men at their various tasks, and often pushing her favourite green-painted handcart full of plants and tools for much of the way.

Sometimes a cloud would lift from the peaks of *Beinn Airidh Charr* or a particularly happy combination of sun and shadow present the contours in a new relationship, and she would point this out to me, saying in her soft voice, 'Look—isn't it lovely! Busy and mentally burdened though she was at the time, Aunt Mairi never allowed the cares of her life to blind her to its beauties: a rare detachment from the purely personal being one of her great qualities.

Occasionally we discussed people not of the local soil. There were many visitors to Inverewe, a number of whom were well supplied with material possessions. I once confessed that I divide supertax payers into three groups—The Lilies, The Spinners—and The Rest. Spinners were those who contributed by some kind of work to the world's good. Lilies did not toil or spin, but were valuable because they added to its beauty and interest. The Rest merely took all they could get, without giving anything in return.

Amused, Aunt Mairi asked where I placed *her*.

'Definitely a Spinner!' I said. 'But something of a Lily too—and, moreover, one who appreciates other Lilies and makes them grow.'

Strangely enough, she seemed surprised and touched by this.

'If all supertax payers were Lilies or Spinners, there would be no envy or discontent to speak of amongst the less prosperous people,' I said. 'It is The Rest who cause Unrest—for you never hear a poor man complain because the Doctor runs a car, the Headmaster a holiday caravan, or the Admiral a motor-boat or a yacht.

'No, because such people *work* for their privileges. Nor could

148

anyone resent —— (a sweet and gracious lady who opened bazaars beautifully all her life). But oh, Mrs. Top Dog, who sweeps about in mink and Jaguar making much noise and expecting everyone to kow-tow as her bank-notes rustle, she sows bitterness and malice wherever she goes—and never guesses how the 'bad blood' of which she complains is manufactured by herself and her kindred spirits.'

'I doubt if people up here are made envious or cross by her sort,' said Aunt Mairi. 'Though they have not been much bothered by moneyed irresponsibles. They regard such individuals as abnormal—or sick—as perhaps they are. Once upon a time there was a certain Mrs. W. X. who bought land and started dictating to her tenants, but they just ignored her. The factor tried to explain to the lady that she could not order Highlanders about merely because they worked for her and lived in her cottages. "Nonsense!" was the reply he got. "Money talks up here the same as everywhere else." The factor's dissent was swept aside. In the end Mrs. W. X. went too far, and her tenants just took their goods and quietly flitted to other homes and jobs away from her estate. No one would work for her at all.'

'It seems as though Mrs. W. X. got some Further Education, too,' I commented.

'I think so. But you know the people were not cross with her. They spoke with pity of her queer ways. One crofter summed it up. "The poor woman, she is *not wise*,"[1] he said. "She needs her head seen to." '

---

[1] A polite Highland euphemism for 'mentally deranged'.

14. *Inspectors and an Article*

MY weekly journeys to the school at *Bualnaluib* took me past a small house on the edge of Loch Ewe, outside which a thin old man used to sit in fine weather, leaning against the white-washed wall of his cottage and puffing at his pipe.

His only neighbour was a little grey-haired woman who bustled in and out of her door with bowls of scraps for the leggy hens which foraged in the sea-wrack along the shore; or perhaps she carried forth a cold tea-pot to empty out on the stones. She always gave me a cheerful smile and a greeting, but the old man (when he wasn't dozing) would silently contemplate me with a look that seemed to come from a long way off—almost another world—some secret place into which I hesitated to intrude. In weather unsuitable for sitting out, the only sign of him was a blue thread of smoke tirling from his chimney.

One dreich November morning I noticed that the smoke had ceased. The cottage, which seemed smaller than usual, had a shabby, poor, almost derelict, look about it. Sudden depression chilled me like a jet of icy water. I asked my driver what had become of the occupant. 'They took him away to the hospital in Inverness,' he said. 'The Welfare man came in his own car, but Angus wouldn't get into it. So they came again with the ambulance and two men, and when he tried to get away from them they just picked him up and carried him off. He struggled hard, but they were too much for him. He was feeble with age.'

'Was he ill?' I asked.

'Well, he hadn't been himself for some time, and he was not getting proper food; and they said he could not continue to live in that way. But he preferred it. He only wanted to be left alone.'

'It is sad for old people when they have no kin to care for them,' I said. 'But I can't help wishing they could be allowed to end their days where they are happy—even though they live on bread and tea, and the kitchen is not swept.'

'Angus loved looking at the sea,' said the driver. 'He had spent so much of his life in ships. He had been round the world more times than he could remember. It was always the sea he cared about. And now he is in Inverness and cannot see or smell the ocean any more.'

The thought of the gaunt old sailor shut away in a city hospital worried me all the week, and on my next visit to *Bualnaluib* school I asked after him. 'Poor old Angus!' was the reply. 'He took a shock [stroke] after being removed from his cottage, and died soon after he got to the hospital in Inverness.'

'That was a merciful things for him,' said someone who was delivering stores to the school kitchen. 'I mind being sent to that hospital myself, when I had the bronchitis. I thought I was a prisoner in that place! It would drive you demented to stay there long. Outside the window there was nothing but a wall to look at. Just *a wall*.'

I looked from the school windows at the vast panorama of hill, sky, and water; and remembered the aged man down on the shore by his wee house, with his far-seeing gaze on the distant Hebridean islands and the Atlantic horizon. Of course he could not live surrounded by walls, however much care and kindness they contained. Some day perhaps a refuge will be provided on the West Coast where old people of the district can end their lives in sight of the ocean and the hills of their home country.

Soon after this I was driving with Aunt Mairi up the little estate road to Kernsary, and as we turned past a row of cottages beside the river I saw an old woman creeping down the bank with a bucket. It was obviously an effort to keep her balance on the rocks whilst bending to scoop up the water, and I marvelled that so frail a body could manage to live in such difficult conditions. Aunt Mairi told me that this woman had gone away to work in cities all her life, but on her retirement pined so much to return to her birthplace that the people of Poolewe built her the tiny wooden cabin in which she now dwelt, with the Ewe tumbling past her neatly curtained casements. She was happy, and no doubt liked doing as much as possible independently of help—for there were many hands willing to assist where necessary.

I hoped that she would be able to stay in her sanctuary and not suffer the fate of the old seaman. Aunt Mairi thought it was usually easier for an old woman than a man to face life alone. 'It is not the aged only who rebel against being shut up inside walls,' she added. 'There is a young man here who suffers from tuberculosis and was sent away to a sanatorium. But he couldn't endure it, and ran off home. Everyone sympathized with him; and the British Legion men built him a better house in their spare time, so that he can have a room to himself away from his family, with good windows and a balcony, where they hope he will soon be well.'

How much pleasanter for the less fortunate members of the community to be looked after by their friends and neighbours than left to the care of even the best of State officials, I thought; unaware, on that fine Saturday off duty, of the impact which inspectors would soon make on my own working life.

Sunday was still between us; and being very keen to learn more of the Gaelic tongue, I planned to copy the example of the late Lady Mary MacKenzie and attend a Gaelic service at the Free Kirk. So, instead of crossing the bridge to the Presbyterian Church on Sunday morning, I turned up past the cottage of the old lady with the buckets and came to a well-built chapel which dominated the little row of riverside dwellings. A tall, bare-headed custodian in black met me by the entrance, where he stood firmly barring admission. 'You have mistaken the kirk,' he said in the most courteous manner in the world. 'You will need to cross the river and walk past the post-office.'

His voice was so grave and his air so authoritative that I meekly turned back without a word and went in the direction he had indicated. Only then did I realize that the speaker had been Aunt Mairi's head man and stalker—whom I well knew in his week-day dress and rôle. I still think he did not wish me to enter the chapel—probably imagining that I wanted to attend the service in a spirit of idle curiosity rather than devotion—though Aunt Mairi was equally certain it was all a mistake. However, the matter was never discussed with him, and I continued to worship in English. My presence might have given trouble to the Gaelic preacher, had he been as thoughtful as the one I heard about in another Ross-shire village.

Two gentlemen from Edinburgh were touring the Western Highlands in connection with some Government survey of life in the crofting districts, their particular duty being that of report-ing on leisure-time activities. When they saw some people filing into a village hall on a week-day evening, they stopped the car and went in to see what was going on. No sooner were they inside than a religious service began. It would have been im-polite to leave, so they stayed—but not one word of the Gaelic could they understand. At the close of his address the dear old minister paused, wiped his spectacles, looked down to the end of the hall where the men were sitting, and said gently: 'Now I will repeat what I have just said, in English, for the benefit of visitors who may not have the Gaelic.'

This is what they heard:

'A little while ago, I was staying in the great city of Dingwall. And I went down to the railway-station. And a train came in. And the doors was opened. And the people got out. And the people got in. And the doors was shut. And the train went

"A-poof, a-poof!"—and steamed away in the direction of the Kyle.

'Another day, I went down to the railway-station. And a train came in. And the doors was opened. And the people got out. And the people got in. And the doors was shut. And the train went "A-poof, a-poof!"—and steamed away in the direction of Inverness.

'And yet another day I went down to the railway-station. And a train came in. And the doors was opened. And the people got out. And the people got in. But the train did *not* go "A-poof a-poof!"—and steam away. And *why* did it not go "A-poof, a-poof! . . . ?" *Because it had no water in its boiler!*

'And unless you have the Water of Salvation in *your* boiler, you will not go "A-poof, a-poof!"—and steam away in the direction of the Heavenly City. . . .'

A sermon composed in the traditional, repetitive story-telling technique of the Highland *ceilidh*[1] and perfectly suited to the way of thought of its usual congregation.

Shortly before leaving England for the North, I had heard an equally pithy and memorable address from an octogenarian Canon in a beautiful little Cotswold church. The gist of it was the splendour of life; the endless opportunities of interest and mental enrichment within reach of the poorest person in these islands; and how it was up to the individual to seize such advantages and make the most of them.

'There are so many things we can learn!' said the old man, his rosy cheeks and bright eyes only just visible above the pulpit rail—for his figure had bowed with the weight of years although his mind was still taut—'take for instance, these admirable little books in the Teach Yourself series. There are now volumes on almost every subject under the sun. Anyone can buy them for a shilling or two, or borrow from the Free Library. What a world of opportunity they represent! I am just studying the latest issue: it is called *Teach Yourself Preaching*. . . .'

Filled with the Water of Salvation, and developing a zest for

[1] A gathering for song and story-telling, pronounced 'Kayly'.

life equal to that of the second preacher, almost any human engine ought to be capable of pulling immense loads up his or her track through this world. But one sometimes puffs along what seems to be a useful line, only to find signals at 'stop'—or rails uprooted by other people. On my next visit to Achtercairn School I learned that I might be coming up against impassable barriers in the persons of Inspectors of Education—who had heard about my teaching of handicrafts in schools and were not pleased. (The Further Education classes, against which I had expected some opposition, continued to thrive and had not drawn any fire from the local pulpits.)

Of course I had simply done as the head teachers asked— switching from needlework to boys' crafts because they were more in need of help with those subjects. But the Education Committee, I gathered, had an idea that I, preferring the crafts in which I was known to have particular interest, had imposed my own choice on the local schools and acquired a free hand to teach what I liked. Inspectors (in the plural) were said to be hot on my track. 'Well,' I said happily, 'if they come here to Achtercairn they will find me working according to the original plan, and if they visit the smaller schools the people in charge will surely explain that I was asked to change over. So what is there to worry about?'

I was hard at work coping with a cookery class and a coal-range that disliked the prevailing wind, when the outer door opened, drafting a chimneyful of smoke into the kitchen, and the Organizer who had first interviewed me entered, followed closely by a man I had not met before. He was introduced to me and I did my best to be welcoming, and to keep the class (and the fire) on their best behaviour although half-choked with fumes. The Inspectors looked very grave, and stood together silently watching my efforts with a distinct air of disapproval. I dusted flour from two high stools and offered them to the visitors, but these comforts were declined. Not knowing what was expected of me, I decided to get on with the class.

The girls were ill-at-ease and clumsy, and I had never found teaching so difficult; but somehow or other the menu was prepared and cooked. I wondered whether to offer the results to our silent watchers, but thought better of it. The atmosphere seemed unsuitable for our usual party, so the disappointed pupils were told to put the food away in the larder. Soberly they complied, cleaned up the kitchen, and departed. I ought to have gone with them in the school bus—but supposed I was expected to stay behind and face whatever music had to be played.

There was an uncomfortable pause after the children had left, and then the Organizer came out of her trance-like mood and asked to see the sewing and knitting. This she examined without comment. Next, she inquired if I was teaching the same work in other schools. I replied that I was not doing so, and explained why.

'You should teach the subjects for which you were originally appointed,' she said severely. She was a head taller than I, and several stone heavier, and had the strong personality her work demanded.

'I am sorry,' I said, 'but I thought I was under the control of the head teachers, and must teach what they wished me to undertake.'

A slight thaw set in. 'Captain K—— and Miss M—— *asked* you to teach handicrafts to the boys?'

'Most certainly! They said they had no one capable of doing it, and almost jumped for joy when I mentioned that I had experience in those subjects.'

'That makes a difference. This is the Art Inspector [he had been introduced by name, which meant nothing to me], and he was very surprised to hear that you were teaching, without his knowledge or permission, subjects which properly come under his department and not mine.'

'I understand that,' I said, 'but did not know that you were unaware of what was happening. The *Bualnaluib* Headmaster intended to write to Dingwall, I am sure.'

'Well, well,' said the Art Inspector, who must have been extremely bored by the afternoon of cookery, 'I think we should go and see the other schools.'

We parted with cordial civilities, and they drove away together in a trim little grey car, while I tottered across to the Headmaster's house and was revived with cups of tea and the offer of a lift home. We agreed that it does not do to keep officials in the dark; but supposed that the teachers concerned had done so in this case with good intent, to avoid taking up the time of busy people with correspondence about trifling adjustments to their own time-tables.

'Or perhaps a letter *was* written and has gone to ground in the offices,' I said, with ten years' experience of the Civil Service behind me. Was there not the unforgettable memory of that fine writer (and war-time administrator) Richard Hughes—under whose benign direction I once had the good luck to serve— saying with immense dignity that a document which seemed unbearably trivial had found its way behind his office radiator? In his case, conscience ensured that a minion, duly informed of its fate, should retrieve and if possible deal with the hapless paper. Other officials I have met provided no such escape for unwelcome dockets, which occasionally hibernated in their cupboards for years on end.

In my present dealings with officialdom I hoped, for the sake of the children, that the work begun with such enthusiasm might not be jeopardized by tangles of red tape. The result of the inspection would not be discovered until my next visit to the schools concerned, so I must needs subdue my anxiety as best I could. Meanwhile, there was a day's work to be done at Inverewe. My current obsession with officials came out when I told Aunt Mairi that *she* would make an excellent Inspector of Shrubs.

It was a time of year when rearrangements took place in the garden, and I had never before seen such large bushes transplanted. If a rhododendron was not 'happy', as she put it, or if she thought a group was getting congested, Roddy Donn and his helpers were summoned, and, after deep and prolonged excavations, the chosen shrub would heel over. Then it was carefully raised, with as much root soil as possible, and trundled off on a large barrow to its new site. Odd effects were to be seen, as when Roddy

Donn's powerful but short figure disappeared behind a dense bush which seemed to be moving with slow dignity along a grassy walk on one wheel and a pair of black boots.

Aunt Mairi couldn't bear her shrubs to be clotted together in a mass. Each one must be given room to grow and to show the shapely figure which expert pruning helped to mould. She disliked people who referred to Inverewe (or any other good garden) as having 'masses' of flowers. 'Those horrible herbaceous borders people *will* try to make me admire in England!' she would exclaim—'I *hate* banks of gaudy flowers jumbled together in what their owners call "a glorious mass of colour".'

If plants, trees or shrubs were worth growing, she thought they deserved elbow-room; and if people hadn't adequate space to give them, they should stick to smaller growths or fewer varieties. 'You don't (or ought not to) herd children, dogs, or even canaries, together in masses, so why treat plants in that heartless way?'

Her influence was so strong that I cannot now look at a crowded flower-bed, shrubbery or wood without a feeling of horror and pity for the victims. Plants have personalities; not only as varieties—just as bulldogs differ in their characteristics from bull-terriers—but also as individual specimens. Most dog-lovers realize that the difference between one dog and another cannot be fully appreciated if they are kept together in kennels: it emerges only when they are singled out as human companions. The difficulty with plants is that one needs to study them individually without for one moment losing sight of their effect on the garden as a whole. Aunt Mairi had the gift of seeing both the wood and the trees.

Much has been said and written during the last half-century about taste in dress and adornment, and also on the subject of house decoration and furnishing. Possibly never before have so many people thought about line and colour, harmony and contrast, the use of pattern and texture. Overloading of ornament is taboo, whether on a woman's person or in her drawing-room. Don't wear a flowered dress and a large fussy hat together;

Don't plaster yourself with jewellery, or your plain suit with accessories; Don't have a patterned carpet and patterned curtains and covers in the same small room. . . . Excellent counsel of this sort is found in every woman's paper and broadcast programme. When will it be extended to the garden outside the windows?

The Englishman in particular is so often a genius at raising plants, but frequently manages to create a sadly crude muddle of his garden as a whole. Many small plots remind me of bargain basements: stuffed with brilliantly coloured specimens which bear no relation to each other, arranged merely to cram as much as possible into the available space.

Garden design is a difficult but rewarding occupation, and can be carried on just as fitly in a suburban rectangle as in some undulating acres. (By 'design' I do not mean the installation of a lily-pond, crazy pavements, or a semi-circle of rocks. Least of all, the purchase of plaster gnomeries or frogs.)

Facile recipes are useless, but Aunt Mairi demonstrated one valuable lesson to me. When planning the clearance and planting of the new area of woodland now known as 'Coronation Knoll', she spent some time pottering round it—getting the 'feel' of the land, noticing contours and soil, the sunny and shady patches, the outcrops of rock which might be cleared of undergrowth and used as features of the glade, the most easy and pleasant line for paths; and, in short, trying to discover and make the best use of natural features rather than imposing preconceived ideas of her own upon the site. No garden-planner could go wrong by following that method at the start.

For the rest, a loving observation of the plants, and careful thought for their separate idiosyncrasies, is a wonderful help to good arrangement. Assuredly Mairi Sawyer looked upon her plants as 'people'. At the time of which I am writing, winter was bearing down on the gardens; nearly all blossom had ceased; leaves were decaying and falling. The many plants of *Agapanthus umbellatus* (the blue lily of South Africa), which grow so heartily out-of-doors at Inverewe, bore quantities of dead or dying foliage in rain-sodden, gelatinous heaps.

A well-meaning visitor thought this looked untidy, and offered to remove the débris. 'Oh, no, please leave it,' said Aunt Mairi. 'Agapanthuses *like* that covering of squashy leaves. It acts as a kind of sealed envelope to protect the heart of the plant until the spring.'

The best sort of gardening is perhaps allied to musicianship. Many years ago I attended a musical festival in Surrey at which my little friend Margaret, daughter of the composer Ernest Austin, competed. She was the youngest and smallest child in a large entry for solo pianists, and played very quietly and simply. Some of the bigger competitors had far more dash and assurance, and a great show of technique; but Margaret won the first prize.

The adjudicator was that well-known Bach player, the late Harold Samuel, and in announcing his verdict he said quizzically to the assembled children and parents: 'I wonder if you know why I put this little girl first? Before I explain, let us ask her to play her pieces once more.' Margaret duly complied, and the great man beamed at her before turning to the audience.

'There! Do you see what I mean?' he said. '*She treats the notes as ladies and gentlemen.*'

. . . . .

In spite of my ardent curiosity as to the outcome of the Inspectors' visit, I managed (as always) to enjoy every minute of the work with Aunt Mairi in her gardens. Nevertheless, I felt glad when the time came for my next journey to the *Bualnaluib* school. The morning was calm and mild, with the barometer set fair, and smoke rising from the white chimney-stacks of Inverewe as though drawn with ruler and blue pencil on the dark woods of *Ploc Ard*.

Rusty bracken on the hills glowed in gentle wintry sunlight; the waters of loch and burn sparkled; the school children ran smiling to greet me as I stepped from the taxi. I went in, and met the Headmaster and his assistant, both smiling also.

'We had a visit from two Inspectors,' they said simultaneously.

'They were delighted with the craft work and are going to send a lot of materials.'

All was well—indeed, far better than I had expected in my most optimistic moments. The Headmaster said he had told the Art Inspector how I had volunteered to give additional lessons to the small fry, and had brought paper and things for them to use. He had said instantly that I must not be allowed to bear the cost of materials, and had made a note for extra brushes, paints, and paper to be ordered as an emergency mid-term supply.

My spirits were at top level when I went in to take the drawing class of some twenty small children. Then I met trouble.

'I'm no' going to draw!' said a round-faced boy in the front row, staring up at me defiantly. I continued to cut up paper and hand it to the monitors without replying.

'I'm no' GOING to draw!' he bellowed at the top of his voice, scowling like thunder. Still I made no sign of having heard.

This was too much for the others, and several hands shot up. 'Well, Iain?' I said casually to the owner of the nearest arm.

'Please, miss, Alistair says he's no' going to draw!' exclaimed the child with mingled horror and delight.

'Oh, yes, I heard him,' I said, with a thoughtful glance at the belligerent Alistair. 'That *is* a pity, isn't it, now? For you see, if he'll not draw, he'll have to go into the next room and sew with the girls.'

From the tail of my eye I saw Alistair grab a pencil and bend low over his paper, a brilliant scarlet flush spreading up to his ears. Presently I wandered round in his direction and dropped some words of praise on his bent and tousled head. He looked up with a grateful grin. The belligerence had been due to nerves.

The rest of the class couldn't wait for me to visit their desks, and soon a mass of small bodies closed round me, each child thrusting a drawing as near my eyes as he could reach.

'*Tha-at?*' '*Tha-at?*' '*Tha-at?*' they inquired, seeking my approval. Whereas small English pupils usually inquire, 'Is that all right?' these Highlanders were invariably monosyllabic. It became so catching that now, when I want an opinion on my own sketches, I find myself pushing them before my friends with the accompanying '*Tha-at?*' of Iain and his classmates.

. . . . .

I heard afterwards that the Art Inspector had looked at some of the drawings and talked to the children about their work, illustrating his remarks with clever lightning sketches on the blackboard. He was inclined to the Bohemian in appearance, with luxuriant hair and a more colourful tie than the crofter children were accustomed to see. One of the little boys, much impressed, went home and told his mother that *a man* had come to the school that morning.

'Was he an Inspector?' she asked.

'No, he was not an Inspector.'

'Perhaps he was a visiting minister, then?'

'No, he was *not* a minister.'

'Well, what sort of a man *was* he?' said the mother, a little bored with these negatives.

'I th-think,' stammered the child, 'I think he was—he was— an ARTICLE!'

15. *The Great Gale at Inverewe*

WINTER came gradually and made many false starts. When the
first gale blew the month of August out and whistled-in September, my friends the weavers of Gairloch warned me to
prepare for seven months of bad weather. This grim thought
reminded me of my farewell to the Government office and the
gloomy remarks of my colleagues.

'What will you do in the winter up there?' they had asked.
'Incessant rain and howling winds, and in December it may be
dark by three in the afternoon!' *Then* I had laughed it off; *now*
it seemed less funny—but I steeled myself to bear whatever came.

As it happened, my first bout of winter was pleasant and I
enjoyed it. Rain there was in plenty, and many days of blustery
wind; but in between squalls we had welcome spells of sunny
calm, when everyone threw off mackintoshes and opened their
windows wide. The air had enough freshness to be stimulating,
but no savage bite in it; and a thin crust of snow on the mountains
added charm to the scene without causing any trouble to road-
users.

Thirteen weeks after the conversation in Gairloch that had seemed so grim, I returned to the house of the weavers and told them I found their 'winter gloom' remarkably cheerful. As we were sunning ourselves on their verandah at the time, they were unable to find fault with my taste. But the weaver himself still had a shot in his locker. 'Wait till we get some *real* storms!' he said with a nasty glint in his eye. This time I refused to quail, and shrugged my shoulders with foolhardy unconcern. (When next we met, I did not consider it necessary to remind him of the incident. By then I knew the worst and could not joke about it.)

The great gale was quite a small wind when it came into our world, and Aunt Mairi and I spent its birthday morning out of doors. After lunch she retired upstairs for the brief rest which she rather shamefacedly said had been ordered her, while I lazed in a chair with a copy of a gardening paper. My attention was vaguely distracted from the articles once or twice by gusts outside, but as all the windows faced south and this wind was not in the usual south-westerly airt, they did not sound abnormally fierce to me. It was Sheena, coming from the other side of the house, who warned Aunt Mairi on her way downstairs that a gale was beginning.

Nothing could be done to help the battling plants outside, so we settled down to spend the afternoon in the smoking-room, where a desk-load of work waited for our attention. Inverewe was to be handed over officially to The National Trust for Scotland in the following spring, and the Edinburgh office clamoured for the manuscript of a guide-book to the demesne. Aunt Mairi's first reaction to this request had not been encouraging. 'What is the use of writing descriptions of gardens,' she said, 'when all the time plants are dying or being transplanted and new ones are taking their places?'

After it was explained to her that Trust properties open to the public always had descriptive booklets on sale at the gates, she turned to me and said, 'Then *you* will have to write one!' Fortunately we had, as a basis for this, an article on Inverewe published in *The Journal of the Royal Horticultural Society* for November 1950, which I had helped her to compile before I left England for the North.

Never shall I forget the task of deciphering the notes Aunt Mairi sent down to me by post—unable as I was to read her writing, and, in this case, too ignorant of the subject-matter to make guesses with confidence. Many of the Inverewe plants are rare in these islands, but even the most ordinary names—such as *Erica carnea*—would crop up in so many disguised spellings that I couldn't decide whether one familiar or three or four strange varieties were intended. *Euryka karmea* might have been an oddity from Patagonia for all I knew—but turned out in the end to be our old friend the Winter Heath.

Assistants in the public library got so used to seeing me deep in the *Encyclopaedia of Gardening* that they fetched it unasked as soon as I appeared in the reading-room. It took me several weeks of spare-time effort to put that article into the form required and fix (I hoped) the correct spelling of the two hundred or more botanical names. Afterwards I wondered how many of the horticulturally well-informed readers would credit the strange partnership that brought it into print. For Aunt Mairi had all the necessary knowledge of plants, but none of spelling, while I could spell ordinary words but was ignorant of botany. Probably the Editor of the *Journal* wrestled with my draft before it went to press; anyhow, we had no damning criticism of our work.

This, then, could definitely be used as a base; but the Inverewe booklet must contain more chatty information, and also lists of plants in greater detail. All these things I had to drag, with dogged, ruthless persistence, from the preoccupied owner of the gardens. That the operation was completed without sundering our friendship testifies to the sweetness of her temper.

On this evening of December 18th, while I worked at the booklet and Aunt Mairi attended to her usual stack of correspondence, the rising gale began to shriek round the house like a pack of were-wolves. The mail bus from Achnasheen was late, and Janet had a strenuous walk to the gates of Inverewe to fetch the letters, which we received with our high tea just after five o'clock.

When we had finished the meal, Aunt Mairi thought I had better go away home before things grew worse. She came along to the entrance porch with me, and as the big oak door swung open such a roar greeted us that there was a suggestion of my staying the night. I said I feared my neighbours might worry if they did not hear me moving around. Privately, I fancied it would be an exhilarating experience to battle with a gale of such magnitude. My little Cairn terrier thought otherwise, and bolted back to the safety of the smoking-room hearth; so I tucked her inside my mackintosh before launching out into the storm.

While we were in the comparatively sheltered custody of the drive there was not overmuch difficulty in keeping my footing, although anyone studying my tracks might have assumed their vagaries to be caused by intoxication. The tumult on the brae above was most alarming. The feeble rays of my pocket torch served to light a path, but not to delineate the trees, and I felt rather than saw how they were contorted under the hammer blows of the wind. A dark shadow in front of me turned out to be a large pine bough, and set me wondering how many more would crash down on the house or the drive before morning. The possibility of whole trees falling did not seriously disturb me, for I knew they had weathered storms for sixty years. (What I did not appreciate was that severe gales from this *northerly* airt were very uncommon, and therefore the plantations, braced to withstand the south and sou'-westerly winds, were unprepared for attack from the rear.)

As soon as we had passed through the small gate beside the drive entrance and turned towards *Tigh-an-Uillt*, I was almost plucked off the ground and carried several yards down the road by a gust which seemed solid—like lead rather than air. Stooping low to offer less resistance to the buffets, and clasping the little dog tightly in my arms, I ran or was wafted down to the gate beside the deer-house in front of my cottage. There I kicked something soft and wet, and slithered into a large bundle of slimy vegetation which tripped me up and received me flat on my face on top of the puppy.

Fortunately this mattress (of sea-wrack cast up by a high tide and hurled across the road by the gale) was soft and the puppy resilient, so no harm was done. I scrambled up, disengaged myself and the dog from the clinging tentacles of weed, and made my way carefully to the gate.

Safely inside the cottage, my first task was to fasten the sashes and put towels along the window-ledges to soak up rain which had percolated through. And of course the skylights were leaking again, demanding the arrangement of buckets beneath various drips in attic and scullery. A fire was essential, so I made a dash for the wood-lodge to procure kindling. I had learned to keep supplies of peat and logs indoors, where the old rusted-out oven served to dry green wood when I had the stove lit to heat bath water. But I had been extravagant with heather on the previous night, and the kindling basket was empty. Luckily the lodge had not leaked, so my main store was dry enough to make a quick blaze.

I had settled down (as I thought) before a sweet-smelling fire of mingled heather, peat, and pine, when a dreadful recollection jerked me to my feet. I had meant to post a very important letter to go by the next morning's mail. If *only* I had taken it up to Inverewe that day, it could have gone into the leather pouch in the little green sentry-box at the gates! To get it there now would mean a trek away to the Big House, and back again, making a disturbance for Aunt Mairi. I feared to leave an important missive loose in the leaky old box on such a night.

The alternatives were to walk to the village post-box, or go up to the Inverewe gate early in the morning and wait there until Arthur or Colin appeared in the bus. But if the gale kept me awake in the night I might oversleep, particularly as the mornings were now not light until nearly nine o'clock. This was indeed a tiresome situation. Somehow that letter *must* be posted; so I decided to attempt the walk to the village. It was roughly one mile from the Big House to the post-office, and I had done about a fifth of the distance already.

My little dog *Busdubh*, now dried and fed, was put into her basket for the night—where she curled up with a deep sigh, while I crept from view and put on my dripping mackintosh and sou'-wester once more. Wellington boots were clumsy to walk in, but remembering the piles of sodden weed on the road I thought it best to wear all the waterproof armour I possessed. My raincoat had a full skirt, with which the gale played tricks; so I put on an old pair of riding breeches instead of my kilt, and tied the mackintosh tightly at the waist with a cord. Thus equipped, and with a better torch in my hand, I slipped out of the back door.

It took me twice as long as usual to reach the great white byre of the Home farm, just one field's distance away down the road, and I was glad to cower in a more sheltered corner to recover my breath. The heavy wind-pressure on my back seemed to squeeze all the air from my lungs, and then whisk round my face to snatch fresh supplies from nose and mouth.

After a short pause I moved on again, but the road surface here was so thickly covered in weed and débris, and the waves of the sea-loch thumping the shingle on my right sent so much spray across the shore, that I had to keep my left hand on the farm wall to steady myself. I reached a bend in the road and turned towards Poolewe village, with the wind on my right cheeks instead of at my back; and now that all shelter from the Inverewe braes had been left behind the full force of the storm caught me.

I was often pinned fast against the wall, which was a rough, uncomfortable prop, but greatly to be preferred to some stagnant ditch. Stone by stone I scraped my way along it until I came to some wire fencing, which was less easy to cling to. Several times I slithered down into the seaweed, and my mackintosh and breeches were soon as slimy as seine-nets. I began to feel tired, and the Wellington boots seemed to add twelve pounds to each foot. Then the high enclosure of Pool House garden appeared on my right, and shut off a little of the wind-power. This helped me to make rather better progress as far as the post-office, where the letter was with some trouble extracted from my inner wrappings and pushed into the posting-box.

So far all was well, and I felt elated at having achieved what I had set out to do. But of course the homeward journey had yet to be tackled, and this would be much worse, with the wind in my face and vicious squalls of bitterly cold rain coming across the loch at a nearly horizontal angle. It would have been pleasant to go into a house or the hotel for a rest and some refreshment before returning, but everyone seemed so well battened down (not a door or window showed a chink of light); and I was in such a messy condition that I decided not to attempt an entry. Also, it would have been harder to turn out a second time into the stormy night afterwards.

This, then, was It! I must leave such shelter as the little village street afforded and set off round the loch again. Although within reach of many friends, I felt absolutely alone in the struggle with that screeching wind and fusillades of rain. It was a long, slow advance—once I had left the hotel wall behind—and often two steps forward were followed by a blow-back of a yard, with a fall to end the run. Some of the gusts had such lifting power that they gave me a sensation of flight—but in an undirected, helpless fashion. It was comforting to remember that were I lifted bodily (as seemed possible) and whirled overhead, this wind could not carry me away from the land.

Exhausted and sobbing for breath I reached the haven of the Home farm, and propped myself up in the shelter of the byre. I had struggled along the last fifty yards or so with a sudden recollection of words spoken to me as a schoolgirl by that wise friend and mentor, the late Sir Francis Younghusband. He had taken me to an enormous cupboard somewhere in the back premises of his home (Currant Hill) in Kent, and there shown me sleeping-bags and other bundles of equipment used on his Himalayan expeditions.

'I give them a pat and turn them over now and then,' he said. 'I shall not use them any more, but they served me well.' I asked him about his long walk through the terrible Gobi Desert, and what he remembered most about that experience. After a thoughtful pause (he always gave his full attention to questions, even from the youngest or least important member of a party) he said, 'I found it the greatest help when I was utterly weary to blot out all thought of my destination or the distance to be covered, and to concentrate entirely on *seeing how well I could walk.*'

This conversation lived in my memory for thirty years, and the advice implicit in his words had stayed me through difficult tasks unconnected with forced marches. Now, for the first time, I followed it in the literal sense—trying to put my feet down firmly and keep to a steady plod in spite of the boisterous wind, blinding rain squalls, lack of breath, and (it must be admitted) fear of these violent elemental forces let loose in the dark.

The sight of my cottage room, with the sleeping puppy in an old peat-basket, the glowing remains of fire on the hearth, and the pot-bellied black kettle spouting steam, made me feel rather sheepish. Who was I, never more than one mile from this comfortable home, to be comparing my thoughts with those of a great explorer? Nevertheless, Sir Francis himself would have been the last to despise remembrance and gratitude from a mere poster of letters.

Although the gale was drumming the tiles on the roof above my bed like all the tom-toms I had ever heard in the Ceylon jungle, I was too tired to notice the din for more than the few moments it took me to undress and get between the sheets, where I dropped immediately into dreamless slumber.

Next morning there was still a strong wind, but the gale's wickedness had departed, and as soon as I got downstairs I went to the door with the idea of running to the gate for a look across the loch at Inverewe. Then I saw Lizbie peering from her window, and went round to speak to her first.

'Oh, dearie me, what an awful night!' she said; 'not one wink of sleep could I get! And the blown trees at Inverewe are a terrible sight, they tell me.' This was alarming news, and I could scarcely wait to swallow my *brose* and tea before setting out for the Big House. The drive was not looking materially changed—just littered with boughs and twigs which could easily be cleared, but when I passed the garage and came to the wide sweep before the house entrance I stopped and stared, aghast.

The wooded slopes of *Am Ploc Ard* behind and to the west of the mansion looked as though some super bulldozer from Outer Space had ploughed a track right across the width of the penin-sula. Large trees lay around in all sorts of ungainly attitudes, roots with chunks of peat clinging to them were silhouetted against the sky, and rhododendrons had been lifted from the soil and perched in the branches of the fallen timber like huge tufts of mistletoe. I could see that the wide walk from the west of the house past the enclosure named 'Japan' to the boat landing was choked with trunks and branches from end to end.

I raced down the path to the back door and into the kitchen, where Janet, unusually pale and hollow-eyed, and old Sheena were at work.

'Och, what a terrible night!' said Sheena, drawing in her breath with a sharp hiss. 'We are lucky to be alive! All those trees crashing down the brae—it was awful! Every minute I thought something was bound to fall on us—but the house not even scratched! It was a miracle.'

Saying that house and inmates had indeed been fortunate, I bemoaned the dismal fate of the garden. Sheena agreed there had been a lot of damage to *that*, adding, 'Mrs. Sawyer's out looking at it just now.'

I ran away out in search of her, and found her clambering through the pallisade of trunks down by the landing jetty. She was quite calm, and her bright eye and fresh complexion bore no trace of sleeplessness. Together we crept under and over the débris, counting the fallen trees and assessing the damage throughout her demesne.

Round about a hundred and fifty good-sized trees had been uprooted or snapped off a few feet above the ground; and fifty or sixty important rhododendrons were uprooted or crushed. It was curious to see how the native trees (or their near relatives, such as Austrian pine) had suffered most, while exotic strangers like the big eucalypts were standing firm. Aunt Mairi said she had no recollection of a severe gale from the north in her lifetime, nor had her father mentioned any. It had swept up from the *Camas Glas* and cut a swathe from bottom to top of *Ploc Ard*, and down the other side to 'Japan'. She feared for the tree-ferns and other sub-tropical plants in that enclosure, now that the removal of so much cover had left them exposed to the north. She felt sanguine about the damaged rhododendrons—for she believed most of these could be rescued and replanted without suffering much harm.

Aunt Mairi was so quiet and matter-of-fact in her assessment and plans for restoration that a stranger could not have divined what a sickening blow the disaster had given her.

'We must hope the gale won't increase again tonight,' she said, 'for once a gap has been cut, the fringe trees on either edge of it are likely to fall with another blow from the same quarter.'

So far as this went, the great gale was kinder than some. Generally we had three rough nights in succession, but this time the gale practically blew itself out in one. Having been face to face with it, I could well imagine that as much force had been released in those few hours as in three days of a lesser storm. When I got home it surprised me to realize that I had not even mentioned my adventure of the evening before. The sight of Inverewe in such a sorry state had swept everything else from my mind.

16. *Stranger at Home*

AUNT MAIRI considered that very little could be done about clearing the blown timber until the ground had had a chance to dry out; and so, as Christmas was less than a week away, she turned her thoughts to preparing for her guests.

The schools closed for a short vacation, and I packed my bag for a journey south to spend the holiday with my family in Somerset. I was in two minds about the little dog *Busdubh*—for by now she had become such a good companion that I was loath to part from her even for so short a time, and feared she might pine for me. But as it seemed senseless to make so young a creature endure the two twenty-seven-hour journeys, I accepted a kind offer from the weavers of Gairloch to have her back.

It cannot be said that *Beurach* displayed any maternal pleasure at seeing her daughter, but barring a few Keep-your-distance growls she was not actively nasty; and *Busdubh* seemed content to settle again in her old home.

Aunt Mairi arranged for Roderick Mor, her head man and stalker, to drive me in her car to Inverness, which was less tiring than the slower trip by mail bus as far as Achnasheen and thence in the Kyle train. We left Inverewe early in the morning and should have arrived well before lunch-time, had not a travelling crane broken down near the hydro-electric works at Loch Luichart—completely blocking the road and holding up all traffic.

It is well to be prepared for this kind of hazard when motoring in the north-west Highlands; for the narrow roads bordered by ditches or boulders allow no scope for edging round obstructions, there are seldom any alternative routes, and usually nothing to be done except sit and wait. That is what Roderick and I had to do, for over an hour until a breakdown gang arrived to remove the inert lump of machinery.

While we waited I told Roderick that I had experienced a similar hold-up on a jungle road in Ceylon—only in that case the barrier consisted of a large elephant. It stood in the middle of the road to Kandy (whether it also thought, or just stood, we could not judge), and as it was impossible to pass, we switched off the car engine and waited to see what would happen. After two hours the great beast seemed to remember an urgent appointment and lumbered off suddenly into the jungle, without betraying that it had even noticed us in our car.

As a result of this latest delay, Roderick and I did not reach the Gaelic greeting *Ceud Mìle Fàilte* (A Hundred Thousand Welcomes) at the bounds of Inverness until just upon two o'clock. How lost and bewildered I felt when he drove the car away, leaving me and my luggage at the station! Inverness is a relatively small, quiet city, but seemed like some roaring metropolis after the remote peace of Inverewe. With a couple of hours to pass before my train, I crept nervously out into the street.

Crossing the road was an ordeal, and I stood on the kerb for some minutes before venturing over to the shops opposite the station. The first restaurant I approached made no difficulty about serving a good luncheon at the late hour of a quarter past two. Caterers in the Highland capital seem most willing to provide travellers with meals at almost any time, and their staffs attend to one's wants with cheerful courtesy. This is the kind of thing people remember—but how many proprietors and assistants realize it? I was so impressed by the pleasant manner of the waitresses that I was tempted to sample the other shops, and ended by making all the Christmas purchases which I had meant to leave until London was reached.

My travelling companions in the four-berth sleeper were an old woman from the Strathpeffer district of Ross-shire, with her daughter and grand-daughter of six. The child's clear voice and perfect enunciation reminded me of wee Jessie at Achtercairn School, whose back grew so sore with 'picking stones' from her father's croft. The little traveller's pithy commentary on all she saw from the train window was worth listening to for both sound and sense. After watching the telegraph lines for some moments, she said: 'Look! The wires go up and up until they hit the pole, and then they have to come down again'—which could hardly be bettered as a description of how the track-side lines appear to behave when seen from a moving train.

The long winter night closed down very soon after we started, and at once the child curled up on the top shelf opposite mine and went to sleep. Then the grandmother asked shyly if I would mind her husband coming to sit with us for a while. Of course I made no demur, and the old man entertained us with stories of his travels in merchant ships when he was young. Australia had particularly appealed to him, and the most memorable thing about it in those days seemed to be the cheap and plentiful food. 'As much meat as a man could eat and vegetables on a plate with gravy for fowerpence,' he said, repeating it slowly so that we might all relish the idea to the full.

Asked whether he had thought of settling there, he said softly, yes, he had—but the wish to see Scotland again had proved too strong.

In a little while he went back to his own compartment and we settled down for the night. I was a long time in getting to sleep, for the rattle and thump of the train distracted me almost beyond endurance and I was disturbed and uneasy in my mind, not having foreseen that life at Inverewe might make me feel a stranger elsewhere. If this could happen in seven months, how should I manage to visit my home after, say, seven years in the North, I asked myself. (The possibility of interruption to my life with Aunt Mairi in less than ten years or so did not occur to me then, for she was so fit and active for her seventy-odd years, and came of a long-lived race.)

After three hours of wakeful reverie I reached the conclusion that British Railways were providing us with far more noise than usual, so that my uneasiness could not all be put down to changes in myself. This raised my spirits, and at last I slept.

When the first light came through chinks in the window-screen my small neighbour opened her eyes and cried, 'I see morning—time to rise!' So I took the hint, climbed down from my hard bunk, and slid aside the door of our compartment. My intention—to go for a wash in that grimy cubicle marked 'Toilet'—met with frustration in the shape of fifty or more bags of Christmas mail piled like a chain of mountain peaks the whole length of the corridor. I wondered whether the quality of the wash would repay the climbing required to reach the basin, remembering how Aunt Mairi had said she avoided railway water because it made her feel much dirtier than she had been before.

Then the thought of my companions nerved me to scale the hills of canvas, as I felt sure it would shock them to learn that I had given up the idea of washing. I trod as lightly as possible, with care for the loving greetings stuffed into the sacks upon which I scrambled. But squashed robins and crumpled yule-logs must have entered many a saddened home that year, for after my journey to and fro had been accomplished all three of my cabin-mates ventured over the mailbags together, led by the little girl.

No doubt some of the night noises I found so disturbing had been caused by this overflow from the guard's van—apparently the mail had been hurled into our coach at a number of stops *en route*. Confirmation that nerves were not entirely to blame for my wakefulness put me into quite a cheerful mood, which lasted until we reached Euston. But once I had seen my baggage off in the Paddington conveyance and gone out to the street, confidence waned—leaving me with the sensation of a hunted rabbit that had mislaid the entrance to its burrow.

Seeing an Underground station which promised some sort of sanctuary I dived down to the trains, but must in my flurry have taken the wrong turning, for the one I was in arrived at the Mansion House instead of Paddington as I expected it to do. Although London's District Railway is not as peaceful as a Highland glen the carriages are steady goers, and once inside you are saved from dodging other vehicles or being hooted at. No driver in the North had ever hooted me off the road, and I resented being the target for such vulgar sounds in London; so I was tempted to settle in a Circle train going round and round beneath the metropolis.

Before long a sharper spur than Fame drove me to give up this soothing plan and break surface again—this time at a station called Green Park, from whence hunger led me down Piccadilly in search of a meal. Feeding-time at the Zoo is a noisy affair, but I doubt if the Regent's Park animals could have added much, pound for pound weight, to the din created by the people in that café; nor would they have pushed and shoved any more fiercely to get at their victuals. I might have hovered on the unfed fringe for ever had not a motherly waitress said, ' 'ere you are, dear!'— and planted me in a single seat almost before a very large lady had lifted her weight from it.

The clatter and chatter reverberated from wall to wall, making my head buzz, and as soon as I had swallowed my snack I took myself off to the slightly fresher air of the park. The bare trees in the so-called 'green' one looked sooty and dead, and the grass beneath them was a jaundiced khaki colour and smelt of cats, so I passed on to St. James's in search of the wildfowl whose cries lured me to the ornamental water. The sight of so many animated water-birds made me feel more at home, and I sat down to watch them from one of the lakeside seats.

A burst of winter sunshine pierced the hodden-grey sky,

prompting other morning strollers to follow suit, and soon two seasoned London women with sore feet came to share my bench. (I knew their feet hurt because they eased off their shoes with grunts of satisfaction before settling down to vet the passers by.) One woman was plump, rosy, snub-nosed and talkative; her companion lean and sallow, with a sardonic beak and voice like a corncrake. Fortunately she spoke little.

I had often heard Cockney before, but now I really listened to it for the first time. For over six months I had lived among people who, whatever their position in life, spoke (with pure vowels and modulated voices) an almost accentless and unclipped form of our language. By contrast, the Cockney version now sounded like some foreign tongue.

Listening at first to the sound alone, I soon became interested in the conversation for its own sake. I had not known until then that it was possible for people to be critical of the accents of others without (apparently) realizing that they themselves employed exactly the same speech. The discussion between the Plump Cockney and the Lean went something like this:

P.C: Thet's a smort piece! Very smort. Blek. Nothink loyke *blek*!
L.C: Naow.
P.C: But thet one—she's hawful commern lookin'! Plorstered wiv poynt and 'er 'air doyed.
L.C: Aow, oi down' knaow.
P.C: *Corse* it's doyed. Never see 'air wot growed thet colour! [sniff] Doyed!
L.C: Spowse ate ase.
P.C: Hand commern! Jest listen t'er. 'Come 'ere,' she sez ter the kid; ' 'old me 'and.' It's a wunner them blinkin' kids unner-stends 'em, the wye thye talks. It's *thet* commern! Hand the kids ser well edjicated naow; spiks ser *noyce*, the kids does. But their ma's! [sniff] 'Come 'ere!' [sniff] ' 'old me 'and! 'OLD ME 'AND'!

After this, it was comforting to hear some mallard duck speaking the same language as those in Wester Ross.

When it was time for me to go across to Paddington for the last stage of my journey, I celebrated the end of my visit to London by hailing a taxi and sitting snug and smug inside while other pedestrians were hooted out of *my* way.

The Bath train looked (even in its third-class sections) very opulent compared with the horse-box sleepers and filthy wash-places of the night mail from the North. I wondered why passengers on a two-hour journey should be cosseted while the long-distance travellers had to rough it—or pay first-class fares. This is one of the mysteries of our British Railways' way-of-life that has not yet been explained.

The gleaming refreshment car tempted me to a mid-morning snack, so I went in at once and ordered coffee and biscuits. My small change had all gone to the taximan, and I paid the waiter with a pound note. He looked at it, turned it over, held it out to me and said, 'What's this?'

'A pound note,' I began rather testily; 'oh, of course, it's a Scottish one. But it is quite all right.'

The man gave me one of those weary Lord-what-fools-these-customers-are glances which I had not received since leaving the South, and said with the exaggerated, pained politeness that goes with them, 'Could you let me have an *English* one, please, madam?'

I took a wad from my notecase and spread out the gaily coloured varieties from four different Scottish banks—but not one of their sober English relations happened to be among them. 'I'm sorry,' I said, 'Inverness hasn't supplied me with any. But these must be legal tender here, surely!'

'Perhaps you have some silver?' said the man, sounding even more pained and a little less polite.

'All my change went to the taximan, otherwise I should not be paying a two-shilling bill with a note,' I replied.

'I am afraid we cannot accept foreign money,' retorted the waiter. 'You should have exchanged it before boarding the train, madam.'

'*Foreign* money?' I began to get heated. 'These are perfectly good Scottish notes; no more foreign than the whisky you serve.'

'Perhaps I can help,' said a courteously amused voice from behind my right shoulder. I looked up, and saw a senior naval officer in whose department I had worked during the war. He held out an English pound, for which I gratefully slipped him a purple and orange edition in exchange. Then I put the green one on the table beside my bill.

The waiter was now a different man. With inclined head he nervously raked up bill and money, saying in a subdued voice, 'Very sorry, madam, but we have to be careful'—and vanished to get my change. I sensed that my acquaintance's uniformed rank, rather than his production of acceptable cash, had caused the startling transformation. This gave me one more jolt, for in the North a man's a man for all his gold lace (or lack of it); and people who serve do not alter their manner under the influence of a hat or tabs, however brassy.

My helpful friend came over to my table and we talked for some time. He asked many questions about life in the Far North, and how it differed from the south of England. I now realized to the full how unlike my old life it was, and in addition, how much it had already begun to alter *me*; but the variations were very subtle and difficult to pin down and sum up in a few words.

I told him that the people seemed much more placid and at ease in themselves; that they were content to be natural, and rarely showed off or kow-towed before others. I asked if he knew the evergreen story of the old Scottish family retainer who became just a little *too* free with his advice and comments to please his master. One day the latter barked at him: 'James! You and I will have to part!' 'Aye, Laird,' replied the man quietly; 'and where are ye gaun?' This is actually a Lowland tale, but illustrates the lack of all subservience found in the Highlands as well. 'They have no trace of what my mother calls "*the feudal system*",' I said.

'This may be due partly to the good education they have had (and prized) for so long; but even more, I believe, to the fact that until after the '45 lairds were not, like the English squires, owners in complete control of the land by which the people lived. For centuries the Highland chiefs were better described as administrators, governing territory and possessions for the benefit of the clan as a whole. So, although they would die if need be in defence of their chief, the clansmen were independent and free to speak their minds to him. A state unknown to most English countrymen until very recent years.'

My friend said he imagined the wild, rough character of the land, the gales and storms coming in off the Minch, the remote, isolated position of many communities, all helped to breed the vigorous independence of which I spoke. He had known Loch Ewe and the surrounding seas during Hitler's war, when serving in a battleship that guarded this assembly point for convoys to Russia. He said he had marvelled at the remoteness of some of the little white croft houses, which seemed to sprout from the rocks and bogs like mushrooms in an English meadow, regardless of means of access.

'On the few occasions when I was able to land and explore the country,' he said, 'I found crofts which could only be reached by boat or the rockiest of hill-paths—miles away from any road.'

I said that what impressed me even more than the inaccessible position of *some* crofts and clachans today was the thought of the MacKenzie family having made, almost within living memory, the very first road into Gairloch—and this when it had a population ten times greater than that of the nineteen-fifties. Before that, life was indeed strenuous for the inhabitants. Aunt Mairi used to relate how the postman, who bore all mail for the district on his back over the steep path from Achnasheen to Poolewe by way of Ardlair, on one occasion carried more than he was paid to do. An official of the Post Office, who came to inspect the work of '*Iain Mór am Posda*' (Big John the Post), attempted the same journey—on foot, but without any burden to transport. Even so, the walk proved too much for him. He fainted, and Big John arrived carrying both the mailbags and the Overseer.

'And the postman did it all on a diet of oatmeal and herring,

I suppose!' my friend commented. We wondered whether, with the money crofters could now earn by working on hydro-electric schemes, and the increased provision of frozen and tinned foods, the people of the North might lose their toughness and vigour. I said that one of the teachers I worked with (a woman still in her thirties) thought the children were being pampered more than necessary, for such tremendous changes had occurred in the few years since her own schooldays.

Then, they had to walk to school—often many miles and in all weathers. Now, the children come in coaches or hired cars, and special motors are sent long distances up the glens, wherever roads permit, to fetch even one pupil. When they get to school their wet clothes (if they have become slightly damp on their way to the car) are dried on hot pipes. The boys and girls have hot milk at eleven, and a cooked meal at midday. In her time, she told me, they had to sit and shiver in soaked clothes—she was never allowed to go near the open fire to dry and warm herself. Her meal consisted of a 'piece' brought from home; and if she did not know her lessons she received a dose of the strap.

'And of course their religious training was rigorous, wasn't it?' my friend asked. 'In many communities that is still true,' I replied. 'The ministers visit houses regularly to catechize children and their parents. Backsliders are reprimanded—sometimes named from the pulpit, and recreations preached against.

'So carefully is the sabbath kept, that when an acquaintance of ours had a motoring accident which delayed his arrival from Saturday to Sunday, the house where he had booked lodgings was closed to him. He could see and hear the family inside, but no amount of rapping would persuade them to open the door. Finally he stood and called to them at one of the windows, and so brought the man of the house to speak to him. To his amazement he was told to go away to the hotel and come back again on Monday, for he could not be admitted to their home on the sabbath.'

This reminded me of Aunt Mairi's travels with an old gillie, whom she and her father took to a Swiss hotel one Christmas. In those days most people went abroad with retinues of valets, ladies' maids, and other servants, and Donald in his kilt and bonnet soon became king of the large below-stairs community.

On Christmas Eve there was a Ball, and Aunt Mairi went to fetch Donald in order to show him the gay scene from a balcony. She guessed he had been brought up to eschew such a frivolous diversion as dancing for himself, but thought he would be sure to enjoy watching other people at it. After he had surveyed the dancers for a moment or two, he turned away. 'That iss the Devil's work!' he announced gloomily. Aunt Mairi thought her trouble had been wasted. Then Donald went back to the rails and gazed raptly at the waltzing throng below. 'But, indeed, *it iss very inter-resting to behold!*' he said.

'And it has been very interesting to me to hear all this,' laughed my companion, 'but here we are at Bath already.' So I was home—if 'home' it could still be called—more than seven hundred miles from Inverewe, at the end of twenty-seven hours of travelling.

This chapter should really be headed 'Stranger on the Way Home'; because, once under my mother's roof, I shed all vestige of strangeness and fell into the relaxed and blissful state of a kitten which has stolen the cream. After ten days of basking in the rays of family warmth and custom, I felt more like the cormorant on the Inverewe mooring-buoy, who preened his wings and hung them out to dry on sunny days in the fashion of a 'displayed' bird on some heraldic device.

17. *Flitting to the Gate Lodge*

BEFORE I left Inverewe to spend Christmas in England, Aunt Mairi had a long talk with me about next year's plans for admitting the public to her gardens. In a ceremony being arranged for the following May, the policies were to be formally handed over to The National Trust for Scotland; but in fact the Trust already had the guardianship, and all moneys received from admissions would go to it in the coming year.

She felt it would be too much for herself and her household to admit visitors in the future. Hitherto, people had been asked to ring the bell at the front door of the Big House, putting their contributions to the Nurses' Fund into a box in the porch. But now that tickets must be issued and records maintained, it was planned to use the Lodge by the gate for the business, and Aunt Mairi had to decide who to install there for this duty.

Visitors were to be admitted on two days only each week (instead of at any time as before), but the Trust would give so much publicity to Inverewe that numbers were expected to rise.

The recorded total for the summer of 1948 was 700, and this had slowly increased to about 1,000 a year since then.

'Now,' said Aunt Mairi, 'will *you* move up from the cottage to the Gate Lodge and become first custodian? We shall be able to open when you are at home, so as not to clash with your teaching days. And I'd so much rather have you there than import strangers.'

This was an unexpected proposal. I had grown attached to *Tigh-an-Uillt*, was perfectly content to stay there, and happy about life in its present form. The Gate Lodge (which had been enlarged into a rambling sort of bungalow to house the family after the original Inverewe House was burnt) seemed much too large for me. How could I clean five bedrooms, two bathrooms, a big lounge, dining-room, and all the etceteras? Hired help was not to be had, unless you could afford (and find) a resident maid.

But Aunt Mairi—who had stores of rosy memories of her young married life in the Lodge—thought it a tremendous improvement on my leaky half of the gardener's cottage, with its rusty stove and lack of central heating. She of course had never tried to run the place, stoke a boiler without assistance, and earn her living as well. I, with some experience of that sort of thing, had vowed 'Never again!—though she was unaware of this.

'I can't bear the idea of people I don't know living permanently in the Gate Lodge and dealing with all the business of the gardens,' she said. 'So you *must* come there and do it! You will be so much more comfortable and warm, too. It is awful to think of you cooking in gumboots in winter because the scullery floor in the cottage is awash.'

There was no more to be said. I hadn't the heart to disappoint her, so I agreed to move as soon as the present tenants vacated the Lodge. It was further arranged that I should break my return journey in Edinburgh, where the offices of The National Trust for Scotland are situated. This meant travelling up by day, spending a night in the Scottish capital, moving on to Perth next night, and joining the train from Euston to Inverness in the early hours of the following morning.

I booked a seat from London in the express known as 'Queen of Scots' which had a faintly Victorian air about its collection of elderly Pullman coaches. These suggested to me a cross between some provincial bank and a Kensington pub of the solid-mahogany sort. Everything was very comfortable—except for the rather stingy space for hand-luggage—and an excellent luncheon was brought to my table; but how weary I got of that journey by day! It is much pleasanter to sleep through the first part of the route and wake up in Scotland with all the hills and lochs ahead in the fresh morning.

Edinburgh looked magnificent, and (for January) was not cold. With clear skies, a slight breeze ruffling the Forth, and glints of snow just visible on the distant high tops, that city is perhaps at its best. But all this appeared to my sight next morning. It was dark when the 'Queen' puffed into Princes Street station, and I slipped through a side door into my hotel and went almost immediately to bed. My slumber must have been sound, for it seemed only a few minutes later that a smiling chambermaid came with the early tea. She drew aside the window curtain, giving from my pillow a perfect view of the great castle sprawling on its crag above the city, with everything looking clear and clean in the sharp sunlight of a northern winter. For once 'Auld Reekie' seemed a slanderous invention; though most Scotsmen dwell on that nickname with fond relish.

I had various commissions from Inverewe to carry out in the Princes Street shops, and spent about two hours after breakfast dealing with these. Then, fortified by coffee and some of those delicious little cakes and shortbreads which the cafés serve in such abundance, I went round to the offices of the Trust.

When I reached the address it seemed vaguely familiar, though I could not recollect having visited Charlotte Square before. Then I took a mental leap back to the place I had just left —Bath! Of course the Georgian architecture had a strong family likeness, and the great Robert Adam was concerned with both cities. The north side of the square, before which I stood admiringly, was designed by that architect.

The men inside the Trust building, though engaged chiefly in restoring and preserving relics of the past, were themselves anything but antiquated; and our discussions proved both businesslike and breezy. Inverewe (the first estate to be taken over solely on its merits as a *garden*) presented the Trust with several fresh problems, owing to their inexperience as garden-owners and the remote position of the property.

It was useless for me to inquire how much work the custodian's duties would mean—when no one knew how many people would make the long journey to see the gardens. Mr. Stormonth Darling, the secretary, thought Aunt Mairi's estimate of 'Never more than twenty in one day' a little conservative. (Subsequent experiences have proved him right to an astonishing degree.) It worried me that, as I couldn't be in two places at once, the responsibility for selling tickets and booklets at the gate might make it impossible to help with the gardening. It was suggested that I should confine my work to the beds and shrubberies along the drive, from most of which an eye could be kept on the entrance. I felt dubious—for gardening needs both eyes and all one's attention. However, there was nothing to be done about it except wait and see.

The forthcoming production of the guide-book was then discussed in some detail. I had completed the manuscript and also a cover design and drawings, and saw a number of photographs from which a selection would be made for inclusion in the booklet. Before I left the offices it was made clear to me that Lord Wemyss and his Committee were anxious that Aunt Mairi should, so far as possible, be made to feel the garden was still hers. To this end, ownership by the Trust during her lifetime would be as unobtrusive as circumstances allowed. The ordinary run of business must be transacted through me, without bothering her at all. It seemed possible that much tact might be demanded of me if the two masters were to be served with success, but I kept this thought to myself.

'Of course we shall have to put up some Trust signs and notices,' said Mr. Stormonth Darling as we parted. I quailed, knowing that Aunt Mairi loathed notices. She had already got me to paint, in the most refined roman capitals, a board requesting visitors to ring at the Lodge and not at the house when desiring admission to the gardens. This was portable, and designed for removal at the close of each open day. Official signs would be more colourful (and permanently fixed) additions to the entrance. I should have to pave the way for their installation when I got back to Inverewe.

The rest of my journey to Achnasheen was uneventful, though the hurried departure from a Perth hotel at 5.30 a.m. required some effort of will on a winter's morning. It was an occasion for gratitude to the inventor of the vacuum flask—without one of those blessings the vital hot tea would not have been waiting to lure me out of bed. I had never tried the method which an old great-aunt of mine (once a co-member of some country house-party with Mr. and Mrs. Gladstone) declared the Prime Minister to have used. On retiring for the night, she said, the Gladstones were in the habit of asking a maid to fill an earthenware hot water-bottle with boiling tea. This flannel-covered article, after warming the toes of the great man and his wife during the night, was fished up at daybreak to provide several cheering cups before Mr. Gladstone began his day's work on State papers.

In those days, unfortunate domestic servants worked until all hours, and presumably the bottle was not filled much before midnight. Waking early, Mr. Gladstone would have found the contents still very hot when he was ready to drink it. This frugal use of one lot of boiling liquid to warm both feet and stomach appealed to my thrifty Highland instinct; but, as a lively dreamer, heavy earthenware warmers are not suited to my habits. Rubber ones (though too flavoursome to drink from) are more practical, as they can be kicked out of bed without waking the entire household or bringing down lumps of plaster from the ceiling beneath.

My return to Inverewe may not have brought the house down, but it certainly elicited the warmest of welcomes; first from Arthur waiting in the mail bus at Achnasheen, and next from one of the Achtercairn pupils who spotted me as we passed the Kerry Falls on our way into Gairloch. Somehow the mysterious 'bush post' signalled the news, and waving children sprang up from behind every wall. I began to feel like a returning heroine or a film star. It was delightful to receive so many cheery smiles; but perhaps my little dog *Busdubh's* excited barks, and the feel of her cold, shiny nose, gave me the greatest pleasure of all. Her joy was unmistakable and for weeks afterwards she avoided letting me out of her sight.

Aunt Mairi thought I had been away too long; which was pleasanter to hear than 'I didn't expect you back so soon!' I told her the little delay in Edinburgh had been worth while, for not only had I succeeded in getting what she wanted in the shops, but I could also bring assurances about the understanding and considerate attitude of the Trust. To this she said airily that as half the Committee (including the Chairman) were her relations, she felt Inverewe had been more or less kept in the family. I touched very lightly on the subject of notice-boards, and then we plunged into gardening matters. I was very keen to try the latest hardy outdoor strain of freesias at Inverewe, and Aunt Mairi agreed that it would be nice to have banks of them; adding that she would order some if I liked, though *she* would not be there to see them flower. This was her second reference in six months to an early departure—but it seemed too fantastic to regard with more than a smile.

We proceeded to the arrangements for clearing the blown timber, on which task we hoped to employ a team of forestry men. Such hopes were soon dashed. A few days later there was a renewal of the northerly gale which had in December torn down so many of our precious trees. This time Inverewe lost about a hundred others. Further south, immense stands of valuable forest trees were mown flat in scenes of utter devastation never known in Scotland before, and to the north the Ullapool fishing-boats were blown right out of the loch and perched in adjacent fields. The Navy rescued the stranded boats; but every available forestry worker was now so heavily committed to clearing the big southern estates, that we had to abandon all thought of assistance with our remote and relatively insignificant fall of two hundred and fifty trees.

Aunt Mairi called a council of war of the Inverewe employees, and her men volunteered to tackle the clearance work themselves. Day after day they sawed and dragged and carted the casualties away, while Aunt Mairi re-planted shrubs and I ran up and down the braes collecting hamperfuls of smaller branches. This was hard on the legs; and as leather-soled brogues became slippery and Wellington boots were too cumbersome, I decided to get a pair of rubber-soled canvas shoes from the shop in Gairloch.

A suitable model was at once produced; I paid the modest price, and went home with the box under my arm. In the morning I put on the shoes and found that one was a size smaller than the other. Next day at Achtercairn I dashed along the strath just before the school dinner-time to return the odd shoes at the shop. 'Dear me, now, they have jumped into the wrong boxes!' said the owner sadly. He managed to make it sound as though his stock was in the habit of growing skittish after closing time, and played at musical chairs behind his back.

'Now, I wonder who bought the other pair of those?' he mused. 'It must have been Isobel MacRae. She may not have noticed that hers are not matched. Well, well, now, I shall have to send a message down to Peterburn with Donnie tonight.' About a week later I received the two sixes, while Miss MacRae got her fives, and all was well. Being residents, we were not in the least put out by such trifling errors; but I wondered what would have been said had a holiday visitor found herself away in Nairn or Glasgow with odd footwear.

On the whole the rest of the winter was fairly kind to our work of clearance, and we began to hope that the masses of débris really would be out of the way by the date of our handing-over in May—when a concourse of guests was expected. All the men worked like beavers, showing sense and adroitness at moving trunks which had fallen in awkward positions. Aunt Mairi doubted whether professional timber men could have managed any better or caused so little damage to growing shrubs. She herself grew very tired; but still, we managed to have fun at times.

I remember in particular one Saturday afternoon we spent laughing together in one of the greenhouses. An energetic lady who stayed in the vicinity had been invited to walk in the gardens whenever she wished—which she did every afternoon unless the weather was exceptionally rough. We were interested in the big rolled umbrella she invariably carried; for when it was dry she did not need to open it, and on wet days there was generally too much wind to hold it up. (Umbrellas are not much used in Wester Ross.)

On this dampish afternoon the lady had met me on the drive and I noticed that her umbrella was missing. This seemed odd, as it happened to be one of the rare, still days with drizzling rain when it would have been possible to make use of the shelter. After we had greeted each other she said with a quick frown that she felt very bad-tempered because her maid had borrowed the umbrella, taken it to Inverness, and accidentally left it behind.

'It was only my *second-best* umbrella,' she said, 'but so very useful up here! I have another—an expensive silk one—but it is too good to carry in the country, and I do not want to let the maid see it if she is going to borrow my umbrellas like this. It is most vexing! Perhaps it will be best, when Morag gets my second-best one back from her sisters, to buy a *third* umbrella. If I got a cheap one and put it in the hall, it would do for her to borrow—and then I could refuse to lend mine.'

She was so absorbed in her saga that it made quite an impression on my mind, and I repeated it to Aunt Mairi while we worked on the potted chrysanthemums in the greenhouse. The thought of anyone in Wester Ross possessing a *second-best* umbrella touched some hidden spring in her and she began to laugh. The sight and sound of Aunt Mairi enjoying a joke set me off, and as I always cry when I laugh, a handkerchief had to be found. This occurred when Aunt Mairi was on the point of collecting herself, and sent her off into another bout of helpless laughter.

So we went on infecting each other until we had to stop from sheer exhaustion. Luckily we were alone and undisturbed all the afternoon—for who else could have fathomed the sight of two grown women prompted to such behaviour by a sober black umbrella?

Such unrehearsed entertainments are part of the best stuff of comradeship, but are seldom understood by others. It was amusing to see Aunt Mairi's face at tea-time, when old Sheena asked how we had spent the afternoon. With the embarrassed air of a naughty schoolgirl she confessed that we had done little, 'because we laughed so much'! This set us both off again, while Sheena ate her scone in superior silence.

Next time I went up to Inverewe it was extraordinarily quiet and deserted-looking. There was no sign of Aunt Mairi: no tools lying around on the terraces; and the garden-house beside the front door was shut. I went through to the smoking-room, but found nobody there. A log smouldered on the hearth, and the two caged canaries brought from Tenerife sat mutely on their perches. The dog *Cailleach*'s basket contained only a very ancient bone. There was something a little creepy about the silence, broken softly by the ticking of a travelling-clock on the mantelpiece. I left the room in a hurry and padded along the Persian rugs in the hall and through baize doors into the back premises.

There was still no sound beyond that made by my feet on the stone-floored passage, but when I reached the door of the big kitchen I found the household within. In the centre of the floor was a wooden chair in which the young maid Janet, with dead-white face and closed eyes, half sat and half reclined, while Aunt Mairi applied a large towel to her nose. On the other side of the girl Sheena was trying to force the larder key, tied to a length of twine, down inside the back of the patient's collar.

'Janet's got a very bad nose-bleed,' said Aunt Mairi, looking rather worried. 'I think I must 'phone the nurse and ask her to come up.'

The patient's eyelids fluttered and she gave a slight groan, while Sheena took over the towel. As soon as we were alone she passed it to me. 'There's no need for a nurse,' she muttered. 'I can cure nose-bleeds if I'm allowed.' She tied the string (from the other end of which the key still dangled under Janet's blouse) to the back of the wooden chair, and went over to a cupboard in the dresser. Taking a reel of black cotton out of her work-basket she hobbled across to us, raised the girl's limp hand, and fastened an end of thread to her little finger. Then she fixed the reel to a door on the opposite side of the room. 'That will soon sort you,' she said with a satisfied nod towards Janet.

Aunt Mairi, returning and seeing the cotton stretched across the kitchen, turned to the old one and said with pretended disgust, '*Now* what have you been up to?' Sheena looked out of a window at the mist frothing down our wooded brae, and replied that cotton had stopped bleeding noses before there was ever a nurse in the village to come and do it.

Then we heard a car speeding up the drive, and a spruce young woman in uniform came in. After a brief examination and some work with cotton-wool from her bag, she removed the key and said brightly to Janet: 'Well, it is over now! You can lie down for a little and have a cup of tea, and you'll be fine.' Then she noticed the cotton trail. 'What in all the earth is this?' she asked, raising her comely black eyebrows. Aunt Mairi chuckled. 'I suppose Sheena thought that Janet needed a tooth pulled!' she said.

She went away with the nurse, and Sheena turned a sharp eye on me. 'The bleeding stopped before the nurse came,' she said. 'It was the cotton that did it!'

Later on, when Aunt Mairi and I were weeding a bed under the dining-room windows, she referred to the incidents of the morning—saying that black thread was a clean and tidy cure compared with another local remedy given to her when she was young. At the time she lay seriously ill with shingles in a ground-floor room in the Gate Lodge, and one of the gardeners came to the window to inquire how she was. Hearing that she felt no better, he said mysteriously that he knew of a certain cure. It would be necessary to get a black cock, and as there were none at

Inverewe he would like to borrow a boat and row across to Inverasdale—where he thought such a bird could be had. He was so set upon this plan that she gave him leave to try it.

Several hours later he appeared again at her window, all smiles, with a live black rooster under one arm and a china bowl in his hand. To her dismay he quickly wrung the neck of the bird, and draining some blood into the bowl, pushed it across the sill and told her to bathe the shingles in the steaming contents.

'I was so mad with the irritation of the rash, and the man so confident about his cure, that I actually did as he told me! And the funny thing was that the shingles began to disappear very soon after that.'

'I suppose it must have been a faith-cure,' I said.

'Perhaps it was,' she replied, smiling, with a characteristic lift of her eyebrows.

The casement near my head flew open and Sheena poked her nose out. 'You didn't tell about the doctor from London,' she said reproachfully to Aunt Mairi.

'Oh, yes, that was strange. Some months after I was well again we had three English doctors up here on a fishing holiday, and I was telling them the story of my blood-bath while we strolled in the garden before lunch. One of them seemed very interested. "To a skin specialist," he said, "I think your Highland remedy would have some significance. We now know that a substance which is efficaceous in the treatment of certain skin troubles is present in the blood of fowls—though I'm not aware that the sex or colour of the bird matters." '

Aunt Mairi looked up at Sheena. 'But how did you know about the doctor?' she said. 'I don't remember telling you.'

'No,' said her old friend, 'but Roddy was working behind a bush and heard the man talking. He got up and came to the kitchen door and told us that the English doctor was a clever one. "He may come from London," he said, "but he knows how to cure the shingles with the blood of a black cock, the way I put Herself right in the springtime." '

The winter tenants had now left the Gate Lodge, together with their forty packages, and it was being made ready for me. Mice abounded, and we put Rufus the ginger tom (grown from kittenhood to a very sizeable cat) in to catch them. Despite his youth and suspected strain of wild-cat ancestry, Rufus looked too fat and indolent to be an agile hunter, so I borrowed seven traps as well and baited them in the loft. Janet found the cat asleep on an eiderdown in one of the furthest bedrooms when she arrived next morning, so he lost face as a mouser; but all my traps were full.

One of Janet's admirers, then working as garden boy, was permitted to help clean the many windows. Provided with a big can of whitening for the job, the two young people had a hilarious time. I moved in at the week-end—with a pound of home-made butter, some potted venison, and an armful of pernettya as house-warming presents. Someone gave me a lump of coal, also, for luck. Janet had done her work well. The whole place was wonderfully clean and tidy. But when darkness fell, rustles and squeaks in kitchen and passages showed that the mouse population was still large.

Hearing them, *Busdubh's* eyes grew bright and her tongue quivered between her sharp white teeth as she gazed up at me open-mouthed on the wrong side of the sitting-room door. This mute appeal was irresistible, so I turned the handle and let her go. The little dog moved so smoothly that she seemed to have the legs of a centipede. Ten seconds later, she dropped a corpse at my feet. I am fond of mice, and sighed for their fate as I shut *Busdubh* into the kitchen to deal with the situation.

Meantime I arranged the beautiful pernettya berries in various jars and bowls found in the pantry. The most delightful winter decoration imaginable, pernettya is the only shrub I know which bears on the one plant berries shading from rose-pink up to carmine of the richest hue, and down the scale to pure white. The berries are large in comparison with the foliage, and do not drop off indoors. A native of the Magellan Islands off Cape Horn, pernettya flourishes and spreads like a weed at Inverewe and bears fruit in generous clusters.

In front of the Lodge a mixed hedge of escallonia and pernettya stretched all the way from the entrance gates to the loch shore, providing blossom and shelter round the broad sweep of lawn and grassy banks. Aunt Mairi feared that the thousands of bulbs with which these banks had been strewn were likely to flower earlier than usual (after a mild winter) and that even the narcissi would be past their best before the ceremony in May. I said she must guard against the regret guyed so brilliantly by Ruth Draper: '*Such* a pity you didn't come *last* week—these daffodils were magnificent *then!*'

The large bedroom I chose in my new home had a range of windows facing south, with a view across the lawns to the loch and Poolewe village beyond the water, and another small one giving a peep of the drive and the Big House at the far end. So many interesting things were visible that my morning began at daybreak, when I sat up in bed to watch sea-birds and herons busy on the shore. At that time the rabbit population had not been wiped out by myxomatosis, and *Busdubh*, perched on my feet, became very excited about various brown shapes bobbing to and fro on the grass. I was about to let her out hunting when I remembered that Roddy Beg had set snares the evening before—and, for all I knew, gin-traps as well. Then I heard the crack of a rifle, and guessed that Aunt Mairi was taking pot-shots at marauders from her bedroom window with a .22. *Busdubh* had to stay indoors, shivering in anticipation of the chase and regarding me with deep disgust for thwarting her.

The Gate Lodge seemed enormous after *Tigh-an-Uillt*, and its long passages made me walk miles in a day. At first, the boiler fire proved unco-operative and went out every night. The dusty work of removing the ashes and re-lighting it soon palled, so I took to setting my alarum clock for 3 a.m. and going outside to the boiler-house to stoke in the silent hours. Rufus was usually curled up on a sack in the corner, and encouraged me with loud purring. Eventually I procured some anthracite which kept the fire going all night and allowed me to sleep in peace. The hydro men had finished installing main electricity, but as no immersion heater had been provided for bath water or radiators, the ancient black stove was still required.

One of my first visitors was a telephone engineer, who came to replace the old instrument with a modern dialling system. Poolewe, with main electricity and an automatic telephone exchange, had suddenly grown very up-to-date. In some ways we regretted the change in the telephone, for the operator had been such a fund of useful information. 'If it's Mrs. Beaton you're wanting, it'll be no use ringing her number until this evening, for they're all away at Inverness today,' was the kind of remark which saved callers so much time and trouble. With a mute dial, one just has to go on twirling the thing round all day until at last the subscriber answers.

At least, he or she does so if the right technique has been used. The engineer told me that the new installations were causing a certain amount of confusion. Repeated complaints of faulty working in the coin-box came from one village. Would-be callers indignantly refuted suggestions that their dialling was at fault. When persuaded to demonstrate their methods, it was discovered that three fingers were laboriously fitted into three holes corresponding to the number required, and the whole sequence then 'dialled' in one turn of the wrist. After these attempts, the instrument made peevish noises, and of course no human voice ever answered the callers.

Aunt Mairi liked having me as watch-dog at her gates. If anyone specially interesting turned up, I rushed to the telephone and let her know. The drive was sufficiently long to allow the shedding of pastry-crumbs and her apron before they got to the house. On the other hand, if I knew she had some particular ploy in mind and did not wish to be disturbed, prior warning of arrivals gave her a chance to arrange matters satisfactorily.

I enjoyed being connected to the outside world, too. Food could be ordered locally or from Inverness, and once a week I put through a call to my home in Bath. The third of these was momentous. In the previous year my mother had given up her house, it being too isolated and surrounded by overmuch land for her to manage alone. I had seen her settled (permanently, as we thought) in a flat before I travelled to Scotland. Nine months later the landlord decided to sell the house; and I now learnt that Mother might be homeless at any moment.

'What about coming up here?' I suggested. There was a long pause—giving me time to wish I had reversed the charges.

'Perhaps I am too old to live in so remote a place,' said a sprightly voice at the other end of the line.

'Too old at eighty? Rubbish!' I responded.

'All right. I think I *will* come!' she said.

18. *Hundreds and Thousands*

ONE day cheeky little Jessie at Achtercairn called out to me at the close of afternoon school: 'Ah'm awa' hame!' The rest of her class went into fits of laughter at this attempt at a broad Scots accent, which she had picked up in Fife during her Christmas holidays there. The children danced round me gleefully, asking if I could guess what wee Jessie meant. They so seldom heard a 'Scotch' (or any other) accent, that it sounded quite as odd to them as a ripe Irish brogue might to youngsters in the Isle of Purbeck.

So little is this realized in England, that a dear old man in Bath told me with great earnestness of his meeting with a Scot who spoke with '*such a broad accent* that he must have come from *the very far north*'! He, I am sure, found it hard to believe me when I said the northern Scots spoke without accent; and he would have been astonished at the ridicule poured on Jessie's acquired speech by her comrades. But if her attempts at Fife dialect were the only broad accents I heard in Ross-shire, I did listen to a great deal of Gaelic: particularly in the spring and early summer when so many children were preparing for the Mod competitions.

These 'Mods' are festivals of the arts in which only the Gaelic tongue may be employed. From January to June the children in the school bus delighted me with their renderings of old Hebridean melodies, which they practised in parts or unison (and unaccompanied) with equal facility. Unfortunately these traditions mostly go into cold storage when the Mods are over; but at least their seasonal appearance is better than none.

In spite of the best efforts of so many devoted teachers the speaking of Gaelic seems to dwindle. Aunt Mairi told me that Janet could express herself very well in the old tongue, but pretended not to know it because English was thought 'grander'. I had seven little girl pupils, all sisters, whose parents I knew were Gaelic-speakers. The eldest child said her parents did not want them to 'have the Gaelic', because then all the little ones would know what the grown-ups were telling each other. I looked her in the eye. 'I expect you *can* understand most of their conversation,' I said. She wriggled, blushed, and replied, 'Yes, we do!'

'Och, well!' said the Headmaster at Achtercairn, 'Gaelic songs always mean that spring is nearly here—whatever the weather may be like.' We were standing at one of the canteen windows, looking across a navy-blue sea to the Island of Skye. Great pillowy clouds came sailing in from the Atlantic, and when they reached the island it looked as though the jagged Cuillins punctured an outer cover and released their feather stuffing, which we could see pouring down upon the hills beneath. Soon the cushions had all burst and the sun came out once more, sparkling on white mountains thickly covered with snow. March, on its way in, seemed as though it might prove the most wintry month of all. But with Skye and the Torridon hills to intercept the clouds on their journeys from south and west, very little snow fell on our part of the coast. We enjoyed the beauty of it without being worried by blocked roads or hungry sheep; although hills such as ours, where much grass has given way to heather and ling, actually provide better sustenance in severe conditions than the finer pastures further south. Sheep can get through quite deep snow to heather and eat it—which they are unable to do in the case of buried grass. (Even for sheep, a Ross-shire winter may not be as bad as some people imagine.)

That is roughly what my mother said when she arrived clad in fur-lined boots and a heavy overcoat. It was a warm and sunny afternoon, and her thick clothes soon disappeared into cupboards while she emerged in garb more suggestive of Winter Gardens at Bournemouth or Torquay. I took her out to the lawn in front of our Lodge, expecting her to admire the sight of *Beinn Airidh Charr* with a cap of snow and deep blue precipices tumbling down to the Fionn Loch. Instead, she looked critically along our road to the village and asked why there were so many bus stops.

Gently I explained that these posts crowned with circles of tin indicated passing-places for motorists. '*We* all know where they are situated,' I said, 'but without markers, strangers wouldn't be able to decide whether the onus was on them or the approaching traffic to pull off the road and allow free passage along the single track. Unless, of course, they meet the mail bus. Her Majesty's mails should always be given priority.'

'Very interesting; but the Council needn't put up things that *look* like bus stops,' she said decisively.

I had been wondering what would happen when Mother and Aunt Mairi lived side-by-side at Inverewe; for Aunt Mairi was the laird, but my mother the senior in years and very proud of her age. In fact, she had begun to cheat a little by the time she reached seventy-seven. 'What do you expect an old woman of *nearly eighty* to do about it?' she would then inquire, with mock self-pity, in any dilemma. Since her seventy-eighth birthday the word 'nearly' had been gradually dropped. As 'an old woman of eighty' she would feel immensely superior to Aunt Mairi's score of seventy-four, especially as the latter looked about sixty.

Sheena soon showed me that I need not have given the question of leadership a thought. She really *had* celebrated her eightieth birthday—and left it some way behind her. In stature six inches shorter than my mother, and several stone lighter than Aunt Mairi, she managed (with the help of a mind and tongue both as nimble as lizards) to retain with ease undisputed pride of place as matriarch of Inverewe. Luckily she approved of Mother.

Soon after the latter's arrival, notice-boards from the Trust in Edinburgh were brought by the station lorry to our gates. Next morning Aunt Mairi and Roderick, her head man, came down the drive to see about their erection. The badge of The National Trust for Scotland had to go on a little grassy island between the road and our main gates—so that motorists would spot it from as far off as possible. It was hung low, and blended quite well with the surroundings. The other sign was a large, lettered board giving details of Inverewe and the opening times. Aunt Mairi seemed less pleased with this, and made Roderick try it in various places in the hope of rendering it inconspicuous. At last she got it into a corner practically smothered by a bush, and then Roderick's critical looks were given vocal expression.

'What is the use of having a notice at all if you put it where people cannot see it?' he asked dourly. Aunt Mairi turned, opened her vivid blue eyes very wide, regarded him silently for a moment, and then moved away from the bush. 'I suppose you are right,' she conceded with a sigh. Roderick rescued the board which she had buried with such zeal, and stood it near the little side gate. 'That will be the best place for folk to linger and read it,' he said—and immediately began to plant the supporting post. Having fixed both notices he went round with his tools to a shed behind our lodge, while Aunt Mairi walked back to the house.

Feeling that this was a difficult juncture for her, I slipped away. However glad she may have been to know that the life-work of herself and her father would be maintained and cherished for thousands to enjoy, this morning—when placards first announced to the world that her beloved home had become semi-public property—must have been a poignant occasion. It would have been inhuman not to feel some heartache just then, and I guessed she would choose to cross her bridges alone.

One of our visitors later in the day was a well-known horti-culturist, who had the honour of being taken round the gardens by Aunt Mairi herself. I was able to make her laugh by reporting what he said to me on his way out: 'Tell me, are *all* Mrs. Sawyer's gardeners called "Roderick"?'

I said there were but three of the same name, and that her head man and stalker was the only one referred to as 'Roderick'. Of the other two, the gardener who helped Aunt Mairi with the shrubberies for forty years answered to 'Roddy Donn', and the third Roderick to 'Roddy Beg' (Little Roddy). He was of good average height, but probably received the epithet because he was an inch or two shorter than the head man.

It was easy for me to sympathize with the bewilderment of this visitor, since I had lately been a guest in the house of three amusing old sisters who seemed, on ninety-nine out of a hundred counts, to be perfectly rational. Yet their single oddity put visitors into a state of confusion. It was simply this: all three sisters addressed each other indiscriminately as 'Jane'.

Another tangle of names came my way at Achtercairn school. Before beginning my work there I had been supplied with class lists, and noticed that in one group of boys there were two Kenny MacKenzies and two Roddy MacKenzies. 'It's really quite simple,' said Kirstie, who happened to be present when I noticed the duplication. 'The lads from Big Sand are never called by their surname. That family is always known as "*An Ruadh*" (Red-headed).'

I went to the first class on the look out for red-heads, but none of the boys present were even faintly tinged. Two of the MacKenzies were very black, and the others almost flaxen. To the last I said doubtfully, 'Are you the *An Ruadhs?*' 'No,' they both grinned, pointing to the black MacKenzies, 'they are!'

When next I saw Kirstie, I said her 'red-heads' had not worked out as I expected. 'Oh,' she said impatiently, 'I didn't tell you *this* generation was red! The nickname has come down from a great-grandfather.'

So I lived and learnt. The next lesson was entirely different. It is said that nature abhors a vacuum. I discovered now that human nature does the same. Directly I took possession of a five-bedroomed house, other people sprang up to fill the four unused ones. Mother came first; then a musician (to whom I was half engaged) flew home from Australia and wrote saying he would so much like to visit Wester Ross—the county of his mother's kins-folk—with of course a glimpse of me thrown in as make-weight.

He agreed to time his arrival for a day when I was at home, but came instead when I was taking a cookery class in Gairloch. I happened to look out of the window at the right moment to behold a familiar and unmistakable head and shoulders beside Arthur in the mail bus as it went slowly up Achtercairn Hill on the way to Poolewe. My yell of 'Fred!' made the whole class jump, but served no useful purpose—since the whine of the bus climbing in low gear would have drowned my voice at that distance even had it been amplified through a megaphone.

Hurriedly I left instructions for the next step in cookery and rubbing flour from my hands rushed over to the Headmaster's house to borrow his telephone. Mother was not at all amused when I told her our guest had come a day early. 'Bother the man!' she said. 'Why is it that musicians (of all people!) have *no sense of time*?' (She was perfectly right: they haven't. Perhaps they are too obsessed by it in a musical sense to bother with clocks and calendars.)

The poor man had rather an unlucky visit altogether; for one of the windows in his bedroom was an old-fashioned 'sash' type without any supporting cords. Not knowing this, he let the heavy pane crash down on his fingers (one was obviously broken), and a doctor had to be summoned in a hurry.

He came at once, bound up the injured hand, comforted the sufferer by saying that he would soon be able to play again, and fixed up for him to be X-rayed in Inverness. I marvelled at the ease and speed with which one could get up-to-date medical treatment in so remote a part of the kingdom. It was the doctor's turn to be surprised when I asked if his son attended the *Bual-naluib* school. On finding that he did so, I recounted the story of little Alistair who refused to draw. His father was delighted. 'You've got hold of the right way to deal with the wee rascal!' he cried. 'He needs a firm hand!'

Next time I visited the school I was able to watch the doctor putting his principles into practice. Alistair, knowing that visitors were expected at home, couldn't wait until four o'clock to see them and receive a longed-for present. He stole away unseen before our midday dinner, and by taking short-cuts through bog and burn got home just as the guests arrived. His father, furious with him for running away from school, picked him up and dropped him into the car—*without* the promised gift.

The rest of the school had just settled down to plates of stewed beef and carrots when there came the sound of swift, determined footsteps on the path outside. Then the door of the dining-room opened and Alistair was hurled in, landing in a heap on the floor. Not a word was said. The Headmaster scooped up the boy, dumped him on a bench, pushed a laden plate in front of him, and continued his own meal as though all this were an everyday occurrence. In the silence that followed, the doctor's car could be heard driving away. Alistair's appetite remained unimpaired by the adventure.

None of the rough justice I saw meted out seemed to do any harm. The strap is nowadays no longer administered to the slow-witted or ignorant, but in the North it is still vigorously applied to disobedient or cheeky youngsters. Most boys (and many girls) are perfectly reconciled to corporal punishment, so long as it is felt to be deserved—and preferably carried out at once.

In a mixed preparatory school where I taught for a time in England, 'order marks' were the only reward of wrong-doing. I caught one fine little boy playing the dangerous, forbidden game of poking paint-brushes at other children. 'John!' I said sternly, '*stop that!* It will sound so babyish if they read out your name with an order-mark "for poking a paint-brush at Angela".' Misunderstanding the point of my remark, he said confidentially, 'Yes, thank goodness I shall be soon in a real boys' school, where you get a *hiding* for being naughty, and none of these *silly old order-marks!*' I wished some of the over-anxious child psychologists and education experts could have heard him.

The only 'hidings' which seemed rather cruel to me were

those given by local parents in Ross-shire to children who were discovered to have had 'the strap' at school. (Some fathers were in the habit of administering a second dose to teach their progeny *not* to get chastised by their masters.) There was also a parent who thrashed his boy for running home in terror at the sight of the school dentist in his mobile surgery. The runaway fled back to the dentist as being less alarming than his father.

Nevertheless, the children were an outstandingly happy, healthy, vigorous collection—well mannered and responsible without being in the least cowed or dull. They were also very kind to one another, and it was charming to see hulking great boys, with five-year-old brothers or sisters, tenderly wiping up tears or noses, washing sticky fingers, and shepherding the small fry to 'the little house'.

One display of motherly solicitude by a small girl amused us all very much. The local doctors were extremely helpful to patients who suffered from toothache and had no time to visit the nearest resident dentist in Inverness. (Children only were treated in our mobile surgery.) The mother of the little girl had recently asked her doctor to extract a bad tooth. Although the most gentle, kind, and helpful physician, he was prone to absent-mindedness at times. When the patient's gums had been well numbed on the side where the aching tooth was, he began to inject the other side as well. 'Oh, do you have to freeze both sides to extract one tooth?' asked the startled lady. 'Dear me, no! I was just for the moment forgetting which tooth you wished drawn,' was the apologetic reply.

The small daughter evidently overheard what was said, and so when a little friend cried out in fear of the school dentist she put her arm round the scared child and said soothingly: 'Don't worry, Margaret. This man is a *real* dentist and will be *sure to pull out the right tooth!*' The dentist had so many patients that after a two-day visit the playground was sown with a crop of white teeth as though someone had been feeding hens with them.

Our musician came back from Inverness full of praise for the treatment received at the hospital, and with the good news that no tendons had been broken in his damaged hand. He could not practise for some weeks; but he was very helpful at the gates of Inverewe. Visitors had begun to flow in in unexpected numbers, and already (before the gardens were officially handed over) we had admitted more in one day than the estimated 'peak' of twenty. It was a pleasant surprise to find that Mother enjoyed taking the money and talking to people at the door. In fact, she sometimes asked them into the Lodge. Knowing her unsociable reputation I commented on this sudden change in her.

'My dear girl, this is the best way to meet people,' she said. 'There is no *need* to talk unless you feel like it, but if you wish to start a conversation the gardens provide a ready-made topic. And as everybody has come a long way to see the place you can ask them into the house *knowing they won't stay very long.*'

The musician (who had an almost professional sociability) vied with her in answering the door-bell, watching while people wrote names and addresses in the visitors' book, and discussing home-towns with the signatories. With visitors from Australia, New Zealand, Canada, Africa or India he came out top—for he had toured all these countries. But Mother usually charmed British callers away from him, and as these were more numerous her conquests exceeded his. Fred's stock rose to the highest level when two delightful ladies from New Zealand, after a long talk about their islands, sent us some delicious tinned fruits out of a hamper they carried round with them. Aunt Mairi pretended to be jealous, saying that in all the years she had shown visitors round none had bestowed such delicacies upon *her*.

While Mother and her colleague dealt happily with visitors, I found time to work in the gardens, and was content. It became a matter for pride that I was allowed to prune the hydrangeas for which Inverewe is noted. These grow so rampantly in the warm, moist climate that some clumps were jungles in which one could be hidden from sight. We cut them drastically, leaving very little of the old wood. Aunt Mairi and I discussed each plant before we started in with the sécateurs. Many of the discarded branches bore fat, new shoots, and as I couldn't bear these to be thrown away

I made a nursery of about two hundred in 'America'. Later, when every cutting had rooted, we planted them out in the woods. 'When *they* grow, you'll have twice as much pruning to do!' said Aunt Mairi. I wasn't worried. Those rich blue heads were worth any amount of toil and trouble.

In the evenings, after feeding the hungry musician, I dealt with accounts for the Trust—sorting out piles of silver and seeing that receipts tallied with tickets and booklets sold. We also had on sale some postcards of house and gardens, and copies of Osgood MacKenzie's book *A Hundred Years in the Highlands*. (All royalties on that publication had been made over to the Trust funds.)

Quite soon the storage of money became a problem, so I wrote to Edinburgh for larger cash-boxes. The Committee of the Trust was very pleased with the 'takings' and also with the steady trickle of new members we enrolled. Membership was (and still is) absurdly small in comparison with the responsibilities of The National Trust for Scotland. I grew into quite a practised advocate for their work, and the signing-on of members became my special part in the trio now operating at the gates of Inverewe. 'Surely,' I used to plead, 'people who care about even *one* of the properties being maintained could afford ten shillings a year towards its upkeep!' Sometimes I raked in extra cash for admission fees, too. It was a lucky day when I recognized (from my Admiralty experience) a well-known shipbuilder, who came with a party one Sunday afternoon—when we were supposed to close the gates. I told him I must not admit visitors on the sabbath on pain of death—adding that I might be open to bribery and corruption. He was amused, and my week's takings went up by a handsome amount.

Aunt Mairi did not mind her siesta disturbed in a good cause, and was very soft-hearted herself about turning people away after hours. It seemed unkind when everyone had come so far. But she told me I was crazy to show some girl students from Canada round the gardens after ten o'clock one night when dusk was falling. They were touring Scotland on a scooter (a longer job than they had bargained for) and I knew very well that she herself would have been melted by their wheedling smiles and transatlantic drawl.

In this early part of the year it was customary for the local men to go out to the hills for the heather-burning. Tracts of old growth were burnt in succession, to encourage the new. At Inverewe the ritual was almost mediaeval, with the men in aprons of coarse hessian, carrying on their shoulders rude torches made of paraffin-soaked rags in tin holders on the end of long poles. They also bore withy brooms to beat out a surrounding belt and so confine their fires to planned areas. At least, I gathered that this was supposed to happen.

They assembled outside the Lodge at eight o'clock in the morning, and the quaint procession moved off down the road in a straggling line on its way to the chosen hill. All day smoke billowed on the skyline and eddied down the glen, filling the atmosphere with a scent at once acrid and sweet. After dark, especially on breezy nights, the red glow, patches of leaping flame, and trails of sparks on the brae high above us suggested giants at play with fire.

Others were playing with material for fire, too, for already the school children were growing excited about the Coronation of Queen Elizabeth, and there was much strenuous carrying up of combustible rubbish to beacon sites. Poor boys, they could not foresee that the heather-burning in our fine spring weather actually provided far more worthy beacons than the carefully planned artificial pyres were able to show on that soaking wet night in June.

At Inverewe we all had to work too hard in preparation for the handing-over party to think much about the Coronation until after May 9th. Our big date brought us one of the loveliest days of early summer the West Highlands could possibly have provided. An ecstatic visitor from the United States exclaimed: 'Say, what gorgeous weather! It reminds me of the Bahamas! Is it *always* like this up here?'

People rolled up in cars until the road looked like Glyndebourne on the night of a favourite opera. Both our local policemen were kept busy, for once in their lives, controlling the traffic. A large marquee had been erected on the lawn in front of the Lodge, but its shelter was not required. It served as a kitchen and food-store, and people dived in to fetch what they wanted and took it out into the sunshine.

The loch was a radiant blue as the cruise-ship *Lady Killarney* came and stood off *Am Ploc Ard* for her hundred and seventy passengers to disembark by boat at our jetty. Some of the women wore high-heeled shoes which slipped on the seaweed-covered stones, but on this occasion I did not see anybody fall into the water—as had happened in the past.

At our gates various officials of The National Trust for Scotland sat at a table, taking invitation cards from the guests, collecting their signatures in a book, and talking about Inverewe and the Trust to anyone who would listen. We turned the Gate Lodge into a wash-and-brush-up hostel for ladies; and Mother had a busy time lining up the queues, finding lost property, and dealing with telephone messages and elderly or delicate visitors who felt the heat too much for them. We had to keep the furnace at full blast to supply sufficient hot water for the basins, and as the antique radiators got stuck and refused to be turned off, the indoor temperature was as high as the outside sun. Luckily there were shady places and seats in the Lodge garden.

Mother said she had always wondered what it felt like to be a cloak-room attendant. Now she had first-hand experience—except for the tips. (Instead of being rewarded for her services, she actually had to foot the bill for some telephone calls which visitors made and forgot to pay for.) But we hoped we had done our bit to help make a success of the day.

During the afternoon Aunt Mairi made a little speech to the gathering, and Lady Elphinstone, as Convener of the Gardens Committee, accepted Inverewe on behalf of the Trust. The Chairman (Lord Wemyss) in the course of an incisive address mentioned that The Pilgrim Trust had given £10,000 towards the endowment of the gardens. The ceremony was sensibly short—allowing plenty of time afterwards for the later arrivals to explore the policies.

I wondered which of the vague-looking clumps of people would most appreciate a guide. The first party I approached was led by an elderly gentleman who growled, 'I've known this place since I was breeched!'—so I moved on hastily. In order to escape repetition of the rebuff I chose next a lissom young couple with a strange accent. They came from Chile, and were interested to see so many familiar plants from their own country. Among these I was able to show them the crinodendron (now known by the cumbersome name of *Tricuspidaria lanceolata*) with its pendant lanterns of coral-red shining out from between dark lance-shaped leaves. It grows conspicuously well at Inverewe, and was acclaimed with great pleasure.

There were guests from so many overseas countries in the throng that almost every imported plant received recognition from somebody. I felt sorry the musician had been called away. He might have come across visitors from a country he had *not* yet explored. And he would certainly have had a whale of a time talking to representatives of the pre-war British Empire in its entirety. Everyone, whatever his nationality, voted the day a huge success and the gardens 'wonderful'. The finale came when Aunt Mairi, in a lovely dress, went off with distinguished guests and Trust officials to dine on board ship, while a regiment of children from the village advanced upon the left-over food at Inverewe.

A last car drove away; the big marquee came toppling down; tired helpers and overfed children dispersed to their homes. Rufus the cat emerged from my bedroom and sat on the drive twitching his white whiskers and yawning in the face of his friend the Cairn terrier. A pair of owls hooted lazily in some big trees behind the house, answered by a heron from below. The calm loch-water nibbled at our pebbly shore, reflecting further out streaks of light from Poolewe village and one pale star. Peace again floated through the gardens.

19. *Leading to a Last Journey*

THE gardens were handed over on a Saturday. On the following Wednesday, four days after our climate had been likened to that of the Bahamas, I opened the gates of Inverewe to some morning visitors and was greeted by a tall, thin Englishman in a long, wet mackintosh. Apparently chasing a marble round his mouth with his tongue, he mumbled: 'What gorstly weather! Is it *always* like this up here?' Without doubt he thought my manners atrocious and my sense of humour perverted, for I had to laugh. I couldn't explain that four days earlier almost identical words had been spoken—but with 'gorgeous' in the place of 'ghastly'. He would not have found it amusing, for he was right: the weather had turned absolutely foul. But that *is* the West Highlands: unpredictable, ever-changing, maddening—and marvellous.

By the week-end it had again improved, and on Saturday afternoon I wandered round the gardens alone before the after-lunch visitors began to pour in. We discouraged picnics in the grounds, because people *would* light fires, causing danger to our valuable plants and trees. Also, they left litter behind. So we tried to clear the policies between one and two o'clock, and settled down to eat our meal in peace instead of rushing about the walks and smelling out fires.

I knew there was nobody about, so the movements I heard as I walked up the path to 'Bamboozlem' attracted my attention. Beside the primula-and-gentian-bordered entrance, just beyond a little wrought-iron gate, I found something which made me stop—and bolt back to the Big House. I burst into the hall, nearly flattening Aunt Mairi and Sheena, who were having a conference inside the door. 'There's a pigeon in a trap in "Bamboozlem"!' I gasped. 'It's struggling desperately and I can't open the rusty great gin!' 'But you could kill the pigeon!' said Aunt Mairi, quietly resuming her interrupted conversation.

'Kill the pigeon, kill the pigeon . . .' ran through my head as I raced back to the scene of terror. How could *I* kill a pigeon? Hadn't those birds seemed special friends all my life? In my student years I used to stay with an aunt in her great Italian villa above Lerici, where she kept a brood of slim white doves in a garden aviary. These were let out in the daytime and would then flutter down on the terraces and tap gently at doors and windows for tit-bits. Their exquisite svelte forms appeared in many of Aunt Helen's paintings, which were shown at the Royal Institute of Painters in Water-colours (of which she was a member) and other exhibitions in London.

Then there was an imaginary pigeon in a poem by my friend Robert Nichols—alas, he died in 1944. Twenty years back he had a beach-hut on a wild piece of the Sussex coast near our summer bungalow. Here we used to meet and talk. He gave me the sort of education I had longed for (and missed) at school. He was continually recommending books I ought to read and music I 'simply must' hear; and to make these proposals practical he allowed me unfettered use of his library and collection of gramophone records. Up in his village home we used to discuss poetry, and I shall always remember his impetuous fingers plucking volumes of Elizabethan verse from the shelves.

Often he would read from these favourites aloud, but he

seldom opened his own books. On the rare occasions when I persuaded him to do so my special choice was called 'Pigeon Song' from *A Faun's Holiday*.[1] In this, a lonely girl sings to her tame dove:

'Little pigeon, grave and fleet,
      Eye-of-fire, sweet Snowy-wings,
Think you that you can discover
      On what great green down my lover
Lies by his sunny sheep and sings?

If you can, O go and greet
      Him from me; say: She is waiting . . .
Not for him, O no! but, sweet,
      Say June's nigh and doves, remating,
Fill the dancing noontide heat
      With melodious debating. . . .'

I could listen for hours to the subtle modulations of Robert's beautiful voice, and watch his sensitive features as he read. Rich food for the mind of an impressionable youngster! His was the most fascinating personality I had ever encountered; and (unlike many creative artists) he was generous and thoughtful—always quietly ready to enter into other people's troubles and give what assistance his warm heart could devise. With these associations, how could I be pushed into *killing* a pigeon?

Reluctantly I unlatched 'Bamboozlem's' gate and went up to the trap. The hopeless struggles of the victim had now loosed a cloud of feathers and down, which floated around the scene like sudden snow. I saw that one of the frail pink legs had snapped under the strain. The bird could no longer enjoy life, even if my strength and skill were able to release the fiendish instrument's grip. This knowledge impelled me to actions I loathed. Desperately I grabbed a heavy fallen branch, lifted it, screwed up my eyes, and brought the weapon down with a crash on the soft head. Memory of the pleading look in the bird's round, red eye before I shut out the sight is with me vividly yet. There was a bout of

[1] *Ardours and Endurances*, pub. Chatto & Windus, 1920.

flapping, from which I turned away; and then the crumpled body lay still. Nobody could find me for the rest of that afternoon.

Nothing seemed quite the same at Inverewe after the death of the pigeon—or perhaps it was I who changed. A sense of foreboding and depression such as I had not experienced since 1939 took charge of my mind in 'Bamboozlem,' and would not be shaken off.

Somebody removed the small remains of the bird from the gin-trap, and Aunt Mairi made soup out of them. I did not refuse to drink it; for, once life had been destroyed, there was no point in wasting the flesh. In fact, to kill for food legitimizes the act. Even the scruples of vegetarians I have known did not prevent them from preying on the lives of plants. Although the well-known experiments of an Indian scientist have shown how sensitive are the reactions of the vegetable kingdom, tender lettuces are not even stunned in boiling water before mastication. Until it becomes possible to exist on synthetic rations alone, flesh-eaters and vegetarians alike must needs destroy in order to live. And that involves some cruelties—whether at first or second hand.

To say that my youth died with the pigeon would reek of self-dramatization; but perhaps those moments of stress, with their lightning flash-backs to gentler days, demonstrated that youth had been left behind. A too-sudden revelation of this might be expected to depress.

Seldom has any generation lived (in its most impressionable years) through such a spate of changes, both material and mental, as that born just before 1914—which reached maturity when Hitler began to broadcast his ravings. Changes in ideas and mental 'climate' were for me epitomized by the difference between the two poets I had known. Twelve years after the completion of Robert Nichols' attempts to educate me, I met John Betjeman. (Though he doesn't, I think, refer to himself as a poet—and may dislike the description.)

Robert, so unworldly and elegant, with his classical (Winchester and Oxford) references, his absorption in Elizabethan lyrics, and his own songs about shepherds and centaurs, seemed in retrospect to have lived in a golden haze of unreality. He had fought in a great war, and seen many of his friends killed, but to those battles shreds and tatters of chivalry still clung. Robert and his friends were not made to annihilate scores of women and children by pushing buttons. And one felt they could never have wasted time filling in forms.

Betjeman, with his tubby figure clad in mass-produced garments (clothes were rationed), writing verses about Edwardian villa-life and Victorian Gothic churches, seemed earthy—or perhaps bricks-and-mortary; and he was streets and lamp-posts away from the ideal of a poet imagined by any maiden born around 1912.

Dear Mr. Betjeman, don't think me rude! Anyone who could make a Civil Service office amusing and lively, as you did, has genius enough to stoke the warmest fires of gratitude and praise. Our essential part in the war effort had been virtually completed before D-day, and until you came we found the ensuing boredom much harder to bear than bombing.

How memorable was that occasion when, finding in your tray some important but dull document about renewals of plant in an armament factory, you embellished the rim with a beautiful little sketch of an item therein—known as a 'bed of retorts'. In fine detail you showed us mother, father, and the whole Retort family, tucked up in a colossal four-poster bed. How aggrieved you were when the V.I.P.s in London returned it with a curt note requesting staff to refrain from scribbling on dockets!

It was that unmerited, cruel word 'scribbling' which got under your skin. I tried to soothe your ruffled draughtsman's pride by feeding you with rich purple plums from our orchard, and you presented me with a copy of one of your anthologies. It lies open in front of me now, displaying your inscription:

> from J. Betjeman
> Hell,
> Bath,
> 1944

Perhaps, after all, under your pink tie you weren't so very different from my first poet. You gave me your book in September. A few days before Christmas in the same year, Robert Nichols died in Cambridge at the age of fifty-one. He, too, would have found that office hell—and said so. *He* never did experience the frustrations of such an existence. *You* escaped quite soon. *I* at last was free.

But *was* I? Even at Inverewe we now had forms to fill up, time-tables to restrict our movements, money to count and check. I am not over-fond of handling cash: and judging by the way it departs, it doesn't care much for me either. But if poverty can be a nuisance, riches so frequently cause people to become obsessed by money that it seems safer on the whole to have none.

A clairvoyant old man in a Hampstead pub once startled my musician by saying he could see organ-pipes jutting from his head—or something of the sort. I wonder how many prosperous brows he sees haloed in banknotes or dividend warrants? An array of pipes—even to a thirty-two-foot *contra bombarde*—would make a sweeter diadem.

Diadems—of a more conventional kind—were much in our thoughts during the month of June. Almost every newspaper, magazine and radio programme contained some reference to the forthcoming Coronation of Queen Elizabeth II, and in each schoolroom walls were covered with pictures of the Royal Family and regalia.

One afternoon, when the mistress in charge of my smallest school wished me to keep an eye on a group of very young children in addition to my usual basketry class, I made a simple chalk drawing of the crown of England on the blackboard and told the infants to draw one like it. Then, thinking that practice in lettering would not harm them, I added a large E and an R to my picture. I knew that nationalists in some parts of Scotland were unwilling to call our Queen Elizabeth the *Second*—because the first Elizabeth had *not* reigned over the Scots. But no hint of this controversy had come my way in Wester Ross. Nevertheless, I omitted the roman numeral to avoid argument.

The children were all very excited about drawing crowns, and set to work without wasting a moment, while I went to supervise the basketry group. These eleven-year-old boys were competing in the handicrafts section of the local Mod, so I spent some time giving them advice about their entries. I did not worry over the younger ones—for I knew that they were used to working by themselves while their teacher attended to other classes. I also knew they had been well drilled into doing exactly what they were told, and would not proceed to the colouring until I had seen the outlines.

During my first term's teaching in Scotland I had found such step-by-step methods irritating at times, for in the southern schools to which I was accustomed big girls who had seamed one side of a garment would not have sat waiting for me to tell them that the other side required similar treatment. After a while I realized that this cautious behaviour had been developed in one-teacher schools to avoid wastage of material, which might otherwise have occurred when the teacher's attention was needed elsewhere. To encourage enterprise would be costly.

Familiarity with this method made it more startling to discover, when I returned to the drawing class, that although not a hand had gone up nor a single word been spoken, every one of those crowns bore the numeral I alongside the letters E.R. The look of righteous triumph on the faces of the seven young artists would have astonished Her Majesty's advisers. Aunt Mairi was surprised, too; for she hadn't known that there was much feeling on the subject in our neighbourhood.

Coronation Day was sadly inclement: wet, cold, and with a strong, blustery wind. My mother retired to bed with a feverish chill, and I sat alone by a log fire listening to the broadcast of the ceremony in Westminster Abbey. Just before lunch-time the front-door bell announced the arrival of a solitary visitor who wished to see the gardens. They were not supposed to be open, but as he had come all the way from Manchester I agreed to admit him to the rain-soaked policies.

After lunch I left the Lodge for a whiff of fresh air during a lull in the rainstorms, and met Aunt Mairi on the drive with *Cailleach*. 'That *poor* girl, it's *still* going on!' she called out with genuine distress in her voice: reducing in a flash all the pomp and dignity to the level of a common shared humanity. The visitor from Manchester, who had come along behind her on his way out, looked shocked. Aunt Mairi wanted to know who he was and why I had let him in—seeming vexed and unlike her usual self. I put it down to the weather.

That night the heavy rain made mock of the chain of hill-top fires which had so laboriously been built to illuminate our wild coast. We did what we could to cheer the scene by switching on every light in the Big House and leaving them to blaze until midnight. Next day people in the village spoke appreciatively of the gay effect this had made, seen across Loch Ewe and reflected in its waters.

As an aftermath of the Coronation, I watched a small girl playing alone on the shore below my window. She seemed to be acting the part of a great lady, robed in a long gown with a train, and making an imperious speech to some imaginary hearers. I crept along the other side of the hedge in time to hear her say: 'I'm the Queen! I know I'm the Queen! I *feel* like the Queen! I shall be kind to poor people and give them nice things to eat!'

Mother's feverish chill turned to bronchitis, and the doctor had to be summoned; so until the prescribed antibiotics had done their work there was little chance for me to see Aunt Mairi. About a week later the patient had so far recovered as to make it possible for me to spend an evening with her at the Big House. It was fine and warm; we gardened together for an hour or two, and I began to feel the old contentment stealing back. Then I repeated the story of the little neighbour who felt like the Queen, and one or two other trifles of gossip. Soon I realized that my companion wasn't listening.

Presently she asked, with the nearest approach to a fretful tone I had ever heard her use, 'Why is it that your little dog comes back every half-hour or so to see you are all right, while mine just goes off and ignores me?' This was true, but it had occurred many times before—and she had not seemed in the least put out by it. In fact, she had more than once pointed to the inquiring face of *Busdubh*, as she peered round a bush to assure herself of my whereabouts before dashing off on another scent, and had said with a smile that *Cailleach* was too keen a hunter to bother about her mistress until it grew dark. The behaviour of the two Cairns was not new, but Aunt Mairi's response had altered.

I wondered what had caused this change in her. It might have been reaction from the strain of the handing-over ceremony and all its preparatory work. Or perhaps the greatly enhanced publicity Inverewe had received, and the consequent increase in the number of visitors, had worried her. I wished she would tell me (if she herself was aware of it)—for when a person means much, it is natural to want to share their troubles as well as delights.

Before we parted that evening she said casually: 'You know, I think there is something wrong with my eyes. It feels all the time as though some *gravel* has got into them.' Alarmed, though pretending to be equally calm, I suggested that it might be advisable to consult an occulist about this; but she thought it was not worth the bother of a journey to Inverness, and instead asked me to get the doctor to see her next time he visited my mother.

Apparently he shook his head when he saw Aunt Mairi, saying that she must see a specialist about her sight. Arrangements were then made for an examination in Inverness. On her return she told me very quietly that the eye trouble could be cured, but would mean an operation. She was even then getting ready to go into an Edinburgh nursing-home to have it done.

We waved her off, with promises to do our best to care for Inverewe during her absence, and of course a shower of good wishes and hopes for her speedy recovery and return to us. Word soon came that the operation had been successfully performed, with the patient in good heart. Summer at its loveliest revived to colour the happy news, and day after day the loch was a brilliant blue below hills of hazy violet and pink. Azaleas filled the garden with scent and colour; bees were hard at work in the laden roses; outside the gates yellow flag-irises put golden rims to every pool and burn.

There was considerable excitement in the schools over the local Mod, and joy when one of the boys in my Primary school basketry class won first prize for his work, in competition with older scholars from Secondary schools. Life would have been perfect if only Aunt Mairi had been safely at home instead of on her sick-bed in Edinburgh. She who so seldom had endured any sickness, even in her own house, found it very trying and wrote saying she hated nursing-homes. Presently we heard that there was a little congestion of the lungs—nothing serious, but enough to prolong her absence for a week or so.

She wrote to me about certain parties of people who were coming to see the gardens, and asked me to receive them for her. Richard St. Barbe Baker brought a Summer School expedition of his Men of the Trees. I knew that they were to be paid for *en masse* by the leader, but as they straggled in by twos and threes, mixed up with unconnected visitors, it was difficult for me to work out who should pay me and who should not. In the end Mr. St. Barbe Baker arrived and we sorted the business out together satisfactorily. I think the Tree people enjoyed themselves.

Aunt Mairi's letters became less sanguine and she seemed to be fretting for home. Sheena told me she had been asked to send down equipment for the journey to be made in an ambulance; but evidently the doctors and nurses persuaded the patient not to attempt anything so rash. Nevertheless, the nursing-home sounded quite satisfied with her progress, telling me by 'phone that she should soon be well enough to return to Inverewe. Her idea that she would never recover unless she first came home was doubtless just a passing whim natural to a convalescent. I tried to feel calm, and wrote her a cheerful letter.

Next morning I was busy in the kitchen of the Lodge when the bell rang, and Mother went into the hall to open the front door.

It was one of our gardeners, and I overheard some words which I thought referred to *Cailleach*—who was in the habit of escaping from Inverewe and getting herself lost for days and sometimes nights: 'She is gone!' Of course it *must* be the little dog. But I walked rather slowly to the door to find out what was being said.

It wasn't *Cailleach*. It was Aunt Mairi who had gone—quite suddenly, without warning, following a heart-attack. The news had just been telephoned to the Big House number. She never would see Inverewe again. It was unbelievable. None of us could credit it.

I stumbled out of the Lodge and found my way to the house. In the kitchen Sheena sat alone, her wee figure looking smaller than ever. The skin of her white face seemed tightly stretched over the bones. She stared through, rather than at, me, with eyes undimmed but full of grief. I slumped into a chair opposite her, and for some moments neither of us spoke. The clock ticked on, and a tap dripped somewhere into a sink. Then Sheena said in a husky whisper, 'To think that *she* should have gone, while *I* am still left . . . it doesn't seem possible.'

It wasn't only the aged who found their survival difficult to understand. To all of us it seemed beyond reason that so vital a personality, rich with warmth and *joie-de-vivre*, and with so much to give the world, should have left it while we stayed. I got a queer feeling that nothing and nobody really *was* left alive any more. Vitality had seeped out of the place with Aunt Mairi's going, leaving only dry husks of plants and people behind. A line from some poem ran in my head: 'The leaves fell from the day'. Although it was high summer, there seemed to come a fall throughout the whole demesne.

Even the animals felt that something was amiss. *Cailleach* (she who hadn't bothered to keep an eye on her living mistress) lay on the drive with her sable ears pricked and her dark muzzle poked beneath the bottom rail of the gate for hour after hour, ignoring food or blandishments and no longer interested in rabbits.

When the hearse stopped outside those gates it looked so trivial.

Had it been painted scarlet, one would have said, 'Here comes another parcel.' Nothing there to suggest the death of a great lady or the end of a long chapter in West Highland history. But the little dog knew. She stepped forward as the vehicle drove in, her smooth silver body alert and quivering. Then her tail drooped and her ears went down, and she turned and walked away into our Lodge. We tried to comfort her, and let her curl up in an old peat basket with *Busdubh*, where they both slept that night.

For me there was no sleep. The day was full of work connected with funeral arrangements and the running of the estate, and the night of memories. It was over a month since the longest day, but in those northern latitudes the curtain of darkness lifted early. By four or five in the morning I could discern dim shapes of mountains from the south windows of my room; and see, as well as hear, small waves sucking at pebbles on the edge of the loch below the garden. A colony of fishing herons punctuated the silent hours with croaks like the tearing of coarse linen.

Her mountains, her loch, her gardens, her home: all of them hers no longer, and yet still and for ever hers.

> Why did you die?—I died of everything;
> Life, like deep water, robbed me of my breath.
> Sorrow, delight, love, music, winter, spring,
> Slew me in turn, and, last of all, came—Death.[1]

Next day people came in cars: relations and friends and the lawyer from Inverness. Smoke from the kitchen chimney of the Big House showed that Sheena and Janet were busy cooking for them. The weather stayed fine and sunny, but the eclipsed look was on land and water still, and no life in anything. A cormorant sat immobile like a black rock on the mooring-buoy, and the tide sucked at the idle motor-boat; gulls picked half-hearted squabbles among the rocks, and at intervals a heron stirred himself to a feeble croak.

The funeral was timed for two o'clock; and it seemed as

---

[1] By Lady Margaret Sackville. From *Collected Poems*, published by Martin Secker.

though that morning would never pass. They had put the coffin (looking very small under the stacks of roses, carnations, and other richly coloured flowers) to rest in the garden-room, where her sécateurs and trowels lay idle among trays of drying pods and tins of seed from last year's harvest. Someone had taken away the caged canaries which had spent the summer there. Perhaps they were thought to sound too gay in the presence of death. I felt sure Aunt Mairi would have preferred them to remain.

When I reached the Big House about eighty people were assembled before the front door, and a row of cars in the drive; and the coffin was brought out of the garden-room and placed on a bier to the right of the door. Elders of the Kirk, in black suits and carrying bowler hats, gathered in a group to the left, and the fourteenth Chief of the clan, wearing the MacKenzie kilt, stood by the bier with the nearest relatives. All the men (but very few women) from the estate and village were present—the old custom of keeping attendance at funerals to the male sex being still largely observed.

The minister came out of the house and began the simple service, accompanied by the drone of bees working in the roses on the house behind him. The Elders sang a long psalm in Gaelic, keeping the pitch and rhythm perfectly to the end. Their slow, sad tune might well have been as old as the hills which surrounded us, and there seemed no reason why the singing should ever cease.

It broke off at last, abruptly, and there was a pause. Then the men from the estate stepped forward and lifted the bier to the shoulders of four of them, while male relatives took up positions alongside, each holding a cord attached to the coffin. The Chief took the leading cord, but being too infirm for the long walk to the burial-ground he relinquished it before the procession started.

Slowly the cortège moved off along the drive by the flaming Watsonias and tall Himalayan lilies, underneath the leaning eucalyptus trees and out of the gates. Then we turned down beside the loch towards the village, completely blocking the narrow road to all traffic. We passed a cairn to the memory of Alexander Cameron, the Tournaig Bard, once shepherd to the estate; and the long white wall of the Home farm, where collies peered through the gates—and came at last to the rough track which leads to the graveyard.

I would not join the rest of the mourners inside the enclosure, preferring to stand by the open gate with the loch in full view. As the words of committal were spoken I saw a large white steam-yacht swing round the wooded point on which Inverewe House stands and come to anchor near the private jetty. Her paintwork gleamed so brilliantly in the sun that light seemed to shine through her sides. I expected to see a dinghy pull away from her, but there was no sign of life.

The last rites of the ceremony completed, people began to file out of the gate in the wall. As we moved away to our homes I saw the yacht slip from her anchorage, and soon she was round the Point and out of sight as silently and quickly as she had come. I asked the men about the craft, but no one recognized her; and later inquiries on the coast bore no fruit.

Old Sheena, who had stayed at home during the interment, said she had never known a big vessel come so far in for so short a stay. 'You would think they had come *to fetch someone*,' she said; '*but no boat came ashore.*'

20. *Farewell to Inverewe*

I COULD not go away after the funeral, nor was there opportunity to wander off for a day alone in the hills, as I wished. The bell rang more and more frequently as summer-holiday visitors to the Highlands flocked to see the gardens. Although Mother did all she could to help, it would not have been fair to let her cope with the crowds alone. The Trust people were anxious to have Inverewe open every day of the week, and as the schools had now closed for the long vacation I was persuaded to deal with the business involved. Soon we actually passed our first 'century'—by admitting one hundred and two visitors to the gardens in a day.

Before long I realized that being a custodian on seven days every week would not be congenial work for me as a permanent arrangement; nor could I easily become reconciled to life at Inverewe without Aunt Mairi. Lord Wemyss said he hoped to get an expert to superintend the gardens by October, and that the botanist they had in mind might perhaps bring a friend to succeed me as custodian in the Lodge. But for the intervening two months he would be glad if we could carry on—and this we agreed to do. Of course there was no more gardening for me. The work at the gates left insufficient time, and for weeks I did not even enter the policies.

The thought of having to relinquish my work in the schools added to the general wretchedness, and at first I played with the idea of finding another house or cottage in the district in order to carry on teaching locally. But when nothing at all suitable turned up I decided to take it as a pointer to the way I should go— which meant right away from Wester Ross, back to England. Life in the far north could never be the same again for me, and it might be less difficult to rearrange the threads of existence in other surroundings—though I dreaded leaving the country and its people.

These decisions were not quickly made, and while they were taking shape we were called upon by someone who did *not* want to see the gardens. To us the bell had come to mean admissions, so that we automatically picked up a reel of tickets before opening the door. It was a surprise when the stranger outside asked to see me. He introduced himself as the Further Education Officer, and had come to say how interested his Committee had been in the success of my handicraft classes. They hoped I would undertake similar work in new centres when the Autumn session began.

It was hard to refuse this invitation, and the official seemed genuinely sorry when I told him that as a result of Aunt Mairi's death I had decided to return to England. He stayed to have tea with us, and in the course of conversation cleared up a mystery that had puzzled me since the previous year. 'Why,' I asked, 'were my craft classes not denounced from the local pulpits, in common with the Women's Rural Institutes, badminton clubs, and other recreations?'

Our guest looked thoughtful. 'Where exactly did you hold your classes?' he inquired. 'In the school at Gairloch,' I replied. 'Och, well, that'll be it! If you had given the same lessons in the village hall you would probably have come in for criticism, and the whole experiment might have failed. Anything held on school premises becomes "education" and cannot be considered sinful.'

'So even the educational films are suspect *because they are shown in the hall!*' I exclaimed. 'Now I begin to understand.' He agreed that it was a tangled skein to unravel, but felt his experiences in Skye had shown the way; and the solution he had found there seemed to fit my problem too.

After he had gone I sat down at the big desk beside the window in the lounge and drafted a letter of resignation to the Education Committee. The appointment I had accepted with so much pleasure had ended as suddenly and unexpectedly as it began. How little I had dreamed, when starting work in the schools, that for me it would all have to come to a sad and early finish.

All the members of the Further Education class gave a farewell party for me, with many kinds of delicious home-baked scones and cakes, and afterwards I was presented with a fountain-pen— still a prized possession. My thanks were inadequate: from excess and not from any lack of appreciative feeling.

Every week I had to drive over to Gairloch to bank the gate-money, and on one of these afternoons there was some excitement in the bay. Several valuable salmon-nets had been damaged by a thirty-two-foot basking shark, and the boat which had been fitted with a harpoon gun for the purpose of hunting these monsters came out from the inner harbour in search of it. Presently a great black fin showed up close inshore, not far from where I stood. There was a loud report, and a harpoon whizzed away from the boat's bows and struck the quarry.

The fish went off at a spanking pace, with a stout line trailing in its wake and the boat following as fast as her engine could take her. Whether the shark had been mortally wounded by the harpoon or not, it certainly tired quite soon after the missile struck. Then the line was brought in, and a last tremendous struggle ensued, with the doomed fish sending fountains of water mast-high. The end came suddenly, and the dead shark was hauled up the side of the boat. The liver, full of valuable oil, was cut out before the carcase went back into the sea with a splash which

rocked the vessel and sent waves curvetting to the shore below
me.

The basking shark or sailfish (called *cearban* in Gaelic),
although the second largest fish in the sea, is a quiet and amiable
creature. It lives on a diet of small surface life in the ocean, which
it takes in through its ever-open mouth, sieving the fluid out
through a number of gill-slits. The stomach contains a kind of
shrimp paste. A shark will sometimes loiter round the inshore
waters of a sea-loch or bay for a week or more, and it is under-
standable that any salmon- or herring-net which happens to
be there may get damaged. It is not a question of trying to
rob the catch: neither salmon nor herring is of interest to the
shark. It is just that the net, if in the way, will be torn asunder.
Whatever the reason, such habits are highly unpopular with
fishermen.

There used to be many fishers of sharks in Hebridean seas,
for their livers were an important source of oil a hundred years
ago. In recent years sharks have appeared again in large numbers,
and some attempts have been made to revive the catching and
extraction of oil on a commercial scale—notably by Major Gavin
Maxwell, with his factory on the island of Soay beneath the
Cuillin hills. But apparently he did not find this an economic
proposition.

.   .   .   .   .

Our next excitement was the arrival of H.M.S. *Vanguard*
with her smaller attendant ships in Loch Ewe, during the summer
cruise of the Home Fleet in northern waters. Soon the roads
swarmed with bluejackets, and local hired cars overflowing with
cheerful mariners raced round the shore of the loch and back to
Aultbea for another load. Trade boomed; and a small store near
the Naval Base disappeared from sight behind ramparts of crated
beer and mineral-water bottles.

One day the Flag Lieutenant rang me up to ask if the Commander-in-Chief and his party could visit Inverewe as a special

privilege on Sunday afternoon, when the gardens were closed to the public. Of course I consented, and a line of glossy Daimlers rolled up in great style at about three o'clock. Tall marines leapt out to open gates and car doors, and the Admiral and his entourage were a picture of naval trimness with all their gold lace shining in the sun. Mother and I enjoyed naval occasions; for my father, the late E. N. Mooney (during what Sir Stanley Goodall has described as his brilliant but tragically brief career), had been a member of the Royal Corps of Naval Constructors and an expert on battleship design. Having shared his interests to the full, Mother found *Vanguard* a sight for sore eyes.

But the plans of men (even naval ones) go agley. The Admiral advanced with great dignity along the Inverewe drive, until he came in sight of the shores below *Ploc Ard*. Then he stood and regarded the scene below him in silence. Whalers, dinghies, and every sort of craft from the anchored ships had been creeping round the Point in dozens, to land parties of Liberty men, in weird garments, upon the rocky verges of our estate. No permission had been sought and none was needed. They just came in by water and landed where and when they pleased. The private Sunday afternoon visit of their Commander-in-Chief was scuttled from the start.

Fortunately Admirals are tough characters—equal to any occasion. This one turned to me with a bland smile. 'I see my men have got here before me!' he said. 'I'm sorry they are not looking their best. Please pardon their intrusion and attire.' We bowed and smiled at one another and his procession went on its way round the gardens.

But sailors were not the only uninvited guests that afternoon. It was one of those warm, still days with excessive humidity— just the weather for midges. Our most pessimistic fears were realized when we saw the entire party coming back enveloped in scarves and handkerchiefs. Even an Admiral cannot be expected to endure unmoved the assaults of thousands of tiny insects which make free of his ears and hair and invade the regions below his collar. I pressed all kinds of salve and preventatives upon the unhappy guests; but it was too late. They departed hurriedly in their black saloon cars with every window closed.

After tea we noticed that a sporadic drizzle had now turned to heavy rain. 'All the *matelots* will be away by now,' I said to my mother. 'If the midges could not drive them off, this rain will.' But on my way to the house to have a word with Sheena, I thought faint sounds of singing came from the direction of *Camas Glas*. Sheena said there were undoubtedly sailors in the gardens still. They had been up to the house not long since for water, bringing a big kettle to be filled at the tap. She feared for the damage they might be doing to the policies with their picnic fires.

I went off to the far side of the gardens, and guided by the voices descended to a green glade by the shore. In the middle of the grassy patch a large fire was blazing, surmounted by a black kettle and an enormous frying-pan filled with potatoes. About a dozen young men were dancing round the fire, clad in a strange assortment of rain-soaked garments which suggested castaways on Crusoe Island rather than naval ratings in home waters. They all held bundles of driftwood collected to feed the flames, and were lustily singing 'What shall we do with the drunken sailor?'— at least, the *tune* belonged to those words, but they seemed to have composed some different verses. The song stopped immediately they saw me.

There was an awkward silence as I walked towards the un-authorized party. Obviously they feared I had come to send them away. Instead, I smiled at them all and apologized for the poor weather we had provided for their picnic. The circle of worried faces broke into toothy grins. As I turned to go, I wished them '*Bon Voyage*' and added a hope that they would make sure no live embers were left to damage trees after their departure. There was a chorus of farewells and a cheer or two as I walked back to the house. Then the song was resumed with much vigour.

Sheena was comforted with assurances that the Navy could be trusted to do no damage. Even if any smouldering wood were left, I felt certain the steady rain would effectively deal with it.

Oasis of the North

But next morning there were no remains of either picnic or bonfire to be seen, and even the scorched ground had been raked over and scattered with leaves and pine-needles. The only reminder of the visitation was a trodden circle where the dancers had moved, and a channel in the stones scraped by the keel of their boat. It was sad and silent without the sailors and their song.

How often, when gardening among those trees or watching for seals in the *Camas Glas*, I had heard Aunt Mairi calling me! It all looked the same—surely she *must* be there still, working just out of sight behind some bush or round a bend in the path. The impression was so powerful that I put my head down and went rapidly home to the Lodge. Until the mariners' picnic I had not gone far into the gardens since the day Colin brought the bad news. Now I felt I should never want to walk in them again.

But of course I did. One September day the first bell of the morning summoned me to the door, where I found a tall couple in tweeds and mackintoshes who inquired courteously if they could be allowed to see the gardens. As I took the admission money I gave them a puzzled glance. Yes, I had known them before—the voices of both were familiar—but when and where had I heard them? The visitors' book was handy, and I asked for their signatures. Then I knew why the voice of the one—heard in so many broadcasts—had stirred my curiosity in the first minute. And for the other—a 'live' lecture in 1951 on the subject of English gardening through the centuries had introduced me to the expressive tones of Victoria Sackville-West, as she unfolded with unaffected ease and humour a little of her unique knowledge. This morning she was accompanied by her husband, Sir Harold Nicolson.

I escorted the visitors for part of their way round the policies, and Miss Sackville-West seemed delighted with the gardens in general and the eucryphias, now in full bloom, in particular. Their large, creamy flowers (like Mermaid roses) were born in wild profusion on the well-grown shrubs of some ten to twelve feet in height. We had both *Eucryphia glutinosa* and the *Nymansay* variety doing splendidly.

These unusual and beautiful shrubs were matched by their name; for, as dwelt on by Miss Sackville-West, 'Eucryphia' contained whole volumes of delight. Her interest was not confined to rare specimens. As she came down the drive on her way out she pointed to a common little bedding plant, self-sown, beside the path. 'The quality of the blues here is so lovely,' she said. 'The flower of even that ordinary lobelia is a clearer, more vivid colour than I have ever seen before.'

Both she and Sir Harold were deeply sorry to have left their first visit to Inverewe too late to meet Aunt Mairi. They were so sympathetic and quick to grasp the difficulties of one left to carry on alone that I felt loath to let them go.

Next day's first visitor made a contrast—and yet in her earthy wisdom had something Miss Sackville-West would have appreciated. The local 'bush post' must have flashed a message round about our forthcoming departure, for the Tinker woman who came to the back door asked me to let her have any old clothes, bits of carpet, or household goods we no longer required. I gave her some oddments we had turned out, and then, over a cup of tea, said I wanted something from her in return.

Her little brown eyes almost squinted as she gazed intently at me over the rim of her big white cup. 'Tell me,' I said, 'how it is you folk manage to live and sleep out in the heather without being driven mad by the midges?'

She smiled. 'You can get rid of them easily enough,' she replied. 'You just want to soak your hat and your necktie in paraffin at times. The smell of it will drive them off, never fear!' And everyone else as well! I thought to myself. The cure for our Highland plague was as distant as ever.

For the last fortnight of our stay the pantry and back premises in the Lodge were in a state of chaos—strewn with tea-chests and cartons into which our electrical equipment, china and glass, books, tools and gardening clobber were packed by my hands. The carriers are not by repute tender towards the packages left in their care; and when I thought of the long journey my parcels would have to make across most of Scotland and England, with many changes, I feared that only mangled remains would survive.

We had saved up hundreds of newspapers, and with these everything was wrapped and cushioned until I felt that the contents would never be unearthed again. This tedious business probably paid in the end, for nothing was damaged. (But the crates and boxes were also unscathed, so the handling may have been more gentle than we expected it to be.)

The packing was carried out in the longer evenings which October had brought, and night after night as I worked alone at the back of the Lodge I could hear the great red stags roaring at each other at the start of the rutting season. To the north of the house the policies (or fenced ground) ended quite close by, and beyond our sheltering wood lay the open moorland. Here the red deer gathered, and their trumpetings sounded eerie in the darkness. It was the more mysterious because for months we had not caught even a distant glimpse of the herds—all were far away on the high tops for the whole summer. Gradually with the approach of winter they had moved lower, and were now congregating almost in our back-yard. Occasionally, if really hard weather comes to the west coast, herds of deer may be seen foraging in farmyards and even roaming through village streets in search of food.

The red deer (*Cervus elaphus*) is the largest untamed mammal in Britain, and has lived in a truly wild state in Scotland since prehistoric times. For most of the year the sexes keep apart, and each herd, whether of hinds or stags, will have a leader. Stags in summer graze the highest tops, where their tender, growing antlers are free from irritating flies. In August the velvet skin peels off, and the hard antlers are ready for the rutting season in late September. From then until it finishes at the end of October, adult stags leave their companies and go to the hind territories, where they announce their presence by the loud roaring we could hear in the Lodge. It is a warning to other stags to keep off.

·   ·   ·   ·

The misery of leaving Inverewe had lain heavy on my mind for weeks; but as so often happens the actual moment of departure came and went more lightly than seemed possible. There was so much to be done, and so little time for thought. The car came to fetch us in good time, but we had so much to pack into it that our start was delayed. I stole a few more seconds to visit Rufus the cat in his warm boiler-house, and left with a prayer that the next inhabitants of the Lodge would care for him. Then we shook hands with the gardeners, and our impatient driver was away with us. Sheena, who had gone to live in my old home, *Tigh-an-Uillt*, came out with her neighbour Lizbie to wave as we passed the gate; and soon we were over the river bridge and up the long hill to Tollie. I squirmed round hastily in my seat in time to have a momentary last glimpse of the white house of Inverewe snug beneath the woods of *Ploc Ard* before everything was blotted out. It might all have been a single night's dream.

. . . . .

In the year 1651 the great Patrick Mor MacCrimmon, most famous member of that celebrated family of pipers, was received by Charles II when the monarch's army lay before Stirling. Inspired by his royal reception, the musician went away and composed a marvellous pibroch to express the rapture he felt. This 'big music' (*ceòl mór*) is still played on great occasions by pipers skilled enough to master it. It is called 'I Got a Kiss of the King's Hand'.

I, too, had got my kiss—an unforgettable, right royal salute—from the people and land of the north-west Highlands, which I came to as a stranger and left as a friend. But no song flows from my pipe or pen; and so in words (pallid reflections of joy though mine are) I have done my best to record the scenes and the people who gave me such royal welcomes.

Any attempt to portray Mairi Sawyer of Inverewe could be rated foolish—or even shocking. If she had one friend, she possessed a thousand. Nine hundred and ninety-nine of these may dislike my references to her—thinking them at best inadequate, and at worst utterly false. The truth is that she was a diamond-cut personality, with a thousand facets to twinkle differently at each one of those who knew her. My sketch-book contains the best pictures I can draw of the face she turned to me. It does not claim to show anything more.

Words invite criticism. Only silence is safe. Yet if mine reflect as much as a gleam they may serve better than none to keep the coloured memories bright.

21. *Epilogue*

To outward appearance I soon settled down in England, found some work, and 'got over' the shock of Aunt Mairi's sudden death. Inwardly, I was alternately numb and incapable of any feeling, or else full of a wild rebellion. Failure to accept what had happened sprang only in part from personal distress at her loss. There was added a strong sense that she, too, had some bitter struggle to pass through; that the longing to return home to Inverewe (of which she had written from Edinburgh) had not been quenched by death. This impression was too persistent and too strong to be dismissed as mere fancy, however hard I tried to convince myself that it was self-induced.

It made me restless and miserable to guess that she had not found peace, and to have no way of communicating sympathy or help. To watch a friend suffering in this world can be terrible enough; but apprehension of distress in someone who has passed beyond reach of word or look is an even greater burden. It had to be endured in silence, alone—for who would understand? I could hear the voice of one wise friend saying: 'You are not

237

alone. You can both give and find help in prayer.' (He had never endured the spiritual desolation which, in a turmoil of grief and bitterness, finds it impossible to pray.)

When the summer came round again some people asked me to stay with them on an island of the Inner Hebrides. They had been acquaintances of Aunt Mairi's and had fished the Inverewe lochs, but we had not met. Although I had never felt less sociable in my life, something impelled me to accept this generous and unexpected invitation. The island—a large one—was quite different from anything I had known in the Far North. It was smoother and greener, with grass growing high up the hill. The dark, volcanic rock had seemingly been deposited in molten layers, and the long, horizontal lines of the terraces so produced gave a calm, orderly look to the landscape. At first I missed the rough, craggy tops and boulder-strewn sides of the older Torridonian formations in Wester Ross; but gradually the green ridges pleased and rested me. My host and hostess were very kind—leaving me free to come and go as I wished. I wandered for miles along the hills, while *Busdubh* alternately got into a lather with hunting and cooled herself off in the burns. *Her* happiness was not in doubt.

One hot afternoon I came part of the way down the hill and threw myself on a bed of bracken beside a burn, with my feet dangling in the swift, cold water. The stream was like hundreds of others: rushing down from high above me, with a thunderous roar caught and echoing in a narrow cleft in the rocks. Patches of creamy foam topping the peat-stained water completed the suggestion of a river of oatmeal stout.

Great white clouds bounced up over the green mountain cone which came between me and the open sea, and far below the shelf on which I sat my host's little stone house squatted on a shingle beach beside an arm of the loch. Tiny specks of gulls whirled mazily over a shoal of fish close inshore.

Quite suddenly the whole scene became irradiated by a light other than the sun which shone so warmly. Hill and burn, mountain and cloud, wee house and loch-water seemed transparent and lit from within as though some unseen hand had touched a switch and caused everything to glow. This I noticed before realizing that I seemed illumined also. And with the strange radiance which banished every dark thought and oppressive fear from my mind, came the certainty that all was now well with Aunt Mairi. Rebellion and unhappiness melted away in the powerful light. I felt confident that she had been able to draw aside some hampering curtain and move into freedom—to find not only a great new world of opportunity, but all the places and people she had loved (and feared to lose) still before her.

From that minute I began to enjoy the island holiday with the old zest. My new friends commented on the improvement in my looks and appetite. Soon they had to leave their cottage and return to the mainland, but asked if I would care to stay on by myself and 'caretake' during their absence. I accepted the offer with gratitude; and *Busdubh* and I were left alone in the little old mill-house beside the water.

We were not lonely. For one thing, there was always the mail arriving with letters, milk, and the latest island news every afternoon. Then there were two dear old ladies living a few yards down the road—my only neighbours. They would make an excuse to wander along past the house—perhaps bring some stale crusts for a pet lamb in our field—and look in to see that I was safe and well. An elderly crofter who mowed their grass for them would slip in to examine my host's boat and look to the few cattle-beasts grazing with the lamb. This man and his friend had permission to borrow the boat for fishing, and I had heard the owner tell them that I was interested in that sort of amusement.

One night I was leaning on the sill of my open bedroom window, looking across the loch in the afterglow of late sunset to the rounded crest of *Ben a Vullin*, and listening to the burn as it guggled out over the rocks. Around its mouth a score of sea-trout leaped and splashed where the warm July sea-water met the colder freshet of the river. I meant to go to bed, but sat on at the window and must have dozed off. As reality faded into dream the hill before me trembled and heaved and great boulders spilled out of it, and the western flank fell silently away, leaving a sheer precipice of rock, and beyond it a row of distant peaks.

Before me were all the well-loved landmarks of my old home; and the mill-house by the island shore melted imperceptibly into a white Lodge guarding the growing treasures planted on *Am Ploc Ard*, and itself protected by the wooded slopes of that High Lump from the worst of the wild weather that came in off the Minch in winter-time. My island casement had turned into the old-fashioned sliding sash that injured the musician's finger, and behind me (I knew without turning my head) was the long room where giant royal-blue forget-me-nots with leaves like rhubarb stood in an old aquarium glass on the table.

It was no surprise to hear men's voices speaking Gaelic down below on the drive. Then it ceased, and they stood still beneath my window. 'Are you sleeping?' one asked in a soft, careful whisper. 'Good evening to you! It's a fine night!' I replied. 'Yess, but we're thinking it iss too bright yet,' replied the bigger of the two men. 'Angus and I will be waiting a little. The tide will be better in another half-hour. We'll be getting the net down to the boat first.'

'The boat will likely need bailing after yesterday's rain,' I said, 'and the oars and rowlocks are in the garage with the net.'

They disappeared round the side of the house and I heard them speaking Gaelic again—which came more easily to them, but must not be used in my presence because it would be impolite to use words to each other which a third party could not understand. I went down to the back door and opened it; and the night breeze, though hardly more than a sigh, had the nip of northern waters in it, making me run for a coat. The little dog stirred in her old peat-basket and lifted her black muzzle at the sound of my Burberry coming off a peg in the hall, but I told her to lie down, and went out shutting the door behind me.

Fish were jumping harder than ever, and I wished the boatmen would hurry; but well I knew they would never let excitement outweigh their wisdom, which had the sureness of long trial. A faint whiff of tobacco straying from the dark recesses of the garage told me that they had settled down to their pipes. I went back into the kitchen and put a kettle on the hob. Presently the hall clock struck one. Then I heard movements in the garage, and the two men came along the path, one carrying a bundle of net and the other the oars and rowlocks.

Quietly and quickly they pulled the boat down the shingle and launched her without a splash. They fixed one end of the net in the shallow water with a kedge anchor, and then Iain Mor, a hefty caber-tosser in local Games, skimmed the boat along as easily as though she were built of paper, while old Angus paid out the seventy-five-yard net gently without a sound.

They put it down in a wide arc round the mouth of the burn; and then Angus climbed overboard and made the end fast, while Iain pulled the lightened boat across the shallows and splashed the inshore water with his oars to frighten the fish away from the burn's mouth and back into the net. I ran down to the water's edge and heaved lump after lump of rock into the dark pool, slipping on seaweed and clots of jelly-fish stranded by the tide. I heard something hit the net, far out in the centre, and saw the floats dip and sway.

The commotion frightened a trio of oyster-catchers from the shore, and they rose and flew out to sea, the anxious parent birds chivvying their child to greater speed than his untried wings were accustomed to, and screaming '*Bi-glic, bi-glic!*' at us so sharply that their sudden cries echoed in my head long after they had gone.

Angus went along the shingle and took up the kedge. Then he got back into the boat and began to haul in the net, handling the dripping folds skilfully so that no fish were lost. The first few yards brought only small ones, but when the float which I had noticed bobbing came aboard I saw him pull something out which landed with a heavy thud when thrown behind his back into the bottom of the boat.

The work went on with few words spoken, Iain Mor easing the craft along quietly as his partner drew in the net and pulled out the catch. Fish were coming thickly now, and when they reached the end of the net I ran forward to ask what the luck had been. 'Twelve good ones and two small,' said Angus hoarsely, 'but there's an awful lot of jelly-fish and crab in the net tonight.' 'Plenty work for me cleaning it in the morning, then; but never mind if you've got fish too,' I said happily.

While they hauled the boat up I ran for buckets, and phosphorescence gleamed silver on the fish as we gathered them up from the floorboards and stuffed them into the pails. The load was heavy, and I trod with care, steadying myself on the flattest rocks until I reached the grass; and went into the house and emptied out the catch. Fourteen sea-trout in a row are a fine sight on the floor of anyone's larder. Together they turned the scale at twenty-six pounds.

By the time I had weighed the fish and washed out the pails the men appeared at the kitchen door; so I called them in, and took the singing kettle from the fire and made a big pot of strong tea, and set it on the table with cake and scones—and handed Iain Mor his usual dram in a glass. Angus, faithful to his tea, had drained two breakfast cups and was at a third when I noticed Iain looking thoughtfully at the table. In his left hand he held a slab of cake, and his right had just put down the empty glass on a shelf behind him.

There was a lull in the conversation. Angus looked at the teapot and then at me. 'Iain is waiting his tea,' he murmured. I flew for the teapot and kettle. 'I didn't know you mixed your drinks,' I said apologetically. Iain accepted a rich cup and resumed his comparison of the night's sport with other catches in the past. 'It is terrible thirsty work,' he said, draining the cup and putting it down in front of the pot for a refill. They emptied the pot again and finished the cake, and rose to leave as the clock struck three.

I made two parcels, each with four trout in, and gave one to each man.

'Will you be coming again soon for the net?' I asked.

Angus thought for a moment. 'It will not be any good with the tides as they are this week,' he replied, 'but next week you might be hearing us again about the same time. I will let you have word so that we shall not be frightening you in the dark.' They shook my hand and went away with their parcels, and there was no sound but the burn and the tide lapping on the stones below the house.

I do not remember going to bed that night; but I woke in my room in the mill-house when the sun was already high and the gulls mewing on the shore. *Busdubh* shot from her basket as though she feared the day would be over before she got out. A family of shelduck were catching crabs in the shallow water. Idly I watched them shaking off the legs before swallowing the little green bodies. 'Crabs!' I shouted, running to the garden wall. Yes, there was a damp net, full of weed and feebly waving claws, and some nasty blobs of jelly-fish.

'I did not dream about the fishing, then,' I said vaguely to the dog, who was more interested in turning over flotsam and jetsam among the rocks. I wasn't sure whether to get breakfast, or to wait a little longer and have lunch—for it was past eleven o'clock. The thought of food led me to the larder—and there were four large trout and two small ones laid out in a row on the stone floor. 'Well, well,' I thought. 'Dreams and reality—who can tell where one slips into the other?'

. . . . .

One dream comes to me often: sometimes at night when I am asleep in a silent Somerset manor house; sometimes when I am wide awake—once I had it in the middle of Piccadilly. It cannot be summoned at will, nor is its arrival predictable. Other folk have it too, and I make no apology for quoting the well-known verse describing the emigrant's dream—written by an unknown

contributor to *The Edinburgh Magazine* of a hundred and thirty
years ago. Its magic can never grow old.

> From the lone shieling of the misty island
> Mountains divide us and a waste of seas;
> But still the blood is strong, the heart is Highland,
> And we in dreams behold the Hebrides.

22. *Care of the Trust*

PRIMA DONNAS are commonly expected to give more than one 'final farewell' performance. Having written my epilogue, I feel that I am following their example by adding yet another chapter to this book. The publisher is responsible for this behaviour: in fact, none of the foregoing pages would have appeared in print but for a chance remark of his. My recollections were put down on paper to ensure that when I grew old and memory failed, the typescript would be there for my pleasure.

Some months after the bundle had been stowed away in a bottom drawer, I read a book in which certain references to the *loud voices* and pronounced *Scottish accents* employed by natives of the far north of these islands annoyed me to the point of protest. I wrote to the publisher, saying that in my experience the inhabitants of Ross and Sutherland were blessed with soft voices and spoke remarkably pure English. In a courteous answer he pointed out that most people expected all Scots to produce 'Scotch' accents. Probably the author had given his readers the traditional characters they preferred. The letter carried a small barb in its tail-end. 'If you know and like the people of the North so well, why not write something about them yourself?'

'*I have*,' I said in reply: thus in two words releasing the string round my bag and allowing the wild cat to leap out. My secret box of papers had to leave the nest and travel in a parcel to London. Almost before I realized what was happening, a contract for publication had been signed. Then it was suggested that it would add interest if I were to visit my old home and describe how the gardens looked after four years in the care of The National Trust for Scotland.

Although early January is an unusual season for Highland

jaunts, any excuse to re-visit Wester Ross is enough for me; and so I went at once to the nearest travel agent and booked a return ticket to Achnasheen. This brought back memories to both clerk and customer, for he who served me had by a strange chance supplied my first ticket to the same station seven years before—and he had not forgotten the occasion. It was high summer then, and crowds of holiday-makers pressed towards the counter while my man hunted feverishly through his reference books in search of the fare to Achnasheen. I spelt it once, then spied him anchored to the letter L as he sought *Loch* na Sheen. I spelt it again, and his finger darted up and down the letter A without result. 'There cannot be a station of that name,' he said at last.

'Oh, yes, there is,' I replied earnestly; 'it is shown on my friend's notepaper: "nearest station Achnasheen 40 miles".' The clerk gave me a suspicious look (magnified by strong spectacles) and evidently feared a hoax. The press of customers round me began to seethe and finger banknotes with a menacing rustle. Things were growing awkward when a very small old lady in black pushed forward and lifted her chin. 'There is a station at Achnasheen,' she said in a militant voice. 'I have *been* there!' After firing this shot, she returned to her rightful pace in the queue stretching behind my back.

But this time there was no queue, and no trouble about the fare to Achnasheen—except that it had gone up. It cost me about fourteen pounds (second class with sleepers) for the return journey from Bath; and that was not inclusive of meals, taxis, porters, or other incidental expenses. By the time I added hotel bills—and there are no cheap hotels in the north of Scotland—a week's holiday cost more than many Continental tours of similar duration. Yet my choice gave me deeper satisfaction.

The train journey was luxurious compared with my first trip to Inverness. No longer does the second-class traveller sleep on a hard pallet in a four-berth compartment, or fight for a grimy communal wash-place. In winter, at all events, the Inverness sleepers are all of the latest twin-berth pattern, with comfortable beds (provided with linen) and a washbasin inside the cabin.

My travelling companion and I were up early, for she was a Highlander who had, as she put it, 'Got stuck in England', and seemed no less eager than I for a sight of the hills. As the train chugged up the steep Drumochter pass in sight of the Cairngorm mountains, we threw open windows on either side of the train and stood greedily sniffing up the cold morning air like the two children in a famous old advertisement for gravy.

Inverness looked just the same as ever, and I could not believe that nearly seven years had passed since Aunt Mairi first met me in the station-yard. There was even a black car bearing the Ross-shire registration letters JS.; but I missed the silver warrior on the bonnet—and I missed Aunt Mairi. This car stood waiting for some other traveller, and was not for me. I made my way on foot to a familiar café and received the usual cheerful service—for I had purposely gone without breakfast in the train so that I might enjoy it here in Inverness.

Soon I was in the Kyle train, and the best of the journey had begun. We left the frosty nip and ice-rimmed roads behind and came into soft, dull weather on the Ross-shire border. Russet bracken on the braes, burgundy-red tops of birch woods, vivid yellow-green cushions of moss and subtle pink and gold lichened rocks put me in mind of a rich Persian carpet. The lochs we passed were grey and still, and the reflected hills might have been modelled in wood-smoke—so fragile and transparent their blueness seemed. On the higher tops ragged streaks of snow suggested cake-icing that some predatory child had nibbled.

We came to Achnasheen before I had taken in a tenth of the pattern on the carpet. I climbed the high bridge over the line, and there below me on the 'up' side was the Gairloch mail with Arthur himself standing beside it. We shook hands gravely. 'You are very welcome!' he said. I turned to whistle for *Busdubh*, having temporarily forgotten that she had been left behind in Mrs. Richardson's kennel near Bath. Then I settled into the front seat of the big mail bus. I was BACK, and it seemed as though I had never been away.

From Achnasheen the narrow road descends fairly rapidly

through desolate Glen Docherty to the eastern end of Loch Maree, and then winds for some twelve miles along the rock-strewn edge of the water. Magnificent and shapely specimens of Scots pine clothe the roadside verges and the hills framing the shore—last remains of the old, vast Caledonian forest that once covered much of Scotland. Arthur pointed out some particularly fine trees, and then looked across the loch to the further hills. 'There's a lot of snow on old *Slioch* today,' he said. I agreed, and there was a pause. Then he said, 'It doesn't matter how often you drive this road, it always looks different.'

That my thoughts happened to be running on similar lines was in no way remarkable; but surprise and pleasure came to me in the discovery that after so many years of daily journeys he could still observe and enjoy the changing beauty of the familiar scene. He was right about the changes, of course. And on my side the old magic soon gripped me as firmly as before. I tried to discover the nature of the spell this country casts, but it proved to be as elusive as the crock of gold at the rainbow's end—though, unlike the gold, it really does exist.

There were only two other passengers in the bus—both men —and it was good to hear them speaking Gaelic to each other, to Arthur, and to various people who came to fetch letters and parcels from the mail *en route*. When we stopped at the Loch Maree hotel a third man joined the couple behind me. He looked blankly at them as they let loose a torrent of their native language. 'Och, you don't have the Gaelic, Percy!' said one of the pair with a laugh; and for the rest of the way English was spoken instead.

Presently we left the shores of Loch Maree and crossed a narrow neck of land to the sea at Gairloch. At the post-office, where we stayed to unload several mail-bags, another woman came aboard to share my front seat. 'The days are growing longer already,' she said to Arthur when we were on our way again. 'Aye, they are stretching, they are stretching,' he said, 'but not in the mornings yet—it is just in the evenings you see a difference now.'

'And with Christmas past we may look forward to spring,'

I put in (reverting to my best southern shopping manners). 'Well, well, there may be storms yet,' said Arthur, shaking his head. 'You know the saying, "As the days stretch, winter strengthens".' This was new to me, and I was pleased to learn a maxim of northern origin.

I asked after the welfare of this person and that, as we passed the long straggle of houses that fringe the Gairloch shore and began to climb Achtercairn hill on the way to Poolewe. Some friends had died, others had left the district. 'Aye, you will see many changes,' said Arthur with a sigh. The alterations I most feared to discover would be in the occupants of my first home— the wee house by the burn. Reports from The National Trust for Scotland had informed me of Colin's retirement from his garden work at Inverewe, and it seemed likely that his half of the cottage would be required for a successor. Without Colin and Lizbie as ever-helpful neighbours, I doubted whether old Sheena could remain in what had been my portion of *Tigh-an-Uillt*.

Then Arthur spoke again. 'There's one house where you need not fear to see strange faces,' he said. 'The people at *Tigh-an-Uillt* are the same still.' Thrilled by this unexpected news, I was glowing happily when we reached the Poolewe post-office and stopped to unload mail. The light of the winter's afternoon was growing dim, and as Arthur had promised to drive me and my baggage along to the hotel I did not stir from my seat or look around at the empty village street. A moment later I was startled to hear a voice and see a welcoming fist thrust towards me. It was Colin, whose hands had tended the soil of Inverewe for over forty years. Finding him inside the post-office, Arthur had said mysteriously, 'Go and see who I have brought in the bus.' It was grand to meet this old friend again, and he gave me a great welcome. Although troubled by rheumatism he looked as young as ever, and he was still putting in some part-time work in the gardens. He gave me all the latest news of Inverewe.

Being the only guest in the hotel I was given tea in the lounge before a well-banked fire; and when it was time for an evening meal they laid a table in the same room. I was very pleased with this practical arrangement, for large, deserted dining-rooms can be grim and cheerless in winter. Afterwards I dozed off for an hour or so in my warm armchair before going upstairs to a bath of hot burn-water—so soft that the lightest smears of soap covered me in froth. The comfortable bed had been well aired with several hot bottles, and I must have fallen asleep immediately. Some time in the small hours I woke—to hear the old familiar clatter of driven rain and hail on my window facing the sea, while a gale ripped in off the Minch and drummed against the glass. I meant to keep awake for a while to enjoy once more the luxury of being tucked up snug and dry, listening to the wild sounds of storm a few feet from my pillow. But the combination of warmth within and the steady roar outside soon lulled me into a deeper sleep, from which I did not stir until nine in the morning.

After breakfast I waited until one or two fierce-looking squalls had come in off the loch and spent themselves, and then I put on the oilskins and rubber boots I had brought and set off round the loch for Inverewe. There was the Big House, looking less white against the dark woods than I remembered it; and the Gate Lodge nearer the road; and another building down on the shore which was new to me. 'They have built a place in the gardens for visitors to have tea,' Arthur had remarked in the bus. Evidently this was it. The Trust had made tentative proposals for such an enterprise in Aunt Mairi's lifetime, but she would not hear of it. 'For one thing,' she said, 'I couldn't allow any competition with the local hotels. In order to keep going all the year round they depend on every bit of trade they can get during the short summer season.' I was glad to hear that this difficulty had been overcome by arranging for one of the hotels to run the new tea-room. Colin had told me it would hold eighty people, and was to be opened in May during a visit by the cruise-ship *Meteor* to Loch Ewe.

This morning the water of the loch was dashing noisily on the shore close to the new building, for there was a high tide with a strong wind blowing off the sea. I walked away from the tide-line and up the road to the main gates, thinking that I had better observe the rules and show my Trust membership card to the custodian in the Lodge. But the hands of my watch had only just reached the time of opening—and in winter visitors would not be expected at such an early hour. The little summer-house now used as an office was untenanted; my ticket remained in its case; the visitors' book bears no record of my name. I began to feel very like an unseen ghost. Then I found Roddy Beg and another man grubbing out a new path to provide access to the tea-room from the higher level of the drive. They saw me; so the ghost was laid.

It seemed odd to be talking to them outside the familiar door of the Lodge to which Colin had once brought the terrible news of Mairi Sawyer's death—and yet to be a stranger in the place, with no right of entry. But it was the gardens I had come to see; so I turned away from the house and went forward under the leaning eucalyptus trees and the Austrian fir with its thirty-foot garland of *Clematis montana rubens*, past the back of 'America' and into 'Bamboozlem'. The drive looked much as it had always done, and 'Bamboozlem' little changed, though I fancied that the famous blue hydrangeas were less flourishing than of old. This may have been caused by less agreeable weather conditions; or possibly they were missing the careful but drastic pruning their owner used to give them.

The great magnolia, which bears pink blossoms like water-lilies before the leaves unfold in late March, looked well—as did all the other varieties of magnolia. Although one eucalyptus tree had been blown, there was more than enough luxuriant growth left to camouflage its loss. I drifted out of the enclosure, noticing with a pang how the gum tree by the west gate was still shedding cigar-shaped rolls of bark on the path. Often on winter evenings I had amused myself at Inverewe by lighting these 'cigars' at the fire and censing Aunt Mairi and myself with the fragrant fumes. I picked one up and put it in my pocket, together with a blown spray of gum foliage. Much agitation in the tree-tops showed that outside a strong wind was blowing, but down below where I stood it was calm and quiet and very mild.

I hovered in the 'Peace Plot' for some moments by the old

gnarled bush of *Rhododendron campylocarpum*, which is covered with delicate primrose bells in May. This patriarch has countless descendants dotted about the Inverewe policies. Near by, I noticed that the memorial stone to Donald Grant, who served Osgood MacKenzie for nearly sixty years, had grown soiled and discoloured with time and weather, and the inscription looked shabby. I remembered how, six years before, I had spent many hours cleaning off similar discoloration with a wire brush, and painting in the letters with black enamel. When my work was finished Aunt Mairi seemed so pleased with the result. Had it been possible to linger now, I would have cleaned the stone again.

The fact that an imposing cairn (erected on the shore below the Gate Lodge) bears a bold and clear dedication to another who served Inverewe for many years, makes it all the more desirable that the earlier memorial should be spared any appearance of neglect. The cairn, which was unveiled by Mairi Sawyer in the summer of 1952, has the following English inscription:

In memory of
ALEXANDER CAMERON THE TOURNAIG BARD
1848–1933
who lived all his long, useful and highly respected life
on the shores of Loch Ewe, and whose Gaelic poems and
songs earned for him a wide and honoured reputation
throughout the north.

Presently I came to the Grey Bay (*Camas Glas*) where seals used to congregate, and where I once found a party of sailors in fancy-dress dancing round a bonfire in the rain. The old chicken-house from whose roof the brush of a wild cat once dangled had disappeared (together with the hens) and the cove seemed to be void of life. Then I went a little closer to the water, and from behind a rock at the foot of the cliff a heron flapped into the air and flew with steady sweeps of its wings towards Cuddy Rock and out of my sight.

I went on round the shoreward edge of the demesne, and when

I reached the walk below the ponds I was surprised to see a fall of rock on my left, where the brae showed up stark and bare, with an avalanche of small fragments scattered across the path and on the beds at each side. On closer inspection it appeared that the interstices of the rock-strewn beds had been planted with young azaleas, heaths, and gentians, and this suggested that the 'fall' may have been artificially induced. I hoped that wild nature would be allowed to clothe the cleared rock face with tufts of moss and fern, for the charm of Inverewe lies in its clever admixture of 'tame' plants with natural background, and too much clearance of the indigenous growths so as to permit of more planting is apt to strike a jarring note. The rocky outcrops are beautiful, and in the past many of these were disinterred from heavy masking trails of bramble and whin; but Aunt Mairi would always leave sufficient natural cover to avoid any of those harsh contrasts which startle and offend the eye.

Beyond this brae I saw that the old path up to the large water-garden had been closed, so I had to take a new route skirting two black peaty pools which are formed by the outflow of the burn from the big pond above, on its way to the sea. Probably visitors are interested in peering into the pools, and some healthy groups of meconopsis and other flowering plants have been put to decorate the verges. To me the small ponds suggested water-holes used by wild beasts, and it seemed a pity there could not be strings of deer to troop down and drink delicately from them. But there would be little floral display if roe were allowed within the policies.

The high tip of *Ploc Ard* has also been cleared of ground-cover in a rather ruthless manner, and the installation of a white-painted railing along the precipitous edge of this cliff does not improve its appearance—though it may be considered necessary as a safety barrier. Fortunately the outlook is too vast a sweep of wild grandeur to be seriously impaired by trifles.

I stood there for some time, and although a strong wind was blowing in off the Minch the trees of Inverewe protected me from most of it, even at this highest point. At first I thought there were no signs of bird life, but suddenly a great northern diver (or sea herdsman, as it is called in Gaelic) appeared far below me on the rough water of the windswept sea-loch. I was wearing a watch with a seconds hand, and was able with this to time a number of the bird's dives. They varied only slightly in actual length, and the average worked out at fifty-five seconds under water.

The smoothness and speed with which he submerged were magical, and I had not been aware until this morning of the difference between the sea herdsman's method of diving and that of many other creatures. Instead of ducking his beak first, he withdrew his body down vertically (or so it seemed), and the head disappeared last. Perhaps this bird's swimming position, which had always reminded me of an overloaded or water-logged boat, assists it to dive in this manner, and makes possible both the speed of submersion and the avoidance of splash.

Reluctantly I moved away from the high cliff and walked back to the full shelter of the woodland gardens, where a bevy of small birds—mostly tits—kept up a cheerful chattering. Down by the boat-landing whins were spattered with brilliant yellow blossom, and above them the fresh greenish-ochre leaves of *Rhododendron sutchuenense* were almost as bright as the whin flowers. With fat yellow buds on top and long clusters of leaves hanging stiffly down below these 'ferrules', the bushes looked like groups of half-furled parasols.

On the shore below the rockery in front of the mansion house I was surprised to see the famous eucalyptus which appears in so many pictures of Inverewe, for I had heard that both it and its companion (a *Cordyline australis*) had been lost in gales during the previous winter. But apparently the gardeners had cleverly managed to salvage and re-plant the gum-tree, and so far it seems to have regained its grip on the rocky soil. The *Cordyline* did not survive. Many new and interesting plants are being tried out on the rockery, but as it is not known how many varieties will endure the salt winds in their exposed position there is little point in referring to their names.

I couldn't bear to leave the gardens yet; so retraced my steps towards the large pond, and was caught in a sudden squall of rain which made me run for the old Norwegian log shelter on the brae above the water-garden. This hut had been in ruins when I left Inverewe; but the Trust has restored it, and no doubt many other visitors will be as grateful as I for its restful bench under cover. It provides an excellent look-out from which to follow the course of rain squalls that may often be seen racing in from the Atlantic, blotting out the crofts of Naast and Inverasdale on the opposite shore, hitting (or missing) the Inverewe peninsula, and then scudding off inland towards *Beinn Eighe* or the hills of Ardlair.

On my way back to the gates I noticed some clearances bordering a walk behind the house, which seemed regrettable to me because they have been filled with seedling plants and shrubs in the straight, parallel strips employed by nursery-gardeners. If parts of the wild gardens are used as nurseries there is no reason why the young plants should not be grouped irregularly—and in this way they need cause no offence to the eye. At present the geometrical effect is unpleasing, because it is out of keeping with the surroundings. Symmetrical rows and regular-shaped plots are suitable only inside the walled garden. There they provide a pleasing contrast to the informality of the woodlands, and visitors are prepared for a change of mood by the enclosing walls and gateways.

The season of my visit was not, of course, a flowering one but in many ways winter (when there are no brilliant colours or rich scents to distract the mind) is a good time for making a critical appraisal of a garden's lay-out. Of the supreme importance of design there can be no question—even if ninety per cent of those who enjoy the result are not consciously aware of the plan as a whole.

As I wandered across the lawns and down towards the drive on my way out I felt that Inverewe was undoubtedly being very well cared for, and had none of the melancholy dead feeling which sometimes creeps in when the creator of a garden leaves it in strange hands. In particular, The National Trust for Scotland is paying great attention to the vital matter of re-planting gaps where timber has been blown. But there is a risk that it may become just one more Botanical Garden—producing all sorts of unusual and beautiful specimens, but losing intrinsic value as an entity unless the unique character of the design is fully grasped and appreciated by those in charge.

Aunt Mairi, when the *Guide to Inverewe* was being prepared, quoted to me the conversation she once had with a well-known horticulturist. Fearing that he might think Inverewe unkempt, she said, 'for he had fifty gardeners and I had only two and a half at the time, I apologized for its lack of polish. But he replied immediately: "*Don't alter it!* It is lovely—it reminds me of some wild corner in Burma or northern China." ' If such an authority were available to give the same advice today, Inverewe would be grateful for it in the years ahead.

That percipient eighteenth-century writer on gardening, Uvedale Price, said this about Painshill:

I was highly pleased with a woodland walk, and I was pleased with it not merely from what had been but from what had *not* been done; it had no edges, no borders, no distinct lines of separation. If it be high commendation of a painter or a writer that he knows when to leave off, it is not less so to an improver.

He goes on to say that although no precept is more generally admitted in theory than that of *concealing* the art which is employed, none has been less observed in practice. Mairi Sawyer was instinctively one who concealed her art, and because of this I suspected that in her lifetime relatively few people gave her credit for the creative genius she possessed. Now that she is dead, I fear that those who have not divined her gift may rush in to make so-called improvements without realizing how destructive these can be of the greater whole. Not that alterations as such are necessarily to be deplored: but they can only be made successfully if the character of the place and the total effect are kept steadily in mind and given precedence over all else.

Those who knew and loved the gardens of Inverewe when they were privately-owned cannot expect them to remain exactly as they used to be—nor should anyone desire a living thing to be static. I do not even grumble (as some do) about the building of the tea-room. Although Aunt Mairi herself would no doubt have regretted the necessity, she was always realistic in her views and endlessly hospitable. It is a tradition of Inverewe that visitors should be fed, and if the large number of people now coming to see the gardens put too great a burden on existing resources she would surely have agreed that fresh provision must be made for them.

Probably she would have preferred to build on the opposite side of the road—perhaps on the knoll where her hens once foraged—but it may be that drainage and water supplies to that position would have proved too expensive. If one assumes that the new structure had to be placed within the policies, the site used is the best that could have been chosen, and the building itself is suitably designed. My only quarrel with it is the harsh yellow-brown colour of the wood. Unlike any of the traditional local tones, this hue shrieked across the loch at me every time I looked out of the hotel window. But so small a blemish could easily be remedied by a coat of dark creosote or green paint.

On my way home to the hotel for lunch I looked at another new building—a farm cottage built by the Trust alongside the picturesque white house of the Home farm ('the oldest dwelling in the parish of Gairloch', Aunt Mairi once told me). The addition has been unobtrusively constructed of materials that harmonize with the surroundings, and is so well sited behind a row of trees in what was orginally a sheep-fank that it might easily escape notice. Whether the occupants will get sufficient sunlight is questionable; but a few branches could be removed (or even one or two trees) without materially harming the landscape.

My next walk round the loch took me as far as my first home at Inverewe. The approach to *Tigh-an-Uillt* (The House by the Burn) showed so little alteration that I half expected to find my own goods and chattels inside the door, and the puppy *Busdubh* asleep in her basket as of old. There was even a deerskin flung over the same rope stretched between two of the trees beside the rushing stream.

Instinctively I looked to see if the hoofs were all in place. For in the days of *Busdubh's* infancy her greatest ambition had been to seize one of the dangling legs of the deerskin and bite off the hoof. At first I had imagined that their height from the ground would preserve them from her assaults, and thought with satisfaction of all the amusement and strenuous exercise the pup was giving herself without doing any damage.

Then one evening I went through into my sitting-room and met with a trail of fat white maggots emerging from beneath the frill of the chintz chair-cover. Disgusted, I pushed the chair aside and disclosed a battered and smelly hoof from which another batch of pallid gentles was about to descend.

By the time I had removed and burnt the horrid mess I felt somehow disinclined to eat for supper the half-pound of tripe with which my larder was furnished. It was too similar in colour and texture to those maggots to be palatable just then; so (with averted eyes) I cooked and gave it to the culprit instead. After she had bolted it with great relish, she sat on the hearthrug gazing up at me with an expression of heavenly beatitude.

'You didn't deserve that extra meal!' I said severely. For reply, she stiffened her body, raised her chin, and emitted a loud noise— of the sort that is looked upon as a polite indication of gratitude in Bedouin circles, but which sounded exceedingly vulgar to my ears.

At that time we were alone; but the little dog's expressions of thanks-for-meat were not always made in such secluded surroundings. I found it embarrassing when the occupants of school staff-rooms insisted upon feeding her. 'Please don't!' I would cry; 'it isn't good for her—and there may be disastrous effects.' 'Nonsense! How can a saucer of milk hurt her?' they would respond, breaking off some chunks of cake for good measure and putting these down beside the milk. Then, stooping to pat the

gorged puppy, they crooned, 'You feel better now, don't you?'
—and were immediately rewarded for their misplaced concern
by an explosion which made them jump as it reverberated round
the room in a manner no hurried conversation could possibly
disguise. Of course they did not make the same mistake twice;
but there were always new members of the community to repeat
the performance.

But now *Busdubh* was far away and our former home,
inhabited for several years past by old Sheena, looked shut and
forlorn. I went up to the front door, tapped with my knuckles,
and waited. There was no sound of movement inside, so I rapped
again—more forcefully. But there was no response. Perhaps
Sheena was upstairs in bed with some ailment, or possibly just
deep in an after-dinner nap. In a matter of seconds I was knocking
at the entrance to the other half of the cottage instead. This was
immediately opened by Lizbie, who ushered me through to the
living-room where a log fire burned brightly. In reply to my
anxious inquiries for Sheena, Lizbie said that she no longer used
the front room or opened the main door, and it would be necessary to go round to the back. Her rheumatism now prevented
her from walking more than a few steps, so she found it simpler
to dwell near the cooking-stove.

I stayed for about half an hour talking to Lizbie, and before
I left Flora came in, looking almost grown-up and very like her
half-sister Janet in the days when the latter had been in service
with Aunt Mairi. Janet had married and gone away south with
her husband and baby to live on the shores of Loch Ness, while
Flora, since leaving school, had taken her place at the Big House
with the new occupants. I was pressed into accepting a glass of
wine and some Christmas cake, and after I had drunk to the health
of all at *Tigh-an-Uillt* we parted with an exchange of good wishes
for the new year that had just begun, and I ran round behind the
building to try my luck at Sheena's back door.

I called out to ask if I might come in, and a thin, high voice—
barely audible outside the door—bade me enter. Sheena was
sitting in an upright wooden chair with arms, and by pressing

down on these with her tiny hands she made an attempt to rise when she saw me. This difficult feat took time, and I was able to persuade her to remain seated. She had probably been dozing, and looked a little dazed for a few minutes, but soon brightened up and showed much of her former mental vigour when we began to share our memories of the old days.

She said how fortunate it was that Colin had been able to stay on at Inverewe after his official retirement—for otherwise he must have left the cottage, and she could hardly remain there without the kind and constant help of her good neighbours. So long as the Trust required Colin's part-time services and he was fit to do the gardening, they all hoped that it would be possible to stay where they were. But the 'tied' cottage is a source of much anxiety to such folk, who may have to give up a home they have had all their working lives—and find themselves without a roof—just when advancing years make the uprooting more arduous, and when finances are less able to bear the strain of rent or mortgage payments.

On the west coast cottages are very scarce indeed, she told me, and unfortunately many strangers buy them up for holiday or permanent residences at prices the local people cannot pay. Not long since, when an estate changed hands, the new owners bought village dwellings to house their extra staffs, instead of building houses on their own land as they could well afford to do. Colin and Lizbie had had hopes of acquiring one of these old cottages —but now it was lost to them for ever. 'It is a pity,' she said, 'that there cannot be some scheme for letting local workers have first chance to get empty cottages when they fall vacant.' Sheena put it in an unemotional way; for she was not in the least given to self-pity or grumbling.

We discussed the news of the day, including the Common-wealth tour of the Prime Minister (Mr. Harold MacMillan) and his wife, which had just started. 'I remember well her coming to lunch at Inverewe,' said Sheena. 'One of her sisters often came to see Mrs. Sawyer, but Lady Dorothy had never been here before. Mrs. Sawyer gave them a meal of her own cooking, with everything off the estate, and Lady Dorothy exclaimed, "What a marvellous feast!" Her sister turned to her and said, "*Didn't I tell you?*"

'Another time,' said Sheena, 'the old Duchess of Devonshire came to Inverewe for a week-end, bringing a manservant with her. We had him with us in the kitchen, and all the evening he was on about the grand house they had, with huge rooms and valuable furniture, and he was telling us about the marvellous pictures and how much money they were worth. That was some years ago, before we had Janet. It was Katie then. The last I heard of them, she was leading the man up the back stairs to his attic at bed-time and saying firmly, "*You'll not be getting any grand pictures up here!*"'

Sheena shifted on her hard chair; and feeling the uncushioned seat of mine cutting into my flesh, I thought what harsh treatment the wood must give her small, thin frame. 'Do you not wish for a softer chair?' I asked her. 'Those in the front are no use to me now,' she replied, 'for I cannot get up from them. I had a lot of swelling in my ankles, and the nurse said I should put my feet up —but how can I? If I got down on the sofa I should never raise myself from it. I don't use the front room at all now. Lizbie usually puts a fire on in the dining-room in the afternoons, so I sit there to get a change from this back place. I wonder where she is today.'

'She had visitors just before I came,' I said, 'and then I stayed about half an hour and possibly hindered her.' I had already seen a little heap of kindling on top of the stove—no doubt put there in readiness for the lighting of the afternoon fire. Sheena's kitchen cooker was a new one supplied by the Trust—who now owned *Tigh-an-Uillt*—and the roof of the lean-to where we sat had been repaired since the days when I used to cook clad in gumboots. But the bare stone floor offered scant comfort to tender old feet.

When asked if her rheumatism was very bad, Sheena told me that sometimes it hurt less and sometimes more, but that she knew it would never be cured at her age. The most she hoped for was short respite occasionally from the nagging bouts of pain in bed which would enable her to get some sleep. On the previous night it had been much less sore, and she had slept for several hours without stirring—which was unusual for her now. She looked up at me and in a louder tone said, 'But I still do all my own cooking!' This sounded like a war-cry—as indeed it was: a challenge to the eighty-ninth year now advancing towards her, and to her infirmities.

She glanced down at her felt bootees with a deprecating smile. 'I can't reach the right one,' she said; 'my leg is too weak and it just won't lift. So that boot stays undone always. Flora comes in to help me put my stockings on and off.' I wondered how gallant old Sheena managed to drag her stiff limbs up the steep stairway to her bedroom, but I did not inquire. No doubt it was often a very slow and hurtful task. Time was now no object to her, and all her energy went into the daily actions of rising, preparing food, eating, and going to bed. If these could be managed without unbearable pain she was content.

She told me that a recent operation for cataract had made it possible for her to read, but that the magnifying glass she held in order to see print was awkward to manage when she tried to write. 'I will write to you when I get home,' I said, 'but you must not worry yourself to reply.' 'I doubt you'd be able to read my writing if I did,' she replied with a sad little grimace.

It seemed unlikely that she could manage to hang on to life alone in the cottage for very much longer. No doubt she preferred it to any strange place; but if only there were some kindly hostel for the aged in the district, people like Sheena would surely gain much from the knowledge that, as a last resort, they could be cared for close at hand without giving extra work to friends or relations. I thought of the old seaman I had known at Aultbea, and of his forcible removal to Inverness. It would be distressing if Sheena had to go away to the same place, and end her days within hospital walls far from Inverewe.

How gladly, I thought, would I help to collect endowments for some place of refuge on the west coast—perhaps to be called The Mairi Sawyer Hostel—for what could be more fitting as a memorial to one whose dearest wish was to end her own days in sight of these hills and the sea? Everything is now done to make life easier and pleasanter for young people; but it is the old who no longer possess the health and spirits to minimize hardship and difficulties, and it is for them that ease and comfort should be provided before any other section of the community. Over-Sixty Hostels should be as common as Youth Hostels, and the residents should feel as free and independent as the Youth-hostellers do— with no stigma of charity attached to them.

It was hard to leave Sheena. Several times I made a move, but always she began another conversation as though loath to see me go. The small, uncurtained window above the sink grew dark, and when at last I saw the hands of my watch nearing seven o'clock I realized that dinner would soon be ready for me in the hotel. Sheena put her bent fingers over mine, and looked up at me in silence. I knew she was wondering if we should meet again. 'I'll possibly manage to get back in the summer holidays,' I said, and pressed her wrists, and went out quickly.

It seemed very black outside after the light within, and I had brought no torch. I stumbled about, wondering where the burn was and hoping I should not end the day with a cold plunge. Then I heard it chattering over the stones, and guided by the cheerful noise I worked my way carefully along the bank.

Six years ago I had been able to stride with confidence down the path at *Tigh-an-Uillt* after dark, for I had made a practice of taking a stroll before bed-time. From the gate I could look across the water to Aunt Mairi's light in the smoking-room, and I used to stand there for a moment and silently ask a blessing on the house of Inverewe and on Herself.

The same window showed an orange glow this evening—but it was no use pretending that she sat within at her desk as of old. Suddenly I felt that, in spite of the pleasure of meeting good friends and seeing the familiar hills again, I had become a stranger here now and must go away at once. I hurried back to the village fast enough to bring to mind my local nickname of The Motor Bike.

263

After dinner I asked if I could settle my bill overnight, as I should be away to Edinburgh with the mail early next morning. Soon I went upstairs and packed my boots and oilskins, together with the roll of bark and eucalyptus spray from the gardens. Then I had another bath in soft brown hill water, and went to bed. I drew back my curtains last thing, and there across Loch Ewe on the wooded peninsula were pin-points of light which marked out the Gate Lodge and the Big House. 'Farewell, Inverewe, once more!' I whispered.

Arthur smiled confidentially when I climbed aboard his mail next morning. 'I've a parcel here for you,' he said in a low voice. 'I was not sure when you would come, but intended keeping it here until the right day.' He bent down and lifted a square package out from under one of the seats. 'I would have put more, but feared to make it too heavy for you to manage,' he said.

These remarks puzzled me, until he added that he hoped the scent would bring back memories. Then I remembered telling him how we always burnt peat at Christmas and New Year at home in England; but that the peats I had taken from Argyll the previous year did not make the house nearly so fragrant as those from Wester Ross. These were the real thing—cut by Arthur himself, and done up in a neat brown-paper parcel with a Christmas seal on it. I was delighted.

'That is very kind of you,' I said, 'very kind indeed! Next Christmas we shall put it on the hearth away down there in Somerset, and I shall set it alight and carry it all over the house on a shovel so that the fragrance will cling to everything. And we shall fill our glasses and drink the health of you and your family and of all old friends up here. "*Slàinte mhór*, everyone," I shall call out; "*slàinte mhór!* Great good health to you all!"'

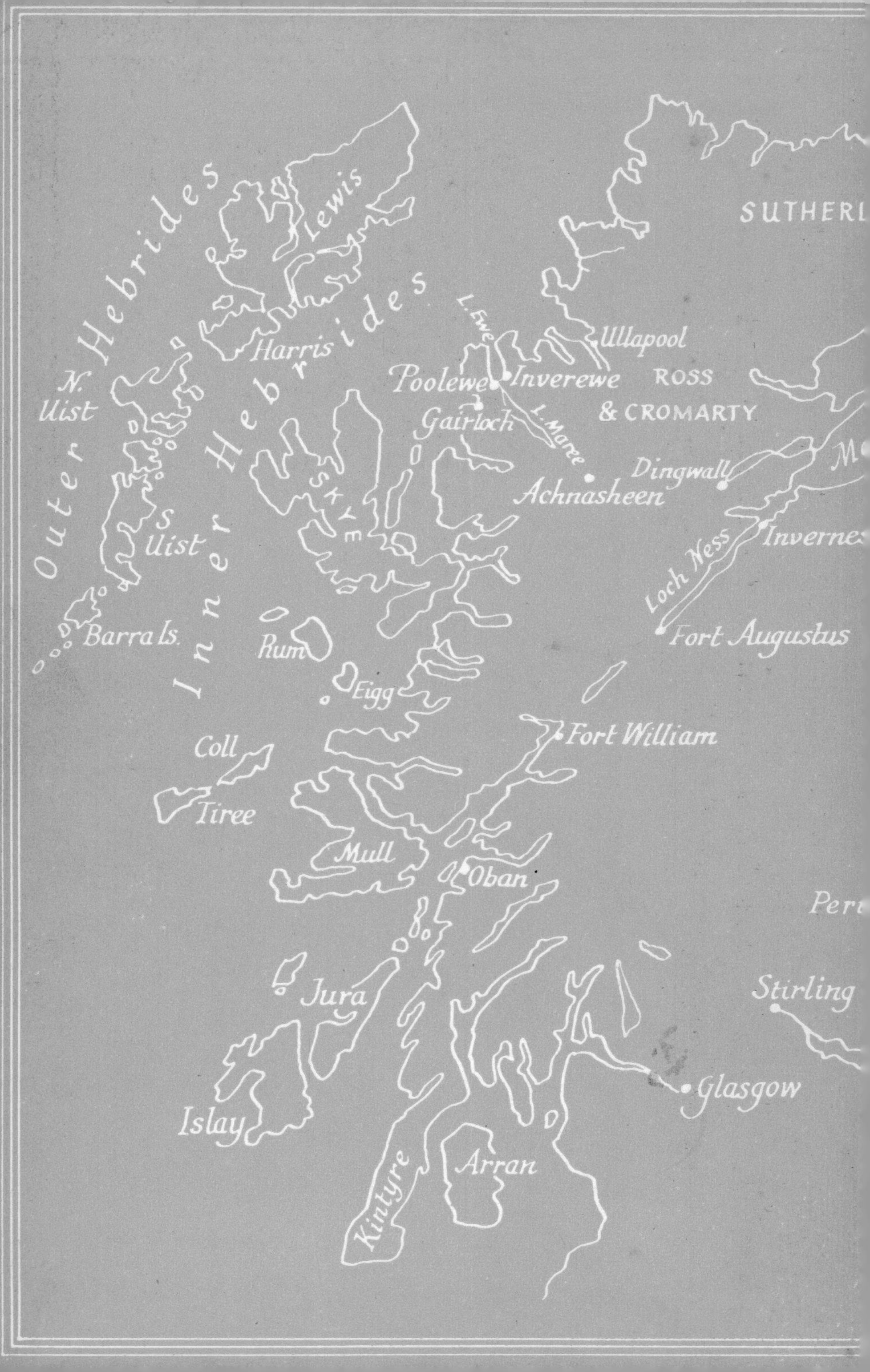

Outer Hebrides
Lewis
Harris
N. Uist
S. Uist
Barra Is.
Inner Hebrides
SKYE
Rum
Eigg
Coll
Tiree
Mull
Jura
Islay
Kintyre
Arran
L. Ewe
Ullapool
Poolewe
Inverewe
Gairloch
L. Maree
ROSS
& CROMARTY
SUTHERL
Dingwall
Achnasheen
Inverne
Loch Ness
Fort Augustus
Fort William
Oban
Per
Stirling
Glasgow